D0891971

THE CRISIS OF POVERTY AND DEBT
IN THE THIRD WORLD

The Crisis of Poverty and Debt in the Third World

MARTIN DENT

BILL PETERS

Ashgate

Aldershot • Brookfield USA • Singapore • Sydney

Published by
Ashgate Publishing Limited
Gower House
Croft Road
Aldershot
Hants GU11 3HR
England

Ashgate Publishing Company
Old Post Road
Brookfield
Vermont 05036
USA

Ashgate website: http://www.ashgate.com

British Library Cataloguing in Publication Data
Dent, Martin
   The crisis of poverty and debt in the Third World
   1.Poverty - Developing countries 2.Debts, Public -
   Developing countries 3.Debt relief - Developing countries
   4.Developing countries - Economic conditions - 20th century
   I.Title II.Peters, Bill
   336.3'435'091724

Library of Congress Catalog Card Number: 99-76365

ISBN 0 7546 1027 6

Printed in Great Britain by
Antony Rowe Ltd, Chippenham, Wiltshire

Contents

Note: Chapters 1 - 13, apart from 1B and 10, are by Martin Dent, and Chapters 1B, 10 and
14-20 are by Bill Peters.

Acknowledgements:
We would like to record our gratitude to those who have particularly helped us in the
preparation of the text; Bill Peters to Mary Ann Roscoe of Eurosec and Martin Dent to Phil
Whalley, Martin Cook and Stephen Roberts for secretarial and computer assistance, and
Patricia Pitts for preparing the final draft. We would also like to thank Sarah Markham and
others at Ashgate for all their valuable editorial assistance.

List of Tables

ERRATUM

Page 4
Lines 18 to 31 this text is repeated on page 5 lines 8 to 19.

Page 23
καὶ ἄφες ἡμῖν τὰ ὀφειλήματα ἡμῶν, ὡς καὶ ἡμεῖς ἀφήκαμεν τοῖς ὀφειλέταις ἡμῶν

Matthew 6, 12
'And forgive us our debts
as we have forgiven our debtors' (past tense);

καί ἄφες ἡμῖν τὰς ἁμαρτίας ἡμῶν, καὶ γὰρ αὐτοὶ ἀφίομεν παντὶ ὀφείλοντι ἡμῖν

Luke 11, 4
'And forgive us our sins
For we also ourselves forgive everyone owing to us' (present tense)

Page 116
Line 18 – Cancun 1981

Foreword

In an age of management cult and focus group politics vision is at a premium: and vision is precisely what Martin Dent and Bill Peters have demonstrated. With a wealth of practical and relevant background experience - one in the colonial service and community development, the other in the diplomatic service - they record in this book how they identified debt not just as a financial burden for impoverished third world economies but as a cruel oppressor of the world's poor in the world's less developed countries.

Their concern was transformed into crusading zeal by a powerful combination of reason and morality. They were dismayed that available resources should be locked into at best helping the impoverished to stand still - at worst to fighting a losing battle against decline - and outraged that the innocent and vulnerable should be made to suffer. They were appalled that a consequence of debt servicing was ruthless cutting of health, education and social services. Their sense of decency and social justice turned them into an obstinate pair, determined that debt reduction should become a central pillar of international development co-operation.

Today, the high profile for Jubilee 2000 and the prominence of debt reduction on the agendas of G7, IMF, World Bank and other international institutions are compelling testimony to the indefatigable tenacity of them both. Awkward and uncomfortable? They have undoubtedly been both! But what of strategic qualitative significance has ever been achieved in the evolution of humankind without these characteristics? Martin Dent is proud of the involvement of his forebears in the abolition of slavery and he makes a number of comparisons between that great cause and their own. It is an entirely valid comparison.

The authors pay warm tribute to the new generation which today carries the campaign forward. Equally generous tributes are due from us all to Peters and Dent themselves for the part they played in originating it all - just as our appreciation is due to others like Kenneth Clarke, Gordon Brown, Lynda Chalker, Clare Short and the more anonymous but indispensable civil servants who have picked up the ball and begun to run with it.

Debt relief is today fairly and squarely on the global agenda. That is only a beginning. As the authors realise, it is now crucial to devise methods of relief, including perhaps periodically reviewed suspension of debt repayment that ensures the benefits really do go into sustainable economic development

The Crisis of Poverty and Debt in the Third World

and social priorities. The poor, who were in no way responsible for the accumulation of debt, have carried the burden of its repayment. The poor must now be guaranteed the benefit of new policies. Internationally agreed principles of conditionality will be essential.

If debt is at last targeted it must be seen in perspective. The latest news is that world poverty is again alarmingly advancing. The campaign will have to be mobilised on other fronts as well: trade, conflict, arms trade, environment, aid flows, technology transfers, and the rest. In a global society dominated by market fatalism there is much talk of equal playing fields, but positive action has to be taken to bring all the players to the point at which they are fit enough to play. The test of good governance will be how the undeniably valuable disciplines and thrust of the market are combined with sane intervention for the common good. The time is long overdue for the debate to refocus on that common good.

Grave events in the Balkans have led to rhetoric about new "Marshall Plans". There were two key elements in the success of the original Marshall Plan which must not be forgotten. The first was that there was the administrative talent, experience and capacity in Europe itself to *internalise* the external assistance and make it part of the continent's own regeneration. The other is that there was a strong ethical context within which it all happened. Responsibility, commitment, fairness, social justice, integrity and care all mattered. Taxation, redistribution and public expenditure were a manifestation of social solidarity. Greed, excessive wealth and corruption were deprecated. Values and ethos are central to the building of a better society - anywhere! It is refreshing that both Peters and Dent challengingly recognise this.

I have enjoyed reading these highly personal - at times idiosyncratic - reflective reminiscences of how they formulated their concern, made their stand, and then irrepressibly advanced. I commend their story to all who care about the future of humanity.

Frank Judd
May 1999

Authors' Introduction

Since we completed our draft texts, two important developments have occurred, which are of the utmost relevance to Jubilee 2000. Ann Pettifor, the Director of Jubilee 2000 Coalition, has prepared a new concordat on debt cancellation. This provides for a demand for an agreement for each severely indebted country that applies for relief. It is envisaged that a separate independent body will be set up to examine the position of each debtor country. This body, to be known as 'a Debt Review Body, would be set up by the UN, on the basis of the UN declaration of Human Rights and of the International Court of Justice, to arbitrate between the debtor nation and its creditors. It would work in a transparent way and give an opportunity for debtor and creditor representatives together, to determine which debts are unpayable. The process would eventuate in a concordat on debt service cancellation and on policy parameters and guidelines, that the debtor country pledges to abide by, with an interval during which payments would not be required and the cancellation would not be final.

The details of this package are still subject to debate, but the objective is a way to grant adequate debt remission to poor countries, while obtaining a public promise from the government of the country concerned, made to its own citizens, as well as to the creditors and to the UN, that financial administration will be honest in future, and that most of the funds released by the remission will be spent for the benefit of the poor, through restoring health, education and other essential services.

The second important development has been the speech of Gordon Brown, the Chancellor of the Exchequer, in St. Paul's Cathedral on 7th March. The meeting which was attended by some 4000 people, was called by the London branch of the Jubilee 2000 campaign to mark the beginning of the last 300 days before the millennium, and of the intense campaigning needed in this period. Gordon Brown came out openly in favour of Jubilee 2000. He promised to work with his fellow Ministers of Finance in the European Community, the Commonwealth and the other G8 members to achieve $50 billion of debt remission. He indicated that he had already obtained support for the sale of a substantial portion of the IMF gold reserves to finance part of this remission and promised a further $1 billion from the British government for this purpose. He asked the people of Britain to match the government's and NGO's help to poorer people in the world, by increasing their own voluntary contributions to suitable NGOs from the present total of £220 million to a sum approaching £1 billion, to which the British Government would add 30%.

This inspiring speech provoked a very warm reception. It is essential to see that it is rapidly implemented in a straightforward way, and that in due course the total of debt to be remitted is substantially increased.

As regards this book the two authors would like to emphasise that they write in a private capacity, and not as one which would seek to state the policy of the Jubilee Coalition Board. Both of them are Vice-Presidents and one of them (Bill Peters) is now on the Board, but that board makes its policy collectively. On most policy issues it has yet to declare its policy. This book contains the views and recommendation of two separate Co-Founders of Jubilee 2000; it is not a joint book, but since we have been involved together in working for Jubilee 2000 from an early period, there is a natural congruence between our views on most subjects. We write as Co-Founders and not as Vice-Presidents, since to speak as Vice-Presidents, might be seen as claiming the approval of the board for everything we say. The authority for our statements is just that of their intrinsic reasonableness.

The order in which our contributions occur is incidental and springs from the timing of our approaches to Ashgate. It does not imply any order of merit or weight. Comparisons are odious; no one should seek to draw from our separate texts any view as to who contributed the most. Jubilee 2000 is a collective effort and its true heroes are not the originators nor the controllers, but the marvellous army of men and women who carry on the battle in local committees and gatherings, in this and in 40 other countries. May God grant victory for the campaign, through the achievement of a true liberation from the burden of unpayable debt.

Bill Peters and Martin Dent

1 The Problem of Debt and Poverty and a Practical Answer

A) The Present Situation of Contrast Between Rich and Poor States

MARTIN DENT

There is an intimate connection between the presence of absolute poverty which is abundantly visible in many low-income countries and that of unpayable sovereign debt. Debt is not the sole cause nor its removal a sufficient cause for recovery, but it is a great contributory factor of lasting poverty of low-income countries. Removal of the debt burden is a necessary cause of escape from poverty. This book describes the origin and development of the campaign for Jubilee 2000, which has already attracted massive support in this country and has encouraged the formation of autonomous Jubilee 2000 committees in 40 other countries.

It is elementary knowledge that there is in the world an immense contrast between the conditions of the poorer nations and those of the richer. The statement of the arithmetical contrasts between standards and consumption in developed countries and that in the poorer developing countries points to a totally excessive ratio, the richest 20% of countries in the world enjoy 84% of the income. The bottom 80% are left with only 16%. This is a ratio of difference of 20 to 1. If we measure the difference at the extremes, say for the top 10% and the bottom 50%, the ratio is over 50 to 1, a grotesque and unjust contrast. These figures may, perhaps, fail to enable the reader to realise the extent to which monies that could be used to meet the bare essential requirements for a decent standard of living in poorer countries are wasted on excess luxuries for richer people in the developed world.

The mere existence of this huge disparity in access to goods and services is an offence against justice. In past centuries, we could say that suffering in a far-off country was none of our business. Only if the juxtaposition was immediate, like that between Dives and Lazarus in the Biblical story, could the richer person be condemned for his failure to help the poorer person living at his gate. Now, however, we live in a global world, and therefore nations with a very substantially higher standard of living have an imperative duty to help poorer nations.

1

This contrast in standards of living is grotesque, it applies not only to Gross Domestic Product (GDP) per head, but also to welfare. The UNDP has prepared a human development index, which encompasses many factors other than income, such as access to education and quality of education, access to health facilities and medicines (free or at a price that ordinary people can afford to pay), numbers of people per doctor, per nurse and per hospital bed, health expenditure per head, percentage of population with access to safe water, percentage of population with access to sanitation, cleanliness of the streets, sewage disposal, life expectancy at birth, percentage of the population in absolute poverty (which is usually defined as income below $1 per head per day), and a number of other factors, as measured by the most important indicators. There is a close correlation between the results of these measurements and the overarching pattern is one of the existence of a group of some 50 countries, who are at the bottom of the scale. This is not because of any congenital deficiencies in their population, but because of the self-perpetuating cycle of deprivation.[1] There is a recurring pattern of inequality in uncontrolled economic relations. It is rightly described in the Biblical verse 'To him that hath shall be given and from him that hath not shall be taken away even that which he hath.' The bare statistics may conceal the extent of the actual suffering involved in terms of unnecessary sickness and pain, hunger and malnutrition and loss of educational opportunity.

A few countries, such as South Korea and Taiwan have moved across the gulf separating the poorer countries from the richer developed world, but in the present crisis are in some danger of falling back again. Some other countries have moved from the category of low-income countries to that of middle-income. This should not, however, make us believe that all low income countries can follow the same route through their own efforts. Their cycle of deprivation is increased and made permanent by the burden of the backlog of unpayable debt, which is not balanced by productive capacity springing from the expenditure in the past of the sums received on loan. The effect of this backlog of unpayable debt is to produce a lock, fastening low income countries into continued poverty as the UNDP Report, 'Overcoming Human Poverty' expresses it:

> Despite recent debt relief initiatives, many of the poorest countries are still forced to direct funds to the richest ones repaying debts that should long ago have been cancelled. Debt burdened governments continue to lose scarce resources that could instead be used to fund the basic services that can serve as a launching pad and for poverty eradication.[2]

The task of enabling these countries to break loose from their chains of poverty and to achieve a state of sustainable development producing a decent level of prosperity is a large one. It requires specific actions and a great deal of imaginative input from countries in the developed world. It requires a great effort from the people and government of the country itself. The obstacles to liberation are as much psychological as material, though the psychological hindrances may well be, at bottom, a product of the physical deprivation.

B) The Historical Context and the Root of the Problem

BILL PETERS

The post-war world's most salient division, already present before 1939, was between governments which broadly favoured a liberal, laissez-faire economic system and those which adopted the Marxist-Leninist line and the type of command economy it fostered. Initially this division was not demarcated throughout the worlds; many countries now recognised as belonging to the Third World were in the mid-forties still colonies of the metropolitan powers, Britain, France, Belgium, Holland, Spain, Portugal and the United States. The last was untypical; indeed one of Roosevelt's principal aims in the post-war settlement, clearly visible in his remarkable correspondence with Churchill about India (edited by Nicholas Mansergh in the vast survey 'The Transfer of Power') was the dissolution of the British Empire, and its associated Sterling Area. The time was ripe. Soldiers in the colonial armies which contributed to the Allied Victory, having seen the condition of people like themselves in other countries, were in no mood meekly to accept a return to the status quo ante bellum. Crucial steps towards India's self-government had already been taken in the inter-war years; the question in 1945 was not 'how much?' but 'when?' As members of the 'Indian National Army' who had followed the Japanese flag returned home and the 'Quit India' Movement gathered momentum, doubts in Westminster and Whitehall about too rapid a transfer of power were overridden; the most significant dialogues[3] took place not in London, but in Bombay, between Mahatma Gandhi and Mohammed Ali Jinnah; and tragically failed to produce a meeting of minds. Once India, Pakistan, Sri Lanka and Burma had gained their freedom the next were quick to follow. Gradations of self-government would not be tolerated. Africa, South East Asia, the Caribbean, the Pacific followed the same course; from the shots fired at a parade of disgruntled ex-servicemen in Accra, Gold Coast in November 1948 to the lowering of the Union flag in Hong Kong in June

1997 the ties were loosened; Empire became Commonwealth. A similar, sometimes less orderly transformation, occurred in the other Europe-centred empires.

Most of the metropolitan powers had foreseen the demand for improved conditions in their colonies. Development Plans were being drawn up in London even before the end of the war. The British Colonial Development and Welfare Acts from 1948 onwards set up the machinery and a financial framework for extended programmes. But the United Nations Organisation supervened, with the World Bank and International Monetary Fund, already formed from the Bretton Woods Conference in 1944; their global programmes soon overshadowed those of the metropolitan countries. The International Bank for Reconstruction and Development embraced the two main post-war economic thrusts; restoration after war damage and economic support to enable countries whose living standards were markedly below a global mean to move closer to the standards of their more fortunate neighbours. In the early stages metropolitan governments' plans for development fitted reasonably well into this wider framework.

Later, as the anti-colonial movement gained momentum within the UN, former colonies began to align themselves with larger groupings such as the Afro-Asian Peoples' Solidarity Organisation and the Non-Aligned Group, and the polarisation in Europe brought about by the Cold War percolated through to almost all the less developed world. During the 1950s and 60s, as alignments within the UN General Assembly were closely monitored, it became apparent that aid and development were useful tools for securing countries' votes for or against resolutions before the Assembly where the interests of the protagonists in the Cold War were engaged. By and large this assisted the development processes; indeed the 1960s and 70s were almost a Golden Age for both the developers and those receiving development and hopes began to stir for a steadily improving world where the extremes of poverty and deprivation might be banished, providing a modest competence for all. Although the origin of today's debt problem is often taken to be the oil crises of 1972 and 1977, when enormous sums of money were loaned to developing countries simply in order to disburse the accumulation of cash from oil profits, patterns of Third World development encouraged (among other things) by the Cold War had already been well established in the post-War world.

The shift in status of developing countries like India from mere colonies to full independence had originated in the inter-War years, but gathered irresistible momentum after 1945. Although most of the European metropolitan powers - Britain, France, Belgium, Spain, Holland and Portugal - had foreseen the demand for improved conditions in their colonies and had set up development plans, in some cases before the end of the War, these were quickly superseded by the United Nations and the subsequent emergence of the World Bank and the International Monetary Fund (IMF), both of whom constructed development programmes of global proportions. Nevertheless, the colonial powers' plans for development often fitted reasonably well into this wider framework. Later, as the anti-colonial movement gained momentum within the UN, former colonies began to align themselves with larger groupings such as the Afro-Asian Peoples' Solidarity Organisation and the Non-Aligned Group, and the polarisation in Europe brought by the Cold War percolated through to almost all the less developed world. It became apparent that development was a useful tool for securing countries' votes for or against resolutions before the Assembly where the interests of the protagonists in the Cold War were engaged. By and large, this assisted the development processes; indeed, the 60's and 70's were almost a 'golden age' for both the developers and those receiving development: Hopes began to stir for a steadily improving world where the extremes of poverty and deprivation might be banished, providing a modest competence for all.

But this benign cycle occurred against a background of persistent danger from nuclear conflict and increasing confrontation between the Cold War protagonists. At this point, in 1972, the Organisation of Petroleum Exporting Countries (OPEC) decided that their cartel was strong enough to challenge the world by raising oil prices savagely. The first 'oil shock', after the near-panic it provoked in Western capitals, was absorbed without intolerable difficulty; the second, in 1977, provoked even more alarm than the first and, according to Dr A Thirlwall,[4] Professor of Economics at the University of Kent, very nearly triggered an economic collapse which might have been as serious as the crash of 1929. The capital accumulation in the main oil producers, once development in their own countries had absorbed a portion of the excess, was so great that the world banking system was almost overwhelmed, as they pushed their surpluses into that system. Interest rates fell to rock bottom. A method had to be found for disbursing the accumulation. It was found, with the IMF and World Bank steering the process, in the great lending spree of 1977-78. Developing countries were in need of funds for continuing their development; interest rates were very low; the lenders discovered a new method for syndicating loans which allowed commercial banks to make sovereign loans, which carried no risk of bankruptcy.[5] In some cases the loans were shrewdly placed and carefully managed; in all too many others the main interest of the lenders was to get rid of their deposits; they gave only passing thought to the effects over time on the borrowing countries of servicing and repaying their loans.

By 1982-83, the credit flows from all sources into developing countries were fast drying up. By that time interest rates, pushed along by the conditions in the US domestic market, had already climbed steeply and were to climb still further. Debt servicing costs, which in 1977-78 had seemed manageable, began to build up; the situation was made worse for the debtor countries because terms of trade began to shift against their interest and have continued to do so ever since. A major contributing factor in this shift was the advice which the IMF and, to a lesser extent, the World Bank and creditor governments gave through visiting teams of experts as the debtor governments began to fall behind in debt servicing.

Within a short time, some 50 governments received forceful advice to shift their production, primarily agricultural, to export crops. The number of crops suitable for this purpose was small, no more than a dozen. Not surprisingly, as this additional produce came onto the world market, gluts occurred, with the normal catastrophic effect on prices. Other elements in the IMF packages generally included advice to devalue currency, tighten budgetary controls, reduce public domestic borrowing, freeze wages and remove subsidies. The total effect of these measures when applied was certainly, as intended, to free funds for debt servicing; but along with that went a harsh cutting back of the governments' inputs into programmes of social support, till then acting to cushion the poorest segments of their populations from new, harsh economic pressures.

Further, because of the concentration enjoined on exports, less land and fewer resources were available for crops needed for domestic consumption. So a small farmer in one of the fifty countries would be faced at the same time with the need to produce ever more crops to obtain the funds needed to buy imported items like fertiliser and agricultural equipment, while supplying less for his own family's and community's needs. Worse still, as his government cut its budgetary provision for social services, he found he had to pay increasing amounts for the education of his children and the health needs of his family, even at rural clinics. The World Bank and IMF have recently awakened to the destructive effect of their advice on education and health in 'heavily indebted poor countries' (HIPCs); less blinkered observers have been aware of this for over ten years, and been vainly calling for remedies.

C) Debt Remission: The Most Immediate of the Ways to Help Poorer Countries

MARTIN DENT

Action is required, both from the developed world and from the indebted low-income countries themselves. It relates to three main areas: aid, trade and debt. Aid from richer countries has to be increased to 0.7% of GNP or above, as the UN recommends, and it has to be wisely directed. The figure of 0.7% of GNP is a moderate one. Religious thinkers in the Christian, the Jewish and the Muslim tradition have suggested that we should tithe, that is to say, give a tenth of our income. This may seem excessive to some in the field of international aid, we are called to give not a tenth nor even a tenth of a tenth, but only seven-tenths of a tenth of a tenth.

The experience of the Marshall Plan after the Second World War shows that an aid programme can, in suitable circumstances, transform the economic outlook of countries reduced to a certain level of poverty by an externally induced disaster. The Marshall Plan involved an expenditure of about 3% of its annual GNP by the United States over a period of a few years in order to enable her allies, who had been wounded in their economies by the War, to make a full recovery and achieve a self-sustaining rate of growth. The initiative originally launched by General George Marshall, the Secretary of State had been welcomed by Ernest Bevin in Britain and was jointly organised by the United States and the recipient countries. The assistance given was in cash and kind. This is a good model for aid to Africa South of the Sahara and other poor countries.

This aid has to be of a kind that will prime the pump of creative national endeavour. Suitable technology has to be transferred to the countries concerned and their entrepreneurs have to enjoy a proper share in the business life of their own countries. These goals are important, but they are also reversible. If we were to choose them as the main task to be achieved in the year 2000, we might well find that the gains achieved in one year could be reversed in another, whereas debt remission, like the abolition of slavery, is a goal ideally suited for the occasion of the millennium because it is irreversible. The debts once forgiven cannot be reinstated. New debts may, of course, arise, but the Jubilee process must be directed to a new beginning, after which the old, inert, unproductive debts will be cancelled and the new debts will be entered into only after very careful examination, and will be of a kind that will create productive capacity for their own servicing and repayment. The strict conditionalities to be attached to the remission will need to be of a kind to prevent large scale corruption and theft in future. The conditionalities of the remission will go a long way to establishing a new beginning in proper financial management from both creditors and debtors.

We need a transfer of technology together with an increase in well administered aid, but this is a continuous process, where technological innovation is continuous, and poorer nations can easily be left behind, if there is no means to enable them to adopt suitable new technologies developed in the richer parts of the world. In the world of international financial relations we have continually to guard against the tendency so common in business whereby the rich get richer and the poor poorer.

One of the major sources of impoverishment in poorer countries has been the deterioration in their terms of trade. This has often greatly outweighed any benefits which they have received from aid. Jubilee 2000, in their evidence to the Select Committee on International Development[6] (this Committee's third report on debt relief) pointed out that if terms of trade had not deteriorated in the last 20 years, the debts of the poorer countries could have been repaid one and a half times over. It is much more difficult to devise means to improve the terms of trade than it is to produce a viable scheme for debt remission. To remit debt we merely have to cancel an obligation to pay. To improve terms of trade we have to create sophisticated buffer stock schemes to purchase from the market, when the price goes below a certain level and to sell back onto it, when the price rises above the maximum we have set. We have to put a floor in the market without putting in a ceiling.

An alternative approach might be like the STABEX scheme operated by the European Community for certain African Caribbean Pacific (ACP) countries, to give compensatory payments to countries totally dependent upon products, whose price has temporarily fallen. Another approach might be to set a minimum price below which producers refuse to sell, and at the same time, seek to allocate a quota to each producer country. This is the approach which OPEC has sought to follow in the oil market. All these methods can and should be explored, but in the past the record of success has been far from uniform. The cocoa agreement collapsed when Côte D'Ivoire withdrew from the scheme because the floor price was considered by them to be too low. The coffee agreement also foundered, as did that for tin. The oil producers did succeed in achieving a large increase in price in the wake of the Yom Kippur War, but the price has since fallen from some $42 per barrel to little more than $12.

There is an urgent need to take action to improve the terms of trade, but this may be a long-term endeavour. In the meantime, we can deal with the urgent problem of the backlog of unpayable debt of the governments of poorer countries. This debt imposes a considerable burden of debt servicing, diverting resources in low-income countries, which are urgently needed to meet the essential needs of the poorer part of the population, and to maintain the essential structure of the state. The debt depresses the self-confidence of these countries and gives them the feeling that however much they earn, it will only go to repay a small proportion of their debt overhang. Furthermore, the presence of this debt burden drives away investors. Just as bad money drives out good, so old bad debts drive out new and productive loans. Only by clearing away the detritus of past unpayable debt can we open the gates to new and productive investment.

Achievement in these fields is likely to be nullified if the country concerned owes a large external debt. In recent years, as Professor Sir Hans Singer has put it in his chapter on debt relief for heavily-indebted poor countries:

> The debt problem has developed into a debt crisis, particularly for the heavily-indebted poor countries (HIPCs) mainly in Africa...As a country's backlog of unpaid debt mounts up, so does debt overhang - the idea that an excessive debt burden deters investment, impedes growth and thus any chance of poverty reduction...The servicing of the debt absorbs a high proportion of export earnings.[7]

The effect of the existence of this unpayable debt overhang has been to create a situation of injustice. It reduces low-income debtor countries to a status like that of poor Indian farmers sunk in perpetual debt to the Banya (the village money lender). The debtors are unable to repay any of the principal, since all they can do is to cope with the continually increasing interest payments; the stock of debt continually increases. The situation of this debt overhang has produced a dramatic change in the power relation between debtor countries and their creditors, both multilateral and bilateral. Much of the liberative effect of political independence has now been nullified by economic dependence. Some of the more or less mandatory advice given by creditor agencies to debtor countries has been beneficial, some has not, but the total situation of loss of control over their own key policy decisions has sapped the self-confidence of many poorer countries. Those who make the decisions do not have to bear the consequences, neither directly nor indirectly through the votes of suffering debtors. They are outside the system and unaccountable.

If we examine the World Debt Tables country by country, we find that most of the low income countries (which the World Bank defines as those with GNP per head below $765) owe upwards of 80% of a year's GNP or 200% of a year's export of goods and services (XGS). The percentage of debt to GNP and debt to XGS of low-income countries is as follows:

Table 1   Total debt of low-income countries as percentage of GNP and percentage of export of goods and services (1996)

Country	Debt as % of GNP	Debt as % of XGS
Albania	28	171
Angola	307	203
Bangladesh	51	292
Benin	74	254
Bhutan	32	76
Bolivia	88	382
Burkina Faso	51	289
Burundi	100	2012
Cambodia	68	257
Cameroon	113	426
Central African Republic	89	455
Chad	88	312
Comoros	89	319
Congo, Democratic Republic of (Kinshasa)	212	638
Congo Republic (Brazzaville)	279	330
Côte D'Ivoire	201	383
Equatorial Guinea	116	156
Ethiopia	169	1224
Gambia	118	200
Ghana	100	349
Guinea	86	418
Guinea-Bissau	352	4074
Guyana (1993 figure)	246	483
Haiti	34	4683
Honduras	111	220
Kenya	77	226

Country	Debt as % of GNP	Debt as % of XGS
Lao PDR	122	486
Liberia (1987 figure)	160	394
Madagascar	105	512
Malawi	107	486
Mali	116	467
Mauritania	228	424
Mozambique	379	1080
Nepal	53	217
Nicaragua	355	650
Niger	80	476
Nigeria	101	200
Rwanda	79	1133
Sao Tome & Principe	638	1991
Senegal	73	213
Sierra Leone	127	1042
Somalia	284	2599
Sri Lanka	53	146
Sudan	212	1766
Tanzania	130	536
Togo	105	283
Uganda	61	492
Vietnam	115	271
Yemen	120	177
Zambia	216	539
Zimbabwe	69	160

Source: World Bank Debt Tables 1998.

I have omitted from this list of 51 low-income countries, suitable for total or near-total debt remission, three large ones - China, India and Pakistan - whose GNP per head is below $765, but whose export potential is powerful, whose currency reserves are extensive and who benefit from very considerable overseas private investment. The ratios of debt to GNP and to XGS for these countries are as follows:

Table 2   Three low-income countries not on our list for debt remission

Country	Debt as % of GNP	Debt as % of XGS
China	16	71
India	25.6	170.8
Pakistan	49.1	352.4

Source: World Debt Tables 1998.

The reasons for excluding these countries from debt remission are examined in detail in chapter 6, 'The Boundaries and Criteria of Jubilee Remission.'

Sudan, Somalia and Liberia have experienced most destructive civil wars and do not have a satisfactory figure for the present ratio of debt to GNP. In 1992, the ratio for Sudan was 273%; that for Liberia in 1987 was 394%, and that for Somalia in 1990 was 284%; these countries have almost certainly deteriorated even further in the years after these statistics were returned, and should be admitted to the list of countries for total or near-total remission.

Of these 51 countries, 37 have a ratio of debt to GNP above 80%; only three of them - Haiti, Bhutan and Albania - have a ratio below 50%. Clearly the debt overhang is so enormous that for the 51 low-income countries listed the vast majority, if not all, of the debt is totally unpayable.

There are also lessons in the ratio of debt to XGS: 45 of the 51 countries have debt of more than 200% of a year's XGS. Only Equatorial Guinea, Yemen, Zimbabwe, Bhutan, Sri Lanka and Albania have debts less than two times a year's XGS. Since low-income countries have no other source except for their income from XGS (apart from grants) with which to repay their debt, and since the export of goods and services income is all desperately needed to meet the needs of the poorer people and to keep the services of the state running, there is no way that countries can divert anything like two years' income to debt repayment. These ratios indicate that the debt is unpayable because of the absence of resources with which to make repayment, and that this situation is in no sense a self-balancing one. These low-income countries can only get out of the well of debt when a rope is thrown to them from above.

It must, however, be emphasised that even those low-income countries, whose ratio of debt to GNP is below 70%, and of debt to XGS is below 200%, require remission of all or nearly all the outstanding debt. The diversion of any substantial sum from their export earnings to debt repayment would be a theft from the poor, for in such low-income countries, all or almost all the export earnings are needed for essential services and help to the poor, as well as for the necessary maintenance of the state. It would be unjust to forgive the entire debt of a country such as Zambia, which owes 539% of XGS and 216% of a year's GNP, while leaving intact the debt of a country such as Uganda, which owes 61% of GNP, Nepal, which owes 53% of GNP, or Burkina Faso and Bangladesh, which both owe 51% of GNP. We must forgive all or nearly all of the stock of debt of low-income countries (which meet the criteria of determination to institute sound financial management, democratic government and civil rights in future), and this means cancelling the debts of countries in this category, which owe relatively small percentages of GNP or XGS, and not just concentrating on those whose debt stocks are defined by the World Bank as unsustainable. This crucially important distinction is further examined in Chapter 5.

There is a radical difference of objective between the World Bank and Jubilee 2000. For the World Bank, the debt problem is one of how they can enable debtor countries to keep up their debt service payments, while for those concerned with the eradication of poverty, it is a question of how we can liberate these countries from the burden of the debt itself. Instead of the banker's perspective of the World Bank, which seeks to preserve repayment of its loans, we must adopt the people's perspective of helping poorer countries, to be relieved of the entire burden of past unpayable debt.

Notes

1   The population of these countries comprise most of 'The bottom 40% of mankind', of whom Robert McNamara, at that time the President of the World Bank, spoke in his landmark address in Nairobi. He pointed out that this segment of the human family were 'unable to enjoy the improvements in income and welfare of modern science and technology, nor could their basic needs be met.' (Morris Miller, *Debt & The Environment*, p.19).

2   *'Overcoming Human Poverty'*, UNDP Poverty Report, 1998, p. 16.

3   Most of them in Jinnah's house, later occupied by the writer when he was British Deputy High Commissioner in Western India, 1974-7.

4   Tony Thirlwall (1990) *'How To Escape The Debtors Prison'*, Foreign Focus, No.23-24, March/April 1990.

5   Harold Lever *'Debt & Danger - The World Financial Crisis'*: New York, Atlantic Monthly Press, 1986.

6   International Development Committee of House of Commons on 'Debt Relief': London, HMSO, 5th May 1998.

7   Professor Sir Hans Singer in 'Proclaim Liberty', Eldred Willey and Janet Banks (eds.): London, Christian Aid, June 1998, p.36.

2 Genesis of Jubilee 2000 - the Beginning of a Debt Campaign under the Name and Pattern of Jubilee

Biblical Paradigm of Forgiveness of Debt

The genesis of Jubilee 2000 was like this. In 1990, like many other people, including Bill Peters, who unbeknown to me had been lobbying in the Foreign Office and elsewhere for debt remission since 1983, I was acutely aware of the terrible effects of the vast backlog of unpayable debt of the governments of poorer countries. This debt has the effect of imposing a crushing burden of debt service, diverting resources desperately needed for government services to the mass of poor people in low-income countries. It also imposes a great psychological burden, comparable to the situation in which I should be if I owed £2 million and knew that, however much I earned, this would only go to pay a fraction of my debt. I should lose confidence and initiative, live from day to day and be always looking for donors to help me out of my ever recurring financial troubles. The endless cycle of rescheduling debt, which I could not pay when it was due, would absorb and exhaust my energies. To be in a position of owing unpayable debt is a kind of slavery. It is not, it is true, quite as vicious as the physical slavery which was abolished in the British Empire on 1st August 1834, after a long campaign involving very many people and headed by William Wilberforce and after his retirement in 1824, by my great great great grandfather Thomas Fowell Buxton; but it is almost equally dispiriting.

It is intolerable that we should go into the next millennium in a situation where the poorer quarter of the human family owes totally unpayable debt to creditors in the richer quarter. In a fair world, monies should flow from rich to poor to help to alleviate their sufferings. The debt burden has been producing a considerable reverse flow, thus nullifying much of the effect of aid. On the other hand, bankers and governments have a genuine case when they insist that the general principle of the honouring of debts must be preserved. Clearly, there is only one way to resolve this apparent contradiction. An incremental process of debt remission would create the assumption that there is remission on demand; a country, part of whose debts had been recently forgiven, would come and ask for further forgiveness. We should never attain the sense of new beginning which is a prime need of poorer countries, especially in Africa.

We need, therefore, to have a special time by which or in connection with which, a radical one-off debt remission is to be made for each country. This debt remission is not to be repeated for a long period. It is essential therefore that the remission should be the occasion for a new beginning for the country concerned, in which self-reliance, productive energy and honest financial management will replace the corruptions and extravagance of the past. Our conditionalities, which must be demanded for the remission, are those which are for the benefit of the country concerned rather than of its creditors; they are to ensure that the country once released from a backlog of unpayable debt does not fall into the same situation again. Any new debts entered into by a country whose debts have been forgiven in the Jubilee, must be of a productive kind and within the capacity of the country to repay in the short to medium term. These conditionalities are to be liberative and the remission must be made a kind of second independence in which the country takes new life upon itself. I took the name of Jubilee as a short-hand description of this kind of radical debt remission, associated with a 'special time' and not to be repeated (if at all) for a number of years.

The book of Leviticus Chapter 25 in the Bible gives us a pattern of Jubilee. The Ram's Horn was to be sounded on the day of Yom Kippur in the Jubilee year to proclaim liberty in the land, the returning of land to its proper owners, if it had been alienated, and the freeing of those within the Jewish community, who had been enslaved through unpayable debt. The consequence of owing unpayable debt in ancient Israel was to be compelled to serve the creditor without remuneration until the coming of the next Jubilee. These servants, however, were not to be treated like slaves, as people of other races could then be treated by Jews in Israel. The name Jubilee comes from Yobel, 'the sound of the Ram's Horn'. It was a Holy Time of restoration of the just economic order and the proper relations between all the members of the community of Israel, which was holy to God. Professor S.E. Finer in his classic work the 'History of Government From the Earliest Times' describes the unique nature of the Jewish political system. The central event in Jewish history was the occasion when the entire community covenanted itself to God. The whole community was sacred and therefore any breach in the just relations which should exist between different members was a serious offence against God's holiness:

> The entire community had covenanted itself to God at Mount Sinai. This is the central event in Jewish history. Everything else was elaboration and commentary. At Sinai, God gave out his law; it was written down and the people covenanted to obey it. [1]

Jubilee is part of the great Jewish pattern in the Torah, from which at a later date there developed the doctrine of Tikkun Olam (repairing the world). Part of the law related to the periodic sweeping away of inequalities and injustices that had accrued over the years through debt. This imposition of suffering upon the poor was an offence to God's holiness. The Biblical period between Jubilees was every 49 years, in the Jubilee provision in Leviticus 25, or every 7 years, in the debt remission command in Deuteronomy 15. The idea of Jubilee occurs, of course, both in the Old Testament and in the New. The New Testament in particular is full of the doctrine of the need to forgive unpayable debt. For our purposes of dealing with the present burden of debt, we need not necessarily be committed to any exact period nor even a doctrine of recurring Jubilees, for the Biblical model is a pattern or paradigm to guide us in our dilemma; it is not an exact template laying down mandatory detail.

I reached the idea of Jubilee through reason (this is often the way that Providence guides us to valuable conclusions). I was, of course, aware of the rich Biblical tradition of Jubilee, but I used the concept as a kind of shorthand for the necessary remission of past, inert debt which alone could clear the ground for a new beginning. If there had not been a resonant doctrine of Jubilee already in the Biblical text, we should have had to invent one. 'We come', as Auden put it in another context, 'because our open eyes can see no other way'.

In 1990, I prepared a general paper to give to Frank Judd, Director of Oxfam, on ways to help poorer nations, and included in it the idea of a Jubilee debt remission. I wrote to my friend, Michael Schluter, the Director of the Jubilee Centre in Cambridge, enclosing a copy. He replied, welcoming the paper, suggesting that it might be a good basis from which to challenge the problem of the unpayable debt of poorer countries, and suggesting that we should take the coming year 2000AD as the 'acceptable year' - the year with which to connect the one-off debt remission. I accepted his valuable suggestion, and the student group working with me for Jubilee agreed with the title of 'Jubilee 2000'. At this time, the year 2000 seemed to be a long way off like low hills on the far horizon. It is only recently that the Jubilee year has come to dominate our view. Michael Schluter's contribution to the birth of Jubilee 2000 was confined to the use of the year 2000 itself and not to the use of the Jubilee pattern for debt remission, which I had already adopted and included in my letter to him. Michael Schluter later, when the campaign was already under way, spoke several times in support of Jubilee 2000.

The year 2000 has a rather different significance for other religious and secular groups, but for all of us it is a most important date in the 'common era.' For Christians and for a number of other people, it is a kind of 'Kairos' time. Among philosophers and theologians, the doctrine of Kairos time (as opposed to 'Chronos' time) is the special or appropriate day or year when we can achieve things, which would be well-nigh impossible in the ordinary moments of Chronos time - 'the petty pace from day to day down to the last syllable of recorded time'. Kairos time is like a mountain top, very different from the lowlands of ordinary Chronos time. A year becomes special, or Kairos time, because we make it so, not because the earth goes round the sun on a different orbit or at a different speed. Archbishop Carey writes of a Kairos moment as one that 'speaks profoundly of hope, of God breaking into ordinary time and filling it with His presence. It is a Jubilee moment in which a new start can be made'.[2] The New Testament is full of such phrases as 'the time has come' or 'in the fullness of time' It proclaims a kind of theology of time when new possibilities are opened for mankind.

The year 2000 will be, for many of us, a special year when we shall rejoice. It is appropriate that at such a time we should also be generous to our fellow human beings. Joy and consciousness of common identity go hand in hand. Schiller's 'Ode to Joy' which is the theme song of the European Community, starts with the ecstatic proclamation:

> Freude, schöner Götterfunken,
> Tochter aus Elysium,
> wir betreten feuertrunken
> Himmliche dein Heiligthum.

(Joy beautiful spark of the divine, Daughter of Elysium, let us enter drunk with fire, Heavenly one, into your temple). It goes on to describe how joy brings brotherhood:

> Deine Zauber binden wieder,
> Was die Mode streng getheilt;

Alle Menschen werden Bruder,
Wo dein sanfter Flugel weilt.

(Your magic binds together again what custom has so strongly divided. All men become brothers where your gentle wing beats). The poem goes on with a general affirmation of the unity of mankind:

Seid umschlungen Millionen.
(Embrace one another oh ye millions).

The second part of the poem follows from the first, for the concept of joy implies and gives rise to the concept of love. It is hard to see, however, how the millions can truly embrace when the poorer part owe unpayable debt to the richer!

Africa also responds from the bottom of its soul to the idea of joy. Archbishop Carey relates how one of his Sudanese friends said to him, 'Believe me, no child will be born unless he is surrounded by song. No man will die without being surrounded by song. This is how we turn our tragedy to triumph'.[3] The Archbishop concludes with the prayer, 'May the spirit of courage, determination and sheer joy fill all our hearts as we seek to fulfil all the expectations of Africa.' This joy, which we feel at the occasion of the start of the new millennium, would be spoilt for us if we knew that the poorest quarter of our human family were still enslaved in past unpayable debt, owed to creditors in the richer quarter, and that we were doing nothing about it.

The Jubilee also implies a great act of liberation. The song of the American Civil War has the refrain:

Hurrah, hurrah, we bring the Jubilee,
Hurrah, hurrah, the flag that makes you free.

I incorporated a similar concept into the 'Ballad of Jubilee', which I composed in 1984 to celebrate the 150th Anniversary of the abolition of slavery in the British Empire in 1834:

Sound, sound, sound, sound, sound the trump,
The trump of Jubilee.
This the day and this the way
That set the people free.
Through the first of nations [i.e., Britain] to repent

Of the sin of slavery.

The rich tradition of Jubilee into which we have keyed has resonance for people of all religious faiths, or of a secular belief in the unity of the human family and the need to help its poorer members. Jubilee has come in the tradition of the Church to symbolise three separate concepts merged into one vibrant whole. It means rejoicing as we see in the Latin word 'Jubilate' - rejoice. There was an old Latin word 'Jube' meaning a shout. This concept of a shout of joy has a separate etymological origin from the Hebrew word 'Yobbeh' and the similarity of sound is probably accidental; nonetheless, the Church has been able to bring together the concepts of joy, of the special year of rejoicing and of liberation into one vibrant whole in the concept of Jubilee.

The remission in Leviticus was announced by the blowing of the Ram's Horn, the Shoffar. This blast was known as Yobbeh and it was used to proclaim liberty throughout the land. The original Jubilee was, of course, only for Jews. Ours is for the whole human family. The biblical Jubilee referred to individual debt. Our Jubilee must deal with sovereign debt. Rabbi Hillel the famous Jewish scholar and teacher (60 BC to 10AD) relaxed the strict law of Jubilee through his doctrine of Prosbol making things easier for ordinary people; one is bound, however, to comment that anything that makes it easier for the creditor may make it hard for the debtor. This doctrine sprang from the fact that Jubilee in the Torah in Leviticus dealt with individual debt and Hillel was worried that the known approach of a Jubilee would stop people from lending.

Jubilee 2000 deals with sovereign debt of states and it is agnostic as to whether this Jubilee is to be a one off event, or whether it can be part of a regularly occurring pattern. The cut-off point, which I have taken, is 1995, five years before the Jubilee. All debt owed from before that cut-off point, plus any interest accruing on it up to the year of remission, is to be forgiven. The problem of disincentive for loans between this cut-off point and the year 2000 is not a very serious one, since the poorest countries to whom we envisage granting remission are at present almost 'unbankable' and unlikely to receive new loans until the old have been forgiven, and are thus unlikely to have received substantial loans between 1995 and 2000.

The Leviticus pattern of remission involved all debt. In Jubilee 2000 however, we seek only for the remission of unpayable debt. A debt is unpayable either because there is no money for the repayment, or because such repayment would impose suffering upon the poorer elements of the population, which no honourable creditor would seek to impose. The Jubilee also implied an ecological purpose, allowing the land to rest fallow and recover its fertility. The reason for the remission of debts is clearly and authoritatively stated in Deuteronomy 15, verse 2: 'It is the Lord's remission'.

Jubilee doctrine is part of Sabbath doctrine in the Old Testament, and Sabbath doctrine teaches opposites. There is a command to work and to avoid idleness, but there is also a command to set aside one special day in seven for the opposite. On that day, we are to devote ourselves to rest, recreation and worship, neither performing nor demanding unnecessary servile labour. Similarly, debt is, in general, to be honoured and the penalties for failure to repay debt were severe. The debtor had to perform unpaid labour for the creditor, until the year of Jubilee reversed this status and forgave the debt. In this way, the community of Israel avoided a continual build up of inequality and provided for a new beginning, when the redeemed community of Israel would re-establish its solidarity with one another in economic terms, and avoid injustice.

These provisions in the Jewish Torah have parallels in some other traditions in the ancient world. Solon in 594 BC at about the same time as the Jubilee legislation in Exodus, pronounced the cancellation of debt and the abolition of debt slavery in Athens. This seems to have been devised as a means of preserving the polity against popular unrest arising from the burden of debt. The act of release was a reform intended to preserve the political system, for Solon was a practical and cautious man as well as being an innovative lawgiver. This liberative act was graphically described by him as 'shaking off the burden'.[4] The Sumerian Prince Urukagina (see 2400 BC) decreed release to the people of Lagesh partly as a means of bolstering his own legitimacy. In the Babylonian kingdoms of Isin (2017-1794 BC) and Larsa (2025-1763 BC) new Kings marked their accession by issuing a partial debt amnesty.[5] The Jubilee in ancient Israel for the forgiveness of debts, the freeing of slaves and the restoration of land to its original holders is the most complete and liberative of all the examples.

Jesus launches his gospel message with a reference to Jubilee. In his first sermon in Nazareth, He quotes the passage in Isaiah Chapter 61 that speaks of the 'acceptable' year of the Lord, which He has been anointed to proclaim. This is a clear synonym for the Jubilee year. It is to be good news for the poor and liberation for the oppressed. It is to put an end to the injustices which oppress God's Holy people. In the vision of Leviticus and Isaiah, the Holy people were especially God's chosen people of Israel, but, as St. Paul has taught, the whole of the new faith community is now 'the New Israel'. We may therefore take it that anything that oppresses the poor anywhere is an offence against God's Holiness. This sermon is the most important, for Christians, of all the references to Jubilee in the Bible.

The expectation of Jubilee is enshrined in the great passage in Isaiah, which He read aloud:

> The spirit of the Lord is upon me, for He hath anointed me to preach good tidings to the poor, release to the captive, the giving of sight to the blind and the liberation of the oppressed; to proclaim the acceptable year of the Lord.

The pamphlet issued by CAFOD on Jubilee to celebrate its own 25 year anniversary in 1990, has pointed out that Jesus follows the text of Isaiah 61 as far as the phrase 'giving of sight to the blind' and then leaves it, before the verse 'to proclaim the day of vengeance of our God'. He goes instead to Isaiah 58 on proper fasting and quotes the command to proclaim liberation of the oppressed.

In applying this doctrine of remission, we have to find a formula which is indeed good tidings to the poor. It must surely imply a total or near-total remission for low-income countries, rather than the reduction of debt to sustainable levels as proposed by the World Bank. We should be surprised if the leader of our prayers in church were to ask God to forgive us 55% of our sins or debts and to reschedule the rest, while reducing them to a sustainable level! The import of this vital principle is that the remission we must seek in the Jubilee 2000 campaign is that of the whole stock of debt itself and not just of the excessive yearly cost of servicing it. Bankers look to the means to ensure the regular payment of instalments due to them. We must look at the extinction of the unpayable debt itself, which also implies the remission of instalments of debt service due each year.

We may find that it is necessary for us to consent to leave a small proportion of the stock of debt unforgiven, and to leave the debtor country to repay this small proportion. This must, however, be small enough for the country to repay, within the short-term, without undue suffering. We can therefore use the phrase 'the total or near-total forgiveness of debt'. The advantage of leaving this small proportion for the debtor country to repay would be that it would make it easier to negotiate with creditors, and that the fact of having participated in a small way in their own liberation from debt, may make the debtor country value the remission all the more.

The Biblical pattern offers its own special approach to debt remission. The Lord's Prayer in St. Matthew's Gospel uses the Greek word 'opheleimata' (debts): 'forgive us our debts as we forgive our debtors'. It is only in St. Luke's Gospel that the Greek word 'hamartiai' (trespasses or sins) is used. The literal translation from the Greek is as follows: [6]

και αφες ημιν τα οφειληματα, ημων,
ως και ημεις αφηκαμεν τοις οφειλεταις ημων

Matthew 6, 12
    'And forgives us our debts
    as we have forgiven our debtors' (past tense);

και αφες ημιν τας αμων,
και γαρ αυτοι αφιομεν παντι οφειλοντι ημιν

Luke 11, 4
    'And forgive us our sins
    For we also ourselves forgive everyone owing to us' (present tense)[7]

Furthermore, the basic mystery of redemption through the death of the Redeemer is often spoken of in terms of the remission of an otherwise unpayable debt. It is true that 'the things which are seen are temporal and the things that are unseen are eternal'. The forgiveness which we are offered by God is in the realm of eternal reality, while the forgiveness of debt which we are bidden to offer to others relates to the temporal and the physical. However, we are enjoined again and again in scripture to remember that faithfulness in stewardship of temporal and material matters is required from us, to fit us for the reception of the eternal riches in the spiritual sphere.

In the parables also, we have a picture of generous remission of unpayable debt. The servant who owes 10,000 talents and asks for rescheduling, i.e., time to pay, is at once forgiven the whole debt by his King (for it is the nature of Kings to be able to give total Royal forgiveness). Through his stupidity and greed, the servant fails to forgive a fellow servant, who owes him a much smaller sum, faces the royal anger at this injustice, and finds his original debt reimposed by the King. In another parable, Jesus tells Simon the Pharisee of a moneylender who had two debtors. Because they had not the means to pay, the moneylender forgave them both. This is related in a matter of fact way as the natural and proper thing to do with unpayable debts. The one who was forgiven most, loved most. The money lender in the parable was far more generous than the IMF or the World Bank!

There is no doubt a general moral principle of conduct that someone who owes a debt and has the means to pay it, should do so, either immediately or according to the timetable agreed when the debt was incurred. Without this principle, it would be difficult to have proper financial transactions, in cases where full cash down payment cannot be made at the time of purchase. The New Testament, however, propounds a second and complementary doctrine of a moral imperative to forgive debts, which cannot be paid. This emerges clearly from the examples that I have quoted above and from the whole tenor of New Testament teaching on forgiveness and the law of love. It applies both to debt instalments that are due and also pre-eminently to the forgiving of the whole stock of unpayable debt. The failure to do so places both material and psychological burdens on the debtor, which no honourable person should impose.

The New Testament parallel, which I have outlined here, differs from our situation in one respect. The sin which has been committed in the cases mentioned in the New Testament is entirely the fault of the sinner and not that of God. In the case of the unpayable debt of poorer nations, however, the fault is on both sides. The creditors are guilty of pressing excessive loans on borrowers in the wake of the dramatic oil price rise after the Yom Kippur War in 1973. They are also guilty of imposing excessive rates of interest on the loans. The third source of blame on the creditor nations is their failure to do anything to prevent the terms of trade from shifting dramatically against Third World producers. This caused a great deal of the depreciation in their balance of payments. One may say that this was due to the unavoidable consequences of a commodity market, where there was oversupply and where the demand for most tropical primary products is inelastic. However, it should have been possible to find some way to stabilise the market and to put a floor in it without putting in a ceiling. The actions of the IMF, as explained in the section by Bill Peters, exacerbated the situation by insisting that Third World producers, who were in serious debt, should increase their exports of tropical produce.

There is also guilt on the part of many leaders of poorer countries and their governments, which have often been corrupt and extravagant. To some extent they have been encouraged in this profligate course by the governments of creditor nations, who have continued to give them loans, even when they were behaving like irresponsible tyrants, wasting the assets of their people. Sometimes, they were persuaded to buy arms which their country did not require for its essential security purposes. It is a fruitless task to seek to apportion the balance of blame. Governments of rich and poor countries are all guilty, and we need a Jubilee remedy where, like Laertes and Hamlet in the end of Shakespeare's play, we can 'exchange forgiveness'.[8] We must also bend our concerted efforts to achieve a new beginning.

The duty of forgiving unpayable debts is further reinforced if those debts are largely the result of overdue interest, as is the case with debts owed to many moneylenders, both on the individual and the national level. The taking of interest is strictly forbidden in the Muslim tradition, and the Holy Koran has many verses proclaiming the punishments which will befall those who impose oppressive interest on debtors. In the modern world, Muslims have found it difficult to follow this rigid prohibition exactly, but have made attempts through Islamic banking to substitute a principle of shared profit for one of an obligation to pay a given rate of interest.

The Christian Church also proclaimed an almost equally rigid prohibition of interest for the first 15 or 16 centuries of its existence, as R.H. Tawney's study of 'Religion and the Rise of Capitalism' points out. Economic necessity, as well as human greed, induced Christians in the modern period to connive at the charging of interest and finally to remove the prohibition altogether. It would take too long to examine the general principle, but it is clear from humanitarian as well as religious criteria, that excessive rates of interest charged to the poor are to be condemned. As we shall show in Chapter 13 on future developments, we may be able to devise a formula to provide for the conversion of a portion of interest payments into repayments of principal, where the cumulative total of interest paid on a loan to a poorer country has already exceeded half the original principal of the loan.

The presence of a large interest element in the unpayable debt makes it all the more imperative to forgive the stock of past unpayable debt. For instance, between 1985 and 1992, the debt of developing countries as a whole rose from $990 billion to $1,510 billion. During that period, just under $500 billion was paid by Third World debtors to creditors in the richer part of the world as interest. Furthermore, just over $200 billion of the $500 billion debt increase was due to unpaid interest.[9] There is a clear moral duty to rescue poorer countries from the treadmill of interest payments. They are like people with weak hearts trying to go the wrong way up a moving staircase. No wonder so many indebted poor countries suffer from the financial equivalent of a heart attack.

It is interesting to note that in the Holy Koran also, the merit of debt forgiveness to those who cannot pay is described. In verse 279 of the second chapter of the Koran (that called Bakara, or 'The Cow'), it is said:

> If your debtor has difficulty in paying, give him time until it is easier, but, if only you knew, it is best for you to forgive him for the sake of 'Sadaka'.

Sadaka is best translated both by our word 'charity' and by our word 'justice'.

Notes

1   S.E. Finer 'Ancient Monarchies and Empires', Vol.2 in *'The History of Government from the Earliest Times'*: Oxford, OUP, 1998, p. 238.
2   George Carey, Archbishop of Canterbury, 'Chains Around Africa, Crisis or Hope for the New Millennium', in *'Proclaim Liberty'*: London, Christian Aid, 1998, p. 24.
3   op. cit., p. 20.
4   I am indebted to my colleague, Gerald Nussbaum of the Classics Department, Keele University, for this reference.
5   Dr. Pat Logan, *'The Biblical Jubilee, Political Economy and Christian Realism,'* op.cit., 1998, p. 58.
6   I am indebted to Mr. David Simcock, a fellow member of the congregation of St. Philip and St. James Church, Milton, for this information.
7   I am indebted to my colleague, Gerald Nussbaum, of the Classics Department, Keele University, for this reference, and R. Wallace, Head of the Classics Department, for the typing of the Greek text of The Lord's Prayer.
8   William Shakespeare, *'Hamlet'*, Act v, Scene II, line 340, Laertes who has grazed Hamlet with a poisoned sword, in a fencing bout in revenge for his father's death, has just been grazed with the same poisoned weapon after an accidental exchange of swords. He absolves the dying Hamlet with the words 'exchange forgiveness with me noble Hamlet. Mine and my father's death come not upon thee nor thine on me'.
9   See M.J. Dent *'Jubilee 2000 and Lessons of the World Debt Tables'*, 1993, p. 12.

3 The History of the Growth of the Jubilee 2000 Campaign

The Beginning of Jubilee 2000

In 1990, there was at this time a dedicated group of Keele students, among whom Simon Flint was one of the leading figures, working for the interests of poorer nations under the title 'Third World First' and 'Oxfam'. I had spoken to them at their request on the general theme of ways to help poorer nations. I covered in equal emphasis the three subjects of aid, trade and debt. We decided that in order not to be a pale copy of major aid charities, we needed to have a special emphasis to contribute to the general campaign for the eradication of poverty in the Third World.[1]

I persuaded them that Jubilee 2000 would be a suitable title for us. We resisted the suggestion that the name should be 'Millennium 2000', since this was too close to the unrealistic expectations of the millennarians, who have arisen at various key dates in human history to proclaim the immediate arrival of a totally new order of society. I was acutely aware of the fact that those who set out to change everything usually end up by changing nothing. Like the anti-slavery movement in Britain, we needed to choose one objective on which to concentrate our somewhat slender forces. Having captured that objective, we could go on to further victories in the fight against poverty in the world. 'Ce n'est que le premier pas qui compte'. The first step is all important, not because it alone suffices to get us to the goal, but because it transforms our endeavour from the field of exhortation and rhetoric to that of action. Many other steps will then follow the first. One cannot assume that the achievement of the Jubilee of debt remission will bring in a new heaven and a new earth, but we do have a real duty to work to achieve at least one practical and important victory for humanity, as we enter the next millennium.

From this small beginning, at an evening function in a lecture room at Keele, and from the parallel efforts of Bill Peters (who had also campaigned on the debt issue), of which I was at that time unaware, grew the campaign which 8 years later brought 70,000 people on to the streets of Birmingham, forming a ring of hands around the leaders of the G8, to ask for debt remission and a new beginning. The campaign which we started has sought to bring together the academic study of the phenomenon of unpayable debt, owed by governments of poorer countries and the practical programme of liberation, that springs from the concept of Jubilee and the results of this study. It is good to be able to bring thought and action together. There is a particular power in an idea whose time has come. In the Biblical analogy of the Kingdom, a single mustard seed, the smallest of many seeds, can be the origin of a great tree which gives shelter and benefit to many people.

At that time (February 1990), I wrote and circulated a short paper entitled, 'Why We Are Founding Jubilee 2000'.[2] I began:

> A movement to be successful and to effect some great and important improvement in human affairs must have three characteristics. It must be bold and inspire the imagination; it must have a single great idea and a simple purpose that can be easily grasped. And finally, it must start from small beginnings and spread to become a great movement, with many branches and advocates with access to publicity and means of influence upon government; it must build up expertise and distinguished leadership as it progresses. Those who start the movement may well not be those who lead it when it grows to larger dimensions. Since the purpose of the movement is to produce beneficial change and not to reflect credit upon its originators, this is altogether fitting and proper.
>
> Among the Tiv people in Nigeria, where I now have the honour to be a Chief with the title 'Asor-Tar-U-Tiv'; 'The One Who Heals the Land of Tiv' there is a saying 'Or Soron Tar A Ye Ga' - the one who heals the land never eats, i.e., if he is looking for personal honour he will not succeed in his high task.

I went on to point out that:

> The duty of richer countries to help the poor is beyond dispute. It springs from the common identity of the human race, of which we have become more and more aware, especially as we see the whole world, like a fairly small thing, through the eyes of the astronauts. It is a categorical imperative which we must obey and a duty which we cannot avoid.

I pointed out that many low-income indebted countries such as Nigeria, having undertaken an extremely harsh regime of structural adjustment causing great suffering to masses of the poor, are like a man giving himself a heart attack by climbing the wrong way up a moving staircase and yet, at the end of several hours of effort, he is no further up than when he started, owing as much or more than he did at the beginning of this harsh process. I appealed to governments and IFIs to break their hitherto invariable practice and to agree to once and for all write off of the debts due to them. I pointed out that if nothing is done to remit these debts, the poorer nations themselves will increasingly get together and begin to renege on them, provoking in turn sanctions from the lender nations, which will set off a bitter and destructive dispute between rich and poor, instead of the sense of unity of the whole of humanity which we seek to achieve as we enter the new millennium in AD 2000. If only we have eyes to see, it is in the common interest of richer and poorer nations to work together to achieve this remission.

I pointed out that the palliative measures so far adopted would merely put off the evil day: ' it is a mere rescheduling of debt. It is like the situation of the villager in debt to the moneylender, who lends him more and more in order to make his overdue payments, and so entangles him increasingly in unpayable debt'.

The student support remained strong for some three years and was invaluable at the inception of the campaign. For the next three years, after the key student activists had left Keele, I was working almost full-time on Jubilee 2000 having retired from my academic work in July 1990 at the age of 65. I received great help and encouragement from the Politics Department at Keele University, who lent me part of a small room in which to work. It was hard pounding and initially I was acutely aware of the fact that though many people were sympathetic, I was working on too small a scale to achieve the great goal which I had set. I wrote to every MP and received a number of letters of support. I wrote to every High Commissioner and Ambassador accredited to Britain to explain the object of the campaign and to seek their support in getting a resolution through the UN General Assembly asking that the year 2000 should be declared a year of Jubilee for the forgiveness of unpayable debt, and received several enthusiastic responses.

I spoke at the Liberal Democrat Party's Conference in Blackpool in 1990, proposing the remission of all the debt of low-income countries by the year 2000. Looking at the bird of freedom, which is the symbol of the party, I declared:

> 'let the bird soar into the new millenium carrying the incomparable gift of freedom to the poorer nations of the earth'.

The amendment was passed with acclamation and remained part of the party's policy for the next six years until it was removed by a new policy document. However, Dr Jenny Tonge MP, the party's Spokeswoman on

International Development, has rendered yeoman service to the cause of debt remission in the House of Commons Select Committee and elsewhere.

I corresponded with Bank Chairmen and received particularly helpful replies from Sir Jeremy Morse, Chairman of Lloyds. This led me to buy Lloyds Bank ordinary shares and to attend the annual shareholders' meeting, to ask if the Chairman could examine Lloyds' 'problem country debt', to determine which parts of it could be repaid by the governments concerned, and which parts were either physically incapable of repayment, or only repayable at a social cost which no honourable banking institution would seek to impose. I received a most courteous reply from the Chairman, who told me that he shared my objectives but was not sure how they were to be achieved. He claimed that any country obtaining debt remission would find it difficult to obtain new loans in future. This is not always true. It is easier for a bank to lend to a country whose debt has been forgiven than to one that still owes an unpayable residue of past debt. I also received an encouraging letter from Lord Runcie, former Archbishop of Canterbury, who happened to be present at the meeting to propose a vote of thanks to the Bank's staff. I wrote to religious leaders of all denominations and was very pleased to be invited to attend the Debt Crisis Network, where both secular and religious NGOs working for amelioration and remission of the burden of the debt of poorer countries met informally every three months to exchange ideas.

My colleague at Keele University, Gerald Nussbaum and I, lobbied Neil Kinnock, Leader of the Opposition by post, to seek for a reference to debt remission in his forthcoming speech to the Overseas Development Institute, on the Labour programme up to the year 2000. We received a most generous greeting from David Clarke in Neil Kinnock's office stating that he appreciated the Jubilee 2000 campaign. Neil Kinnock made some reference to the need for debt remssion in his speech, but did not explicitly mention Jubilee 2000, although he sent us a letter of thanks for the way we had put the case.

Meanwhile, unbeknown to me, Bill Peters CMG, a former High Commissioner in Malawi and subsequently in his retirement, Chairmen of the Society for the Propagation of the Gospel, had also been working on the debt issue. He had put forward the case in his valedictory dispatch in 1983 as retiring High Commissioner. Bill Peters and I have been for many years fellow members of the South Atlantic Council. In 1993, I joined with him in a joint Jubilee 2000 campaign; he accepted my invitation to be Co-Chairmen with me. This followed a conference at Tirley Garth MRA Centre on 'Unselfish Motivation in Economics', to which he had invited me and for which I had prepared a paper comparing the Jubilee 2000 campaign with the 'Holy Cause' of the campaign in the nineteenth century to abolish slavery in the British Empire. Bill Peters' paper dealt with a number of issues connected with unselfishness in economics, but did not concentrate on debt remission or mention Jubilee except in reference to my paper. He referred, however, to my paper and wrote

> Beyond that a form of state altruism like a biblical year of the Jubilee, possibly fixed for 2000A.D might be possible. Martin Dent's paper goes into this in detail. He compares the debt issue with last century's slave trade issue: abolition of that looked impossible before middle-class and church opinion was raised. I hope that a tide is running which may sweep in the changes which Martin suggests could be achieved by the end of the century.

Jacob Bowman-Larsen, Director of the Centre for New Economics in Norway, said in his paper for the conference,

> A third element could be Martin Dent's Jubilee 2000 campaign. That campaign should be a world-wide campaign, which could have tremendous effect and could easily mobilise large groups of people. His message is easy to understand.[3]

Bill Peters is therefore rightly considered to be a Co-Founder of Jubilee 2000 with me.

From 1993 onwards, we worked together with great effect. I persuaded him to join the Debt Crisis Network. Bill was able to win substantial funding for the campaign from various trusts. Through his contacts with decision makers we were able greatly to increase the tempo.

In 1996, we were joined by Isabel Carter of Tear Fund, who helped us to win further financial backing from donors and to distribute 90,000 copies of our first leaflet through Tear Fund. William Reid, a retired banker, joined us and rendered invaluable service. A charitable trust called Jubilee 2000 and a campaigning company was set up by Isabel Carter, Tim Greene, William Reid, Ann Pettifor, Bill Peters and Martin Dent. Our relations with the Debt Crisis Network became progressively closer, and partly through the efforts of Ed Mayo, its Chairman, we eventually merged, appointing as our co-ordinator Ann Pettifor, who had been the network's co-ordinator and lobbyist. She eventually became the Director of the Jubilee campaign. As a result of this great infusion of talent and skill, the Jubilee 2000 campaign took off and became a most influential movement. The Jubilee 2000 office in lower Marsh Street, became an effective dynamo of the campaign and helped to spread its influence in this country, and in 40 other countries which have just founded their own Jubilee 2000 committees, which met recently in Rome. Adrian Lovett, the Deputy Director, Nick Buxton who deals with Jubilee committees at home and abroad, Barbara Withstandley the administrator, and the other members of staff - Marlene Barrett, Eva Otero, Angela Travis, John Garrett, Karen Joyner, and the Africa team Kofi Mawuli Klu, Toure Moussa, Mesmin Grazaley and Affiong Southey - have all given yeoman service, as has Charles Aniagolu, Communications Officer, and many dedicated volunteers.

In 1997, the management of the campaign was transferred to a coalition of many NGOs, both secular and religious, with Ed Mayo as the Chairman. This is the change, which Bill and I had suggested some two years previously in a paper on the need to create a coalition for Jubilee. We realised that the individual members of the Jubilee 2000 campaign could not by themselves bring in the great change for which we sought. It was urgently necessary to enlist the help of organisations bigger than ourselves, who were working for the eradication of poverty and unpayable debt in the Third World. We used the analogy of an army of Highlanders in the seventeenth century. They could be enlisted in a great common cause, but would need to fight each in his or her clan identity and with their own clan head. This sort of organisation requires considerable skill to create and to maintain, but it has great potential for mass mobilisation and contact with key decision makers. As it has turned out the coalition has given the campaign access to the resources of bodies far more influential than we could have been on our own. It is a development greatly to be welcomed. The coalition was launched in a large meeting in the Jubilee Room in the House of Commons. Bill Peters and I, to whom particular tribute was made as the original founders, were created the two Vice-Presidents. The President is Michael Taylor, formerly Director of Christian Aid and now President of the Selly Oak Colleges, Ed Mayo, the Director of the New Economics Foundation, is the Chairman. The campaign has had remarkable support from the whole community, secular and religious. Christian Aid has been particularly vigorous in support of Jubilee 2000.

In our original committee we rejected a proposal that the name should be changed from 'Jubilee 2000' to 'Debt-Free 2000', and, subsequently, we have derived enormous momentum from the support of all the churches. They have acted like the leaven in the lump to help produce the present extensive level of support for Jubilee 2000. They have been effective inspirers of action in the secular field and have brought to the campaign a dimension of the call for justice and compassion.

The Catholic Church has had a long tradition of support for a more just deal for poorer nations, and CAFOD[4] had already produced an excellent pamphlet on Jubilee, to which reference has already been made. Furthermore, the 2000th Anniversary of the Word made flesh and the birth of the Redeemer has obvious meaning for that Church. In his Apostolic letter, Tertio Millennio Adveniente, section 51 (The Coming Third Millennium), the Pope asked for the millennium to be a time when Christians should

> Raise their voice on behalf of all the poor of the world proposing the Jubilee as an appropriate time to give thought, among other things, to reducing substantially if not cancelling outright, the international debt which seriously threatens the future of many nations.

When I had the opportunity of submitting a written question to Cardinal Etchegaray (the Cardinal formerly in charge of justice and peace, and now also of the Catholic millennium celebrations) at a conference in Swanwick, I expressed my appreciation for this passage, but pointed out that we must do more than just think about debt remission; we must work for it with the same vigour that the anti-slavery campaigners in the last century fought for their goal. In his 1996 Pope Paul the Sixth memorial lecture for The Tablet, Cardinal Etchegaray described how the commitment to resolve the question of international debt has become for many 'the barometer to measure the level of solidarity present in today's world'.

The Anglican Church has given equally wholehearted support to the Jubilee concept, passing unanimously a resolution of commitment to Jubilee 2000 at the General Synod, and introducing a major motion on Jubilee 2000 to the Lambeth Conference later in the year. The support from Bishops and from congregations has been overwhelming. The Free Churches also have expressed their support through their governing bodies and have been most active and effective in the campaign. The leading role of the churches in this matter was further emphasised by the fact that when James Wolfensohn, the President of the World Bank, came to Britain recently, he made a point of having a long discussion with the religious leaders - Cardinal Hume, Archbishop Carey and the Free Church leaders. In this campaign, the church has a special role of leadership. Therefore we welcome the headline in the leading article in the Church Times, (6th December, 1996), 'After 2000 years, it is time to think big.'

In the excellent pamphlet on A Chance to Start Again, prepared for the Churches Together In England by a committee of an Anglican Bishop, a Catholic Bishop and the Free Church President, we are advised what we should do to celebrate the great Jubilee of the year 2000 which presents us with the 'challenge of the time.' [5] The booklet specifically asks for action to remove unjust debts. This is the feeling of very many people as we approach the millennium. We are in the position described by James Russell Lowell in his poem 'The Present Crisis' (1845):

> Once to every man and nation
> Comes the moment to decide,
> In the strife of truth and falsehood
> For the good or evil side.
> Then that choice goes by forever
> Twixt that darkness and that light,
> Then it is the brave man chooses
> And the coward stands aside
> And the multitude make virtue
> Of the faith they had denied.

Bill Peters and I have addressed many meetings, large and small, in various places. One of them was organised by Moral Re-Armament (MRA), Christian Aid and the World Development Movement in the Westminster Theatre London. I also addressed two meetings of the Caux Assembly, on Jubilee 2000 in successive years. MRA have been only one of many organisations who have supported Jubilee 2000, but their enthusiastic support has been most valuable.

Meanwhile, Ann Pettifor and her staff of over 12 paid and unpaid helpers have established an office in Lower Marsh Street, London, and by their Herculean efforts, have given a new dimension of effectiveness to the campaign, making use of professional advice and public relations techniques, as well as entering into dialogue with government and International Financial Institutions. The World Bank have been courteous and informative, but there is still a wide gap between our positions on debt remission. We had a similarly courteous and informative meeting with senior officials of the Export Credit and Guarantee Department at their head quarters in Harbour Tower. We prepared a thorough study of the lessons of the ECGD annual reports and accounts.

The Anglican Bishops' meeting in the Lambeth Conference in July and August 1998 made a point of including a special section and a day's plenary debate on the Christian duty of debt remission for poorer countries. James Wolfensohn, the President of the World Bank, who has a close relation or friendship with Archbishop Carey, flew over specially from Washington D.C. to address the plenary session. The argument with the World Bank is no longer on the principle of debt remission, which they now accept, but on the conditions, the extent and the number of countries to whom it should be granted. The bishops appointed a special committee under Bishop Peter Selby of Worcester to concentrate its attention on the debt issue, which it has made a major part of its conference report and of its continuing activity.[6]

The campaign is now entering a new phase with a high profile to mobilise the necessary opinion to win victory by the end of the year 2000. The Jubilee 2000 campaign is essentially connected with the whole year 2000, just as the Jewish Jubilee was concerned with 'The Acceptable Year of the Lord'. The Jubilee was announced on the day of Yom Kippur and it lasted for one year. Our Jubilee badly needs the extra propulsion of the enthusiasms that will be released during the year 2000. Strictly speaking, although the early chronologists may well have got the year of the Lord's birth wrong, it is the 2000th Christmas that we should be celebrating as the memorial of the birth of the Redeemer. This would mean that for us Christmas 2000 is at least as important as January 1st 2000. We must regard the Jubilee year as ending on January 1st 2001 and seek to achieve our goal of debt remission by that year. The staff in the Jubilee 2000 office have contracts which run until 31st December 2000.

However, since it is unlikely that we shall have achieved all of the necessary remission by that date, we must try to obtain by that time the promises of specific remission and continue the Jubilee 2000 campaign after the year 2001, until all these promises are redeemed. A great deal of dialogue is taking place with MPs and MEPs, with the Treasury, with the Department For International Development (DFID), with the World Bank in London and in Washington, with the UN and with the Commonwealth. There is a thriving Jubilee 2000 Group among MPs of all parties in the British Parliament, chaired by Bill Cash MP. It is impressive to see how MPs of different parties who disagree on many other issues combine in this great cause. I spoke recently at a meeting in Trentham Gardens chaired jointly by Bill Cash, the Conservative MP, and Mike Tappin, the Labour MEP. Partly as a result of the representations made to him, Gordon Brown, the Chancellor of the Exchequer, announced at the Commonwealth Finance Ministers Conference in Mauritius in September 1996, his commitment to a programme to remit the bilateral official debt of two-thirds of the poorer countries owed to Britain. He described this policy as the 'Mauritius Mandate', and later called a 'Mauritius seminar' of 25 representatives of churches and NGOs committed to helping poorer nations. In February 1999, he announced the remission of $30 billion, later increased to $50 billion.

On May 16th 1998, a public display of our concern with the plight of HIPCs took place in Birmingham, where the leaders of the G8 - USA, Canada, France, Germany, Italy, Britain, Japan and Russia - were meeting. Clare Short, on behalf of Tony Blair, received the 1.4 million signatures collected. By June 1999 the total has risen to 2.5 million in the UK and over 10 million from other countries. At the same time, a gathering of some 70,000 people held hands around the meeting place of the leaders of the G8 to demonstrate the ill effects of the chain of debt and the need to break it. This was a truly remarkable occasion. As Clare Short later said in a broadcast, it was one of the great days for Birmingham. The gathering was accompanied by a series of presentations by various speakers. Although the G8 leaders, for motives either of security or of timidity, left Birmingham on the day to go to Weston Park in Shropshire, Mr. Blair returned to meet the Jubilee President, Chairman and Director. The gathering was not a failure for it focused attention on the plight of the debtors. Five months later representatives of 40 Jubilee 2000 committees in other countries met for a conference in Rome.

In a broadcast in February 1999, Clare Short stated that the Birmingham meeting had had a real beneficial effect on debt negotiations. She subsequently became critical of some aspects of the Jubilee 2000 campaign. She addressed the General Synod of the Church of England and presented the case for the campaign to eradicate poverty. For this initiative she quite rightly received a standing ovation. However, she then went on to criticize the Jubilee campaign on three spurious grounds.[7] She said that remission to other low-income countries would be unfair to Bangladesh and to Malawi. As we have pointed out on page 17, it is most important that the creditors should forgive the debts of Bangladesh (and Burkina Faso), which are low-income countries, but owe respectively 56% and 51% of a year's GNP. The sums are a considerable burden for the two countries. As regards Malawi the Secretary of State got her facts wrong. She said that Malawi did not owe substantial debt. In fact, according to World Bank figures for 1996 Malawi's total debt stock is $2,312 million which is 485.6% of her year's export of goods and services. The total debt service for 1995 was $118 million and for 1996 $89 million. The World Bank of which Clare Short is a Governor, had inexplicably omitted Malawi from the list of 41 HIPC countries who are potentially deserving of debt remission. Malawi's position is examined in detail in Chapter 9. However, the World Bank/IMF website of March 3rd 1999 has just included Malawi among the 41 HIPC countries. This is a most welcome reversal of a patently unjust situation. It may well be partly a response to the arguments put forward by the Bishop of Birmingham and me, and may also owe something to the good offices of Clare Short.

She complained that Jubilee 2000 has asked for unilateral action on debt remission from the UK, rather than waiting for all the creditors to act together. This is a tactical matter; the debt owed bilaterally to UK is substantially less than that owed to Japan, Germany, USA and France. If we can more effectively persuade them to remit debt by waiting to act in unison, we should do this. If, however, we are more persuasive by giving a good example through our own actions, we should remit on a unilateral basis.

Her third criticism was that Jubilee 2000 would favour corrupt tyrants, who have no interest in helping the poor. The number of such corrupt tyrants still in power in poor countries is steadily reducing, but we have made it abundantly clear that the acceptance of a low-income country into the list of those potentially eligible for debt remission does not imply implementation of that remission, until its government has met certain vital conditionalities, as explained in Chapter 7. These include return to democratic civilian rule, maintenance of fundamental rights and the implementation of proper audit. Even the World Bank accepts such a rationale, it has included Myanmar (formerly Burma) in its list of 41 HIPC countries to be considered for debt remission, but has no doubt made remission dependent upon the end of the present corrupt and oppressive military dictatorship.

There has been strong resistance to radical debt remission for low-income countries from Germany and Japan. Recently, however, Heidmari Wieczorek-Zeul the Minister for International Development in the new Schröder government in Germany, announced that Germany would be implementing the Jubilee 2000 programme and would seek for a shorter waiting time for debtor countries, and a rate of remission above 80%. This support is most welcome, but it will require a great deal more pressure and persuasion to induce the G8 and the World Bank to change their stance. Clare Short announced after the Birmingham meeting that the G8 and the World Bank had agreed to extend to 21 the number of countries potentially qualifying for HIPC debt remission. The Birmingham demonstration failed to achieve immediate results, but it signalled the massive support for the campaign in both religious and secular circles. It is our task to turn this great potential into effective pressures and persuasion on political leaders and decision makers.

A further most gratifying personal letter of support came to Bill Peters and me from Kofi Annan, the Secretary-General of the UN, and a more detailed letter followed from Nitin Desai, the Under-Secretary-General for Social and Economic Affairs. He expressed his pleasure in the fact that 'the goal for which you have fought is now beginning to be realised', (through the Mauritius Mandate) and he asked us to continue our efforts for 'our shared goal'. We had originally sent a 2000 name petition from Keele University to the then Secretary-General of the UN, asking for the year 2000 to be declared a year of Jubilee. In their appreciative reply, the office of the Secretary-General advised us to approach a member government to propose this in the General Assembly. We still await suitable governments to propose a resolution to this effect in the General Assembly; the British Foreign Office who were approached by Bill Peters, have given us useful support, without as yet coming forward as a sponsor for the resolution.

We have also had warm support from the Secretary-General of the Commonwealth, Chief Emeka Anyaoku. Sir Leon Brittan, Vice-President of the European Commission, wrote to me asking for 20 copies of the pamphlet by M.J.Dent on Jubilee 2000 and Lessons of the Debt Tables to discuss with his ministerial colleagues at a meeting in Los Angeles in 1994. He subsequently wrote to say that he had asked his staff to research on Jubilee 2000 and other means of dealing with the debt problem.

Notes

1   In this decision I was helped by the advice of my colleague in the Department of Politics, Keele University, David Throup.
2   M.J. Dent. *'Why We are Founding Jubilee 2000'*, unpublished paper, Keele University, 1990.
3   The text of these two papers is given in *'Economics and Unselfishness Theory and Practical Application'*, Report of Consultation held at the Tirley Garth Conference Center 13-14 March 1993 (circulated but unpublished).
4   CAFOD Proclaim Jubilee, 1988.
5   Reverend Kathleen Richardson, Rt. Reverend Crispian Hollis, and Rt. Reverend Gavin Reid, *'A Chance to Start Again: 2000, Marking the Millennium'*: London, Churches Together in England, Easter 1996.
6   See the Lambeth Conference report.
7   *Times* article *'Clare Short Warns Against Quick Fix on Debt'* November 19th, 1998.

4 The Debt Situation of the 51 Low-Income Countries Whom it is our Task to Liberate from the Chains of Debt

We have a daunting task, since the burden of debt is not one from which the poorer countries will be liberated by their own efforts alone, or by any self-balancing mechanism in world trade. The situation of most low-income countries is like that of an absent minded man who has lost his bathplug. As the water gurgles down the plughole in the form of principal and interest payments, the two taps marked grants and new loans are turned on to keep the bath filled at a rather unsatisfactory level to wash in, while the bill with the water company goes up and up. There must be more intelligent ways to help Africa and other poorer nations!

The total debt of all developing countries is $2,171 billion (World Bank debt tables, 1997 figures preliminary) - a colossal sum which could not possibly be remitted. We should, however, fix our attention in Jubilee 2000, at least in the first instance, on the low-income countries with a GNP per head below $765 (the latest World Bank definition of low-income). There are just over 50 of these and most of them owe 80% or more of a year's GNP, or 250% of a year's XGS. The total face value of the debts of the 51 countries who are (in my view) eligible for 100% remission is $269.219 billion, as indicated in Chapter 8. This debt dates, for the most part, from liabilities incurred before 1990 and from interest on those liabilities. The low-income countries have no possibility of repaying this debt. It is either physically impossible for them to do so, or the social consequences of such repayment in terms of diversion of funds from essential needs are so horrific that no honourable creditor would seek to demand repayment of these sums.

The countries concerned are in a situation of 'debt overhang', like that of people who have fallen down a deep well, and cannot escape by their own efforts. We could have a most fascinating academic argument as to whether they were pushed into the well by wicked capitalists or imperialists, whether they fell in because their leaders were drunk, or careless, or whether it was just that the head of the well was very slippery and unmarked, while there was an economic blizzard blowing on a dark night. All three of these elements may

39

have been present when the debt was incurred. Rates of interest were low, but they subsequently rose. The terms of trade were reasonably favourable when the debts were incurred, but rapidly got worse. Professor Sir Hans Singer has estimated the deterioration in the terms of trade for primary products and low-tech manufactured goods - the main source of export earnings for the HIPCs - at 20-25% over the past few decades.[1] Furthermore, the oscillation of primary commodity prices from year to year has been at a level which precludes efficient economic planning. Finally, much of the money received in loans was misused or misappropriated by leaders of governments of debtor countries.

Our task is not to linger over this academic debate, but to throw down the rope to help debtor countries escape. Only one poorer country has got out of the well through its own unaided efforts, and their case is a cautionary tale, teaching other countries not to attempt this. The late Nicolae Ceausescu, dictator of Romania, determined to repay the $10 billion external debt of his country and achieved this in eight years, from 1982 to 1990, through treating the whole population like underfed and unpaid animals, whipped to work. Romania has still not recovered from this ordeal. It is an example that no sane country would seek to follow.

The country which made the second-largest reduction in the total of debt stocks between 1985 and 1992 was Yugoslavia. Its external debt stood at $22,470 million in 1987 and $16,482 million in 1991, a reduction of just under $6 billion, around 26%. This very substantial reduction was achieved at the cost of considerable economic hardship and disappointment. This was not the major cause of the subsequent break-up of Yugoslavia into warring factions, but it was a contributory factor.

This situation of imbalance is in no sense a self-correcting one. It locks the debtor countries into a vicious cycle of exclusion from the global market and increasing poverty.[2] On the contrary, the heavily-indebted low income countries have often only been able to meet their yearly debt service payments by rescheduling. The process is extremely tedious and wastes a great deal of the time of the relatively few qualified financial administrators in low income countries. The rescheduling has to be approved by the Paris Club and by the creditor country. It requires a detailed report and a considerable expenditure of time, through detailed and lengthy negotiations. It has been said (whether truly or not, I do not know) that one rescheduling operation carried out in Paris by the emissaries of the Nigerian Government saved less money than the emissaries spent in their generous allowances for overseas duty! The reschedulings made between 1987 and 1996 by low income countries and by

Table 3 Debt reschedulings and arrears

Debt reschedulings (US$ Million)

Country	1987-9	1990	1991	1992	1993	1994	1995	1996	Arrears (1996) interest	principal
Albania	0	0	0	0	35	1.1	255	0	25.1	83
Angola	2137	252	0	0	0	322	437	1545	536	1423
Bangladesh	0	0	0	0	0	8	0	0	1	25
Benin	385	22	58	49	12	8	6	128	8	72
Bhutan	0	0	0	0	0	0	0	0.7	0.3	0.2
Bolivia		153	138	125	115	0	196	433	26	64
Burkina Faso	0	0	43	14	6	0	0	44	10	38
Burundi	26	0	0	0	0	0	0	0	5	15
Cambodia	0	0	1363	0	0	0	246	12	5	708
Cameroon	470	21	0	988	0	1298	642	656	788	774
Central African Republic	38.7	6.3	0	0	0	38.5	7.6	0	39.5	82.7
Chad	40.2	7.8	3.9	0	4.9	5.6	55.4	33.4	8.1	35.4
Comoros	0	0	0	0	0	0	0	0	9.9	17.7
Congo, DR	2058	446	0	0	0	0	0	0	3008	4679
Congo Rep.	391	780	146	15	2	1044	108	269	283	1011
Côte D'Ivoire	1184	930	568	399	0	645	381		953	2551
Eq. Guinea	13.3	0	0	0	0	0	0	0	39.6	93.7
Ethiopia	0	0	0	185	140	47	28	0	481	4303
Gambia	22.8	0	0	0	0	0	0	0	0	0.2
Ghana	45	0	40	0	0	0	0	0	62	40
Guinea	155	110	29	156	0	0	131	228	103	332
Guinea-Bissau	99.7	27.1	11.2	1.1	16.1	25	13.7	277	61.5	157
Guyana	405	474	90	41	53	50	1	2	92	97
Haiti	0	0	0	0	0	0	107.7	66	0.7	1.3
Honduras	101	310	88	134	83	45	25		55	130
Kenya	0	0	0	0	0	517	0		16	30

Debt reschedulings (US$ Million)

Country	1987-9	1990	1991	1992	1993	1994	1995	1996	Arrears (1996) interest	principal
Lao, PDR	0	0	1262	0	0	0	0	0	0	1
Liberia	0	0	0	0	0	0	0	0	617	956
Malawi	79	0	0	0	0	0	0		5	15
Mali	87	12	11	38	57	15	0	21	33	380
Mauritania	138	12	0	0	177	67	59	68	85	162
Nepal	0	0	0	0	0	0	0	0	2	4
Nicaragua	588	30	1920	100	119	50	253	761	475	971
Niger	120	29	27	0	15	120	5	65	24	58
Nigeria*	22173	1480	2615	2497	0	0	0	0	4967	9298
Rwanda	0	0	0	0	0	0	6	0	19	51
Sao Tome & Principe	4.9	0	0	4.3	0	0.7	29.5	0	4	19.4
Senegal	367	111	73	33	0	212	220		15	14
Sierra Leone	20	0	0	195	47	107	31	24	3	21
Somalia	133	0	0	0	0	0	0		533	1167
Sri Lanka	0	0	0	0	0	0	0	0	35	42
Sudan**	35	0	0	0	0	0	0	0	5683	7467
Tanzania***	402	158	27	358	67	8	0	33	929	1630
Togo	228	81	31	40	12	0	141		28	61
Uganda	204	6	6	108	40	0	172	0	49	202
Vietnam	0	422	0	283	752	0	90	160	2865	10672
Yemen	360	98	0	0	0	0	0	80	487	2561
Zambia	22	879	268	269	192	146	20		591	710
Zimbabwe	0	0	0	0	0	0	0	0	0	0

Source: World Bank Debt Tables 1998.

*Although Nigeria had no officially approved reschedulings from 1993 onwards, it in fact built up cumulative arrears of interest and principal of LDOD of $4,967 interest and $9,298 million of principal in 1996.　** Sudan built up arrears of $5,683 million of interest, and $7,467 million of principal by 1996.
*** By 1996, Tanzania had built up arrears of $929 million interest and $1,630 million principal of LDOD. **** Yugoslavia, which reduced its debt so significantly between 1987 and 1991, owed $1,298 million in debt service to the World Bank at the time of the outbreak of the civil war and the break up of the country.[3]

countries which are almost low-income have been as shown in Table 3; arrears are also extremely common, and in some places very substantial. During the decade 1985-94, the debt actually paid by HIPCs was only 38% of the scheduled payments, yet even this debt servicing payment absorbed over 22% of their export earnings.[4]

This list is sufficient to show that rescheduling has been the rule rather than the exception, and that the majority of low-income countries have failed to keep up debt repayments. It has been calculated that in 1995, despite high and rising actual debt service, at least 43% of scheduled repayments by some sub-Saharan Governments went unpaid. Such non-performing loans lead to breakdown in debtor/creditor relationships and undermine the international lending system.[5] This surely indicates a structural imbalance that can only be cured by debt remission by the creditors. The figures in table 2 for interest arrears and principal arrears also show that very many low-income countries have been unable to keep up debt repayments. If, in a class in the university, just one or two members fail to produce their essays or produce them late, one may blame those individuals. However, if all of them fail one might surmise that there were too many essays in too little time. Similarly, in these tables of debt reschedulings and arrears on debt, we find that almost all low-income countries cannot keep to the repayment schedules. It is surely a fair conclusion from this that the whole structure of required repayment is at fault. When one fails to get blood out of a stone, it is more sensible to conclude that blood is not to be found in stones, than to blame some fault of the particular stones examined.

These figures of reschedulings and arrears of debt demonstrate the untenable nature of the present debt relations. Two contrary arguments can be made from the fact that countries have not made their debt servicing payments on time and have had to have them rescheduled. The World Bank and the IMF would argue that the existence of these arrears gives the country concerned a bad record, and renders it ineligible for debt remission. Others, however, might draw the opposite conclusion that the rescheduling and arrears indicate the inability of the country to service its debt, and that therefore the debt should be forgiven. In several cases, relating to multilateral debt, this inability to keep up repayments has been remedied by the transfer of the debt from high interest IBRD (World Bank) debt to IDA debt (International Development Association), which bears a rate of interest of only 0.75%, and has a grace period of 10 years before principal repayment is due at a rate of 1% per year, and a further 10 years before the rate rises to 3% per year for the next 30 years. IDA funds are mostly drawn from the aid budgets of richer countries, unlike the IBRD funds for World Bank loans, which are mostly raised on the commercial market by the World Bank (with some contributions from World Bank annual profits). The World Bank administers both these two 'windows' (as they are called) of the different types of loan, and the President of the World Bank is also the President of the International Development Association. However, the need for debt forgiveness goes deeper than the requirement to reduce debt service payments, although this is important. It also involves liberation from the unpayable debt itself, both bilateral and multilateral as well as the smaller amounts owed to private creditors. If a 100% remission cannot be obtained from the financial authorities, it might possibly be acceptable to leave a small residue of, say, 5-10% of the debt still to be paid by the debtor country itself, so that it could be seen to have had a part in its own liberation from debt.

If the debts owed by an individual were as unpayable as those owed by the 51 poorest countries, the individual would be declared bankrupt and would thus obtain a merciful release. The bankruptcy proceedings would probably involve a degree of disgrace and loss of reputation, which we would not wish to see imposed upon debtor countries. It would also involve the transfer of most of the assets of the debtor to the receiver acting on behalf of the creditors. In the international sphere, we need some equivalent to this procedure, though it would be harsh and injurious to include the compulsory transfer of assets and the element of disgrace. On the contrary, we need to bring a joyous liberation creating self-confidence and full participation in the trade relations of the global community.

It must not be thought that these 51 countries are at the bottom of the pile through the inherent psychological defects of their people. This is not the case. They are in a situation similar to that described by Thomas Gray in his elegy on the dead inhabitants of the village of Stoke Poges, whose graves he found in the churchyard. They contained in their number perhaps a 'mute inglorious Milton' or someone who 'the rod of Empire might have swayed or waked to ecstasy the living lyre'. All their potential, however, had been nullified by their poverty:

> Chill penury repressed their noble rage and froze the genial current of the soul.

It is the same with the majority of the inhabitants of poorer countries, only when we are able to remove the burden of absolute poverty will we see their full creative potential.

Archbishop Carey, in his chapter 'Chains Around Africa' in the recent volume 'Proclaim Liberty' (produced by Christian Aid for the Lambeth Conference) has drawn attention to the failure of many commentators from outside Africa to realise its great potential:

> The beauty, tenacity and hopefulness in the vast majority of African communities is never conveyed, nor are their own efforts to transform the economic and political structures that perpetuate the inequalities that sustain chronic hunger. [6]

No economic force other than the deliberate action of the creditors is going to get the 51 nations out of the well of debt. The bland assurances that I received, from some ministers and from some civil servants, concerned with international finance, suggested that this imbalance of debt was a temporary phenomenon. In fact, between 1985 and 1996 (the last year for which World Bank figures are at present available) we find an increase in every category - economic and geographical:

Table 4 Growth of total debt owed by various categories of countries

Area	1985 Debt (US$ Bn)	1996 Debt (US$ Bn)	Increase (US$Bn)	Increase %
All developing countries	990	2,095	1,105	112
Sub-Saharan Africa	99	227	128	129
Latin America and Caribbean	388	656	268	69
E Asia and the Pacific	166	477	311	187
Europe & Central Asia	158	370	212	134
N Africa & Middle East	110	212	102	93
South Asia	68	152	84	123

By income categories also, the debt has risen remorselessly:

Low-income countries including India, China and Pakistan	251	537	286	115
Middle-income countries	739	1,558	819	110

We have omitted India, China and Pakistan from the list of countries recommended for total or near-total remission. The debt of these three countries rose in the period concerned, and in 1996, the totals were as follows: China, $129 billion; India, $90 billion; Pakistan, $30 billion, making a total of $249 billion, and leaving a total for the remaining low-income countries of $288 billion out of $537 billion.   From this total of $288 billion we must deduct the debt of Myanmar which though it is eligible for debt remission on economic grounds and is in fact on the World Bank list of 41 HIPC countries, is at present under so well entrenched and corrupt military dictatorship that it is unrealistic to include it in my list for remission; thus we are left with a total of $270 billion from the 51 countries suitable for remission

Source: World Debt Tables 1998 Vol. 1 and 1990 to 1991 Vol. 1.

For every category and every area there is a similar pattern of an increase in the region of 100%. Between 1991 and 1996, the debt of 89 countries increased, while that of 24 countries decreased, although some of the countries whose debt went down had benefitted from debt remission, e.g., Nicaragua.

The debt owed by low-income countries is of three kinds. A relatively small amount of it (about 20%) is private debt owed to private creditors, primarily banks. The remaining 80% is public debt owed to public creditors. Of this public debt, the multilateral debt owed to international financial institutions, primarily the World Bank, the IMF and some regional development banks, constitutes $55 billion in 1996 out of a total debt of sub-Saharan Africa of $179 billion. $29.5 billion of the $55 billion multilateral debt has been transferred to the International Development Association (IDA) from commercial World Bank debt, which now totals only $6 billion from Africa South of the Sahara. IDA is a relatively favourable concessionary 'window' of the World Bank, bearing a rate of interest of only 0.75% and a ten year grace period for principle repayment. For the HIPCs as a whole, multilateral debt totalled $51 billion out of $232 billion. In Africa South of the Sahara, the proportion of multilateral debt has grown from 35% in 1990 to 41% in 1996. This indicates the extreme importance of negotiations with the IMF and the World Bank, both as regards debt owed to it directly and as regards debt owed to the IDA, which the World Bank administers.

Bilateral debt owed by the countries of sub-Saharan Africa in 1996 to individual governments, administered by the informal gathering of the Paris Club, constituted $80 billion, which is 59% of debt owed by the same countries. This is still the most important category of debt for remission purposes. Its remission requires only the decision of the creditor governments. It is a question solely of political will. It has been decided that all forms of the official debt of each country will be dealt with on a comprehensive basis, i.e., the various forms of relief on offer from the World Bank and the Paris Club shall be applied together. The rates of remission are, however, considerably different.

4 The Debt Situation of Other Countries in the Developing World

The debt problem is not limited to these 51 low-income countries, but they are the ones for whom it is practicable to launch a Jubilee 2000 campaign for total or near-total remission. Politics is 'the art of the possible' and we are in a political situation as well as in one resting on a categorical imperative of justice. By and large, at least in the first instance of Jubilee 2000, we have to make the working assumption that countries outside the low-income category should be able to deal with their own debt situation without large-scale remission. Some of them, however, whose GNP is between $765 and $2000 per head may well require partial debt remission as we have described in Chapter 6.

The total debt of developing countries is over $2100 billion (preliminary estimates 1997 $2171 billion; World Bank figures). The debt has risen from $603 billion in 1980 and $1444 billion in 1990, a huge rate of increase of $1568 billion or 260% over a period of 17 years. One is bound to ask whether such a high rate of increase is sustainable and the present wave of financial crises involving potential debt default would tend to suggest that it is not. The present financial collapse in so many countries in the Far East and South America has been due to a number of causes, including loss of confidence, but over-extended debt has certainly been one of them. Investment on an equity basis creating share of ownership for the lender does not create a debt problem. If the enterprise in which the investor has put his money fails, the investor loses his stake and that is the end of the matter. However, if a large loan is made to a client, who promises to repay in a certain period with a certain rate of interest, a collapse of the client's economy creates a continuing problem of debt overhang.

By far the largest volume of debt is owed by countries whose GNP per head is above $2,000. Some of them have large pockets of extreme poverty, but in general this is due to mal-distribution of income rather than to total shortage. The only country with an income above $2,000 for whom we could realistically propose any debt remission of a Jubilee kind, on economic criteria, is South Africa, whose case is examined in detail in Chapter 6. As we have shown it may be possible, beyond the confines of the Jubilee campaign proper, to recommend remission in the exceptional cases of debt for ecology, as in Brazil. It may also be possible to designate South African debts arising from transactions, contrary to the UN prohibition on loans, as odious debts part of which could be remitted.

As a further development we may be able to put in place some overall limit to the element of compound interest on the original principal of the debt. This is particularly necessary for countries such as Brazil or Mexico, whose total interest payments made and unpaid interest added to the total debt, constitutes more than 100% of the present debt liability. We may also be able to give some ecological remission to countries such as Brazil or Mexico, whose GNP per head is higher than the level where we can grant Jubilee remission, on the grounds of the poverty of the country as a whole.

There are a relatively small number of countries which are poor but not among the poorest, with GNP per head between $765 and $2000. In Chapter 6 we have named 12 of these. Among these 12 are four large countries whose debt, is considerable; Algeria ($33 billion), Egypt ($31 billion), Morocco ($22 billion) and the Philippines ($41 billion); (1996 figures). There are a variety of means of measuring the partial remission that should be granted, but if we were to take a rough estimate of 50% remission the cost for these four countries would be $63.5 billion. Some of them, such as Jamaica and the Philippines, have considerable areas of acute poverty and also strong campaigns for debt remission. The problem of dealing with the colossal debt burden of middle-income countries, which are poor but not amongst the poorest extends beyond the limits of what we can realistically achieve in Jubilee 2000, although our debt analysis may throw some light on the problem. In the follow up to Jubilee remission this problem will need to be addressed.

Notes

1   Professor Hans Singer, 'Debt Relief for the Heavily-Indebted Poor Countries - the HIPC Initiative' in *'Proclaim Liberty'*, Eldred Willey and Janet Banks (eds.): London, Christian Aid, June 1998, p.37.
2   Ibid., p. 36.
3   World Bank Annual Report, *Table of principal and charges overdue to World Bank*, 1997, p. 206.
4   Ibid., p. 37.
5   Global Development Finance: Washington DC World Bank, 1998, quoted in theme six of the Lambeth Conference, International Debt and Economic Justice, section led by Dr Peter Selby, Bishop of Worcester, July 1998.
6   George Carey, Archbishop of Canterbury, *'Chains Around Africa: Crisis or Hope for the New Millennium?'*, op. Cit., Willey and Banks, 1998, p. 20.

5 Efforts Made So Far by the World Bank and the Paris Club to Deal with the Problem of Debt

From the Jubilee pattern we derive the need for the debt remission for the 51 poorest countries to be total or near-total. We cannot expect the fresh start and the new discipline unless we shock the debtor countries with the good news of a total remission. We cannot leave some bad apples in the basket to turn the new ones rotten. Loans incurred after the Jubilee must be those which can be honoured. We cannot leave unpayable debt after the Jubilee, for this would destroy the whole psychological effect. Furthermore, we must have a realistic cut-off point, and this must be later than that of the Paris Club. The remission should involve all debt owing on (say) 31st December 1995, five years before the Jubilee, together with any interest due on that sum.[1]

The Jubilee remission which we seek has a two-fold emphasis. It has to correct the indebtedness of poorer countries by changing the balance sheets, but it has also to produce a psychological effect of introducing a new beginning where self-reliance can flourish. This will require conditionalities for the remission which must be part of a detailed plan for the future running of the economy of the debtor country concerned.

Some measures have already been taken by the Paris Club consortium of richer creditors to deal with **bilateral debt**. These creditors meet informally to reach a consensus so that they can deal with debt owed to them in a united way. The Paris Club is serviced by a secretary seconded by the French Ministry of Finance. Bill Peters and I had the pleasure of meeting the then incumbent Monsieur Jerome Haas for lunch in Paris in 1996. He impressed us with his competence and his genuine concern for poorer countries. However, as we shall see, the remission package which the club has at last produced leaves room for improvement. It involves a cut-off point for remission of debt incurred before the first application for remission was made to the club.

This gives rise to unnecessary variation depending on the unimportant date of the first submission of an application, rather than on a uniform functional date such as 31st December 1995. The Paris Club date is in many cases far too early. We need only a small interval between the cut-off date and the year 2000, sufficient to avoid creating a situation where potential investors or givers of loans during this period will not be put off by the news of a coming remission.

It will also be necessary to forgive interest arising from that debt between the cut-off point and the time of remission. Of course if any of the debt were to be reduced through repayment between 31st December 1995 and 31st December 2000, the amount to be remitted would be calculated on the reduced balance.

Multilateral debt is due to a number of creditors of whom the largest are the World Bank and the IMF. The total of debt owed directly to the World Bank for loans issued by them at more or less commercial rates of interest, from funds which they have raised on the money markets is considerable. On June 30th 1996 outstanding loans owed to World Bank totalled almost $110 billion. Of that sum, however, only $6.1 billion was owed by the 51 low-income countries for whom we are seeking total or near-total debt remission, and $13.2 billion was owed by countries with GNP between $765 and $2000, for whom we have suggested a 50% level of remission (totalling $6.6 billion). Thus the total debt figure for which we should seek for write off from the World Bank is $12.7 billion. As we shall see this is not an impossible sum, when set against the World Bank reserves of $23 billion. In any case, probably not all these countries would succeed in fulfilling the conditionalities.

The present position of heavily indebted poor countries remains most unsatisfactory. As late as its 1996 accounts, the World Bank boasted that it had never remitted any of the principal owed to it.[2] When the Bank belatedly introduced its Heavily Indebted Poor Country initiative (HIPC), it only proposed to deal with 41 countries, it offered far too low a rate of remission based on reducing debt to a so called 'sustainable' level of 80% of a year's GNP, 220% of a year's XGS and a ratio of debt servicing payments to XGS of over 20%. It also imposed a six year interval before implementation and a ridiculously severe list of conditionalities. Tomaz Solamao, the Finance Minister of Mozambique, which has just emerged from a long and tortuous process before obtaining debt remission, described these conditionalities as 'very, very crazy' and said that it is important for other countries that the system for debt relief should be simplified.[3]

The World Bank has been in a position of irreconcilable aims for a long time. It was set up partly as an aid institution to help European countries badly damaged by the effects of the 1939-45 War to make an effective recovery. It was also enjoined to help poorer undeveloped countries to catch up with the rest of the world. This latter goal became increasingly emphasised as the need for help to developed countries became less acute, due to their recovery from the effects of the 1939-45 war. The World Bank was rightly regarded as a body having a special responsibility for the welfare of poorer countries. Successive Presidents emphasised the World Bank's role in the elimination of poverty.

At the same time, however, the Bank was strictly commanded to run on good commercial lines. This involved close attention to the criteria, which affected the money markets' assessment of the World Bank's financial position. The assessors for the money market have commented on the excessively high level of World Bank reserves.[4] This level of reserves has inhibited the Bank's potential to grant remission of unpayable debts on a sufficient scale to help low-income countries. World Bank Presidents had been terrified of losing their triple 'A' status, and have maintained that were they to do so, the rate of interest at which they could borrow money on the money market would go up. This in turn would increase the rate of interest charged to World Bank borrowers.

The World Bank has been far too cautious. Even hard headed political leaders such as Truman were aware of the danger of the influence of the financial market in the US and elsewhere on the Bank's policy. At the very beginning of the Bank's history, President Truman sent a warning to the Bank President, 'I hope you will make it perfectly plain to our friend McCloy, that the Wall Street crowd are not to control the operations of the International Bank'.[5] Cynical observers have suggested that that is just what Wall Street was able to do in the subsequent history of the Bank; its influence has produced a stern attitude to those countries who had difficulty in servicing their debts. The World Bank has been excessively conscious of the possible effect of its actions in producing an unfavourable response from the money markets. These are notoriously volatile and can bring down the value of a country's currency on evidence which, on examination, is found to be insubstantial. One would hope that the World Bank could be insulated from fear of these kinds of psychologically based oscillations, since it is not an authority with responsibility for any currency, and relies only on the money market for its triple 'A' status and its ability to borrow at lower level of rates of interest. The IMF has been harsher than the World Bank, and has refused to participate in any schemes for remission of debt, until its recent decision to grant 80% remission to Honduras and Nicaragua, in the wake of the hurricane Mitch disaster.

One may ask why the sums committed to debt remission by the Bank are so inadequate, springing as they do only from the yearly profit which the Bank makes from its role as a financier for poorer nations. Much of this yearly profit springs from the half percent difference between the rate at which the Bank borrows and the rate at which it lends, but some of it comes from these $10 billion original deposits made by the members of the Bank. These deposits do not earn interest for the Bank members, but are available interest free for investment or for loans. However, this sum of about $10 billion dollars is relatively small compared to $110 billion total of World Bank loans.

The Baker Plan, introduced in 1985 by James Baker, then Secretary of State for the Treasury in the United States, dealt more with South America than with Africa. He sought to persuade banks to provide $20 billion of new commercial capital to enable countries in danger of default to keep up repayments. At the same time, he persuaded the World Bank and the IMF to become more deeply involved and to make short-term loans where needed in situations of the extreme cash-flow difficulty of debtor nations. At this time, the idea of debt remission was ruled out as a breach of the harsh and unforgiving 'bankers' culture' which then inspired the governments of richer countries. Within five years, however, it became clear that the mere putting off of the problem of debt repayment through the making of new loans was not sufficient. The idea of 'debt reduction', which is in fact partial debt forgiveness by another name, came to be reluctantly accepted in policy-making circles in the creditor countries.

The debt reduction approach was two-fold. For the 'middle-income' countries which are moderately poor, the **Brady Plan** put forward by Nicholas Brady, then United States Secretary of State for the Treasury, provided a complicated process of partial debt remission. This remission applied to commercial debt to private creditors, which has been so enormously important for South America, where it constitutes $210 billion out of $381 billion of public and publicly guaranteed debt. South America (including Central America and Mexico) has borne a colossal burden of interest; a total of $352 billion between 1985 and 1996 - a total of some $660 for every man, woman and child of the continent where the total population is about 536 million (including Mexico). The great majority of this interest has been paid to private creditors. The various menus offered in the Brady Plan are somewhat complex, but basically it involves a remission of 35% or more of the debt of selected middle-income countries, in exchange for the conversion of the balance of the debt into prioritised bonds, partly underwritten by the US Treasury.

The second prong of the attack upon debt has been that of the Trinidad Terms, launched by John Major when he was Chancellor of the Exchequer, at the meeting of the Commonwealth Finance Ministers in 1990. The initiative for this plan originated from among some civil servants in the British Treasury and elsewhere at an earlier date. Action on this plan was slow, due to the fact that the British Government was not willing to go ahead on its own, since this might result in 'free-rider' creditors drawing advantage from British generosity through the appreciation of the value of debts still owed to them.[6] In 1996, an agreement was achieved and produced the slightly different terms of the 'Naples Agreement', offering remission at a two-thirds or better level to a list of low-income countries, who had a satisfactory record of following the IMF structural adjustment terms.

Meanwhile, the World Bank had broken with its previous position of principle against any write-off of principal debt owed to it, and in October 1996 produced its much vaunted 'Heavily Indebted Poor Country' (HIPC) initiative providing for the remission of some $8 billion of debt owed by selected HIPCs. This represented a great advance in the acceptance of a new principle of the forgiveness of debt. This new initiative owed a great deal to the efforts of the British Government and is also to the credit of the President of the World Bank, James Wolfensohn, who seems to have a genuine desire to do more to help the poor, but who is often inhibited by the timidity and inertia of the large World Bank organisation.

The $500 million per year allocated to this scheme is no more than a portion of the $1 billion profit, made yearly by the Bank from the difference of 0.5% between the rate at which it borrows on the money market and the rate at which it lends to governments in the developing world. The profit also derives, as we have shown, from the fact that the $10 billion deposits made by members of the Bank do not bear any interest. Prior to 1997, the first year of contributions to the HIPC initiative, the World Bank built up $16 billion in cumulative accrued profit, referred to in the accounts as 'retained earnings',[7] over the years since its creation. This sum is now part of its reserves, which as James Wolfensohn told us at the Lambeth Conference, now total $23 billion. The Bank prides itself on having reserves equal to 14% of its liabilities. This is a suitable ratio for private high-street banks, but the World Bank is in a much more secure situation. It enjoys a triple A status from the assessors for the money markets, which it is terrified to lose, but it is reported that the assessors themselves have suggested that the World Bank reserves are excessive.

The Bank is supported by almost all the major financially powerful countries; furthermore, unlike most high street banks, who have deposits from customers which could be withdrawn immediately by them should they lose confidence in the bank, the World Bank's borrowing is almost entirely on a long-term basis. This does not offer those who have lent to it the right to withdraw their money outside a long agreed time frame. The World Bank's position is further reinforced by the fact that of the contributions made by its members, a small proportion was paid in hard currency, but the remainder is 'callable capital' and would only be paid should the IBRD be unable to meet its obligations, a situation that has never arisen. The conduct of the World Bank in respect of its retention of so large a reserve is analogous to the behaviour of the servant of a strict lord, described in the Biblical parable who, out of fear enegndering excess caution, took his talent and hid it in the ground, rather than use it for the trading purpose for which it was given, thereby earning the wrath of his master for having made no use of the opportunities presented to him. The enormous World Bank reserves are to be used for the benefit of poor countries, rather than stored up in unused balances and investments.

The World Bank claimed that its HIPC initiative was a blueprint for steering HIPCs to what its authors called 'sustainable debt', after consideration case-by-case. The World Bank scheme has four grave weaknesses. It seeks to reduce the debt servicing burden to 'sustainable levels' rather than to remove it totally or almost totally. What constitutes sustainablity? The Bank defines the sustainable level as a total debt not more than 80% of a year's GNP or 220% of a year's export of goods and services (XGS). It also regards as sustainable any volume of debt, whose annual debt servicing burden is not more than 25% of the yearly income earned by the debtor country from its XGS. This is an impossibly high level at which to fix 'sustainability'.

In addition, the World Bank HIPC remission process is far too slow. It usually involves at least six years from first consideration to final implementation. It also involves strict compliance with IMF terms, which are sound in some respects, but deficient in that they place an excess emphasis on free market forces. Malawi, for instance, which has benefited very greatly from improved hybrid types of maize which require generous application of fertilisers, was told firmly that it could not subsidise fertilisers to the farmer since this broke the free market criterion. Furthermore, the IMF conditionalities forbid import controls, despite the fact that some form of protection is often valuable to foster infant industries.

The World Bank only envisaged a maximum list of 41 low-income countries, (reduced to 40 by the deletion of Nigeria but restored to 41 by the subsequent admission of Malawi), potentially suitable for remission, whereas some 51 such countries desperately need remission. Instead of increasing the number, the Bank has reduced it by one, excluding Nigeria which owes some $30 billion and has a GNP per head of about $300. The list of 41 HIPC countries potentially eligible for debt remission had always excluded Malawi whose case is dealt with in Chapter 9. I was recently told in a letter from the Director of the London World Bank Office, that Malawi was on the list of countries potentially eligible for debt remission, but other letters, including that to the Bishop of Birmingham, indicate that it was not. We must have a more open and consistent policy from the Bank. The latest World Bank/IMF website of 3rd March 1999, settles the issue; Malawi is at last included!

Too often, the World Bank spoils the ship for a ha'pence worth of tar. In Mozambique, for instance, the recent large reduction of the overall level of debt has still left that country with a yearly debt service burden of $100 million in place of the $104 million which they had been paying hitherto. The World Bank initiative is now combined with that of the Paris Club of bilateral lenders, under the Naples terms, to produce a comprehensive debt remission package. It is not clear, however, exactly how the sustainability criterion fits into this package. Paris Club remission is often at a far more generous level than that of the World Bank. We can only describe the action towards debt reduction so far taken by the World Bank, the Paris Club and the G8 as 'a good beginning, but only a beginning'. Given the World Bank's $16 billion cumulative accrued profits in 1996, it should surely be possible for more generous terms of remission to be offered. The World Bank could well follow the advice of Wordsworth in his ode on the roof of King's College Chapel:

> Give all you can,
> High Heaven rejects the lore,
> Of nicely calculated
> Less or more.

To take another analogy, we could imagine how Mr World Bank would have behaved if he had chanced to stray into Bunyan's story of Pilgrim's Progress. The Pilgrim was running down the road, much impeded by a burden which he carried. At a certain place where there was a Cross, the burden fell off, and in Bunyan's lovely language, 'the pilgrim gave three leaps for joy and his heart felt very lightsome'. I would like to see governments and peoples of poor indebted countries feel very lightsome at the removal of their burden; if, however, a certain Mr World Bank had chanced to come down the road, he would have said to the pilgrim, 'My dear man, why are you getting rid of your burden? I have here a patent rucksack that will enable you to carry it for the next 50 years without suffering as much as before'. We need a more radical solution, which will provide for an exit from debt and not just a palliative.

The role of multilateral official debt in Africa South of the Sahara has increased dramatically over the last six years. In 1980, multilateral official debt constituted only 13% of long-term debt. In 1988, it had risen to 21%; thereafter it rose every single year until it reached a total of 31% in 1997. The burden of servicing this debt would have been totally prohibitive, if it had remained at the IBRD level at 0.5% above the ruling rate on the money markets at which the World Bank borrows. In order to alleviate this burden, a great deal of the debt of low-income countries has now been transferred from ordinary World Bank terms to International Development Association (IDA) terms. In Africa South of the Sahara, for instance, the total of IDA debt in 1996 was estimated to be $29.5 billion, as compared with $6.4 billion ordinary World Bank debt.

This IDA 'window' of the World Bank was started in 1960 in response to the proposal of US Senator Monroney asking for further aid to low-income countries to help them to deal with their debt. Some people in the World Bank were in favour of outright grants or remission, but the final plan provided for a loan fund on concessional terms for low-income countries. The objective of the scheme as stated in 'Article 1, Purposes, Articles of Agreement of the IDA', was:

> To promote economic development, increase productivity and thus raise standards of living in the less developed areas of the world... To meet their development requirements on terms which are more flexible and bear less heavily on the balance of payments than those of conventional loans.

The Association was expressly provided with powers of modification of its terms of financing:

> The Association may, when and to the extent it deems appropriate of all relevent circumstances, including the financial and economic prospects of the member concerned and such conditions as it may determine, agree to a

relaxation or other modification of the terms of which any of its financing have been provided. (Article 5, section 3).

The IDA terms provide for loans at only 0.75% interest on the outstanding balance (described as an administration charge). They carry a ten-year grace period, when no repayment of principal is required. This is to be followed by 10 years at a level of principal repayment of 1% per year and then by 30 years at a level of principal repayment of 3% per year. This schedule has so far placed only a light burden upon debtors, but in due course, unless the terms are modified, the burden will become heavy.

Malawi, for instance, with an income from XGS of only $428 million (1995 figure) is already meeting a debt service payment of $108 million (1995 figure). Its IDA debt is now $1251 million, which is increasing year by year. If 3% of this figure were to be added to the already considerable yearly debt servicing burden, the consequences for a country as poor as Malawi would be serious. We have, therefore, to obtain assurance that IDA debt is included in the general HIPC or Paris Club remission programme. It is most important that these IDA loans to low-income countries should be converted to grants, before repayment at 3% per year becomes due. This matter is very serious for sub-Saharan Africa.

Commercial debt is far less serious for the low-income countries than it is for the middle-income. It constitutes less than 20%, and is mostly concentrated in a few low-income countries. It is interesting to note that in the Nigerian case, in 1991, the private bankers from Britain, USA and elsewhere, who were owed $5.6 billion in that year, struck a deal with the Nigerian Minister for Finance, Alhaji Abubakar Alhaji, which provided for the remission of $5.6 billion of bank debt and a further $2 billion overdue interest, in exchange for the Nigerian government entering into some $2 billion of bonds which it promised to honour.[8] Yearly payments have been kept up meticulously by the Nigerian government on these bonds, with only one rescheduling, in contrast to its very considerable arrears on official debt. The fact that the banks granted a Brady-type deal with an 80% remission level shows a generosity or realism on the part of the banks in refreshing contrast to the rigidity of Nigeria's official creditors.

However, if we turn our attention to the lower middle-income countries beyond the scope of Jubilee 2000, we find that the burden of commercial debt is indeed crippling. The two countries with the largest debt burden in the developing world are in Latin America. Brazil owes $179,000 million, of which $68,000 million is publicly guaranteed debt owed to private creditors, and $49,000 million private non-guaranteed debt owed to private creditors. Mexico owes $157,000 million, of which $64,500 million is owed to private creditors, and a further $20,000 million is non-guaranteed private debt.

The countries with the next highest debt are India ($81,000 million) of which debt to private creditors is $21,159 million and private non-guaranteed debt is $7,382 million, China ($128,000 million) of which $25,000 is short-term, $62,828 million is guaranteed debt owed to private creditors, and only $1,550 to private non-guaranteed creditors, and Indonesia ($129,000 million) of which $32,000 million is short-term debt, $13,900 million publicly guaranteed debt to private creditors and $36,694 million private non-guaranteed.

In Latin America and the Caribbean as a whole, the share of private long-term debt of all kinds is $250,000 million out of $413,000 million total long-term debt. Short-term debt is $121,000 million, most of it owing to private creditors. Thus private debt comprises 60.5% of the total debt. Interest payments in 1996 totalled $42,448 million. In contrast, sub-Saharan Africa's debt to private creditors in 1996 totalled $42,000 million ($10,000 million of which is owed by South Africa); total interest payments made by sub-Saharan Africa in 1996 were $5 billion. The debt problem of South America is therefore a much larger one in terms of the amount owed, especially to commercial creditors. It also involves eight times as high a burden of interest payments as that of Africa South of the Sahara. However, in terms of the burden upon the countries concerned and their ability to provide essential services to the poorer people in their area, the South American debt is not quite so severe. With a few exceptions (such as Guyana, Ecuador, Honduras, Nicaragua and Bolivia) the ratio of debt to GNP and of debt to XGS is considerably less than that for sub-Saharan Africa. The average ratio of long-term debt (EDT) to GNP for the whole of Latin America and the Caribbean is only 37.4% (1996), while the ratio of EDT to XGS is 198%. For Africa South of the Sahara, however, the ratio of EDT to GNP is 78%, while that of EDT to XGS is 222%.

For the purposes of the Jubilee 2000 campaign, it is necessary to focus on the 51 low-income countries to obtain total or near-total remission of their debt outstanding in 1996. This is the urgent goal of our campaign. As a follow-up to it, however, serious study is needed on how the debts of lower middle-income countries can be addressed. Among the five largest creditors, only India has reduced that debt during the last two years 1995 to 1996 (a reduction of $12,800 million, i.e., about 10%). The debt of Indonesia has risen by $21,000 million in this period (just over 20%) and Brazil's by

$28,000 million (18.3%). Mexican debt rose by $17,119 million (12%). These highly indebted middle-income countries clearly need help from the IMF to resolve their immediate financial crisis. In the long-term, they will need consideration beyond the strict criteria of Jubilee 2000. As a result of the 1998 financial crisis the debt totals have been further increased.

Notes

1   The cut-off point for debt remission to the Paris Club has been taken to be the date when the country concerned first approached the Club to ask for debt remission. The House of Commons International Development Committee asked for the date to be changed to that on which an agreement is reached on exit ratios and timing of relief (p. X1.B Third Report on Debt Relief).
2   World Bank Annual Report 1997:   Washington DC, World Bank, p.188.
3   Ottawa Channel Africa, published from South Africa.
4   This point was made very strongly by a banker at the Jubilee 2000 conference of Financial and other experts, at Lichfield Cathedral on July 17th, 1998.
5   Jochen Kraske et. al. 'Bankers With a Mission': New York, OUP, 1996, p. 60.
6   This point was made very strongly by Lynda Chalker, Minister for Overseas Development, in a reply a question asked by Martin Dent at an Oxfam lobby of Parliament.
7   World Bank Accounts 1996, prepared by Peat, Marwick and Mitchell, from World Bank Annual Report, 1998.
8   Interview with Alhaji Abubakar Alhaji, Nigerian High Commissioner, London. In an interview with the Lloyds Bank General Manager for risk management, I was told that the motive for this deal was realism, for if no deal was made, Lloyds might have lost the whole debt. I believe, however, that an element of generosity and a sense of justice was also present.

6 The Boundaries and Criteria of Jubilee Remission

In this and subsequent sections, I write as the Co-Founder of Jubilee 2000 and not on behalf of the coalition of which Bill Peters and I are Vice-Presidents. The coalition has yet to pronounce its policy on this matter. There is room for a lot of debate on the precise details, but a broad pattern emerges from the Jubilee concept and from the statistics of debt, GNP and XGS of individual countries. It is essential for the general concept of Jubilee 2000 to become operationalised in a specific list. Only in this way can we set the agenda in a practical manner. If the campaign were to remain as a general exhortation to forgive debts, we might well meet with the defensive response from financial decision makers of an agreement in principle and a refusal to implement it in practical detail.

If commentators disagree with specific recommendations in this list, they will at least be provoked into producing their own specific recommendations. Clearly there is room for analysis and discussion of the cases of a number of countries on the margins of suitability for total or near-total remission. There is also a need for flexibility in deciding whether to opt in the campaign for total remission for low-income countries or whether to recommend the acceptance of proposals for near-total remission at a rate of (say) 90 to 95%, leaving the debtor country to find the last 5 to 10% needed to achieve a total deliverance from the burden of past debt. It may prove tactically wise in the final negotiations for proponents of the full Jubilee 2000 remission for low-income countries to ask for 100% remission, but be prepared ultimately for 90 to 95%. There can, however, be no argument on the point that our goal must be a situation where the old past inert debt is removed to allow a new beginning. If a portion of the debt is left intact, it must be small enough to be able to be repaid in the short term, without undue suffering. The World Bank's plan for HIPC countries involves reducing this debt to a sustainable level, where it can be serviced year after year but never be repaid; this cannot be an option for us.

When the negotiations for radical debt remission take place among decision makers, the final result may well be somewhat different from the details of our proposals, for this is the nature of most great reform programmes. We seek for a total answer and achieve a less than perfect solution. It was so in the great anti-slavery campaign under Wilberforce and Buxton from 1820 to 1834. They sought for immediate total emancipation; they got emancipation followed by a period of compulsory apprenticeship. They had to accept compensation from the British Treasury for former slave owners, although several active members of the anti-slavery movement, including Buxton, pointed out that it was the slaves themselves rather than their Masters who deserved compensation. Nonetheless they had achieved the substance of the liberation for which they sought. It will no doubt be the same in the liberative campaign of Jubilee 2000. We may lose on some details but we shall win in substance. Our situation is like that of Buxton and the anti-slavery leadership in 1832. They stood on the major point of principle of winning emancipation, but in order to win this greater goal they were ready as a necessity of negotiation to concede on lesser matters, which others regarded mistakenly as points of principle.

My role in this is analogous to that I once had in Tiv land in Nigeria, when leading a community development project building a road. If the work did not seem to be proceeding fast enough, I would leap into the laterite pit, seize a pick from a protesting volunteer and begin digging. He would complain in a jocular manner, 'You are no good at digging, D.O. (District Officer), it is not your job.' To this I would reply, 'You are doing it so slowly that I've got to do it myself!' With a laugh the volunteer would say, 'Give me back my pick!' He would seize it back and begin to work with renewed vigour. By this kind of camaraderie we pushed the road-building project ahead. A little competition often does wonders for the development process! It is important to provoke the large number of competent economists employed by the World Bank into working out the details of a radical debt remission, sufficient to set the debtor countries free from their burden, instead of spending their time working out excessively complicated minor modifications to an intolerable debt regime.

The problem of debt involves a consideration of many countries in the Third World and a few outside it, such as Russia, and other states of the former Soviet Union. In due course, something may be able to be done for most of these countries, which are poor, but not amongst the poorest. For the moment, however, and for the purposes of our campaign, we have to focus upon the need for total or near total remission for the 51 poorest countries with GNP per head below $765.[1] We have also to devise a formula of partial remission for special cases of countries between $765 and $2000 per head, which I take as a suitable cut-off point. Countries with a GNP per head of above $2000 often have severe pockets of extreme poverty. However, for the purposes of our immediate campaign, we must adopt the working hypothesis of leaving them (with the single exception of South Africa) to deal with this by themselves.

The extent of a country's debt does not, of course, provide a sufficient reason for its remission. At the top of the scale of GNP per head we find countries such as the United States and Australia, which both owe very large sums in external debt. One would not dream of including them on any list for debt remission since, through simple if costly actions of their own governments they are entirely capable of paying off their external debt themselves. When we come to consider Third World countries with GNP per head over $2000, we find only one country, South Africa, which for reasons of its past history under Apartheid, should qualify on economic grounds for partial remission. This case is dealt with later in the chapter. Other countries are more able, if they have the will to deal with the problems arising from their own debts. Many of them have substantial pockets of high levels of poverty, but if their overall GNP per head is at a level above $2000, they probably have the potential to remedy the poverty by measures of redistribution of income and property.

The President of Brazil, for example, rightly pointed out that his country is not a poor one, for it has a GNP per head of over $4000,[2] but is an unjust society. The rich in Brazil are very rich and the poor very poor; the Gini coefficient of the Lorenz curve for inequality of distribution of income is, in the case of Brazil, one of the highest in the world at 60%. One therefore cannot include Brazil in a list of countries qualifying for Jubilee remission on economic grounds. It does, however, present a very great long-term problem because of the huge extent of the debt, which is a great burden for the country to bear ($179,000 million). $68,000 million of this is public and publicly guaranteed debt owing to private creditors and $49,000 million is private non-guaranteed debt owed to private creditors. $35 billion is owed in short-term debt, $9 billion in multilateral debt to official creditors and $16 billion in bilateral official debt. Thus we see that the percentage of debt owed by Brazil to private creditors is much higher than that of any of the low-income countries for whom we have recommended debt remission. As regards debt owed to official creditors, Brazil does not benefit from any low-interest IDA loans. Its multilateral debt of $9,427 million is partly owed to the IBRD ($5,876 million) and partly to continental and other official banks; $16,803 million is owed to bilateral creditors, including $1,000 million to Britain on ECGD debt. Brazil has only a moderate level of arrears on long-term debt - $741 million to official creditors and $2,204 million to private creditors.

Brazil's burden of debt servicing is crippling. Interest payments of $10,637 million were made in 1996, while principal repayments totalled $14,435 million, giving a total debt service payment of just over $25,000 million. This was a major factor in the huge budget deficit, which was partly responsible for the recent economic collapse. The debt service represents 41% of Brazil's income from XGS, a figure almost three times the average of sub-Saharan Africa in the same year (11.5%). The figure for the ratio of total debt service to the XGS for Latin America as a whole is high (32% in 1996). Brazil has the most unfavourable ratio in the entire continent. Brazil presents us with very difficult problems in assessing any possible debt remission. The basic remedy for the large pockets of extreme poverty in Brazil lies with the Brazilian government itself. Furthermore the very large sum in monetary terms owed by Brazil is only 24% of the country's GNP of $732 billion.

There will continue to be considerable problems of repayment, but these will need to be dealt with separately outside the parameters of the Jubilee 2000 remission. Brazil's export of goods and services is only one-twelfth of its GNP; an unusually small ratio. Therefore the problem of finding hard currency to repay the debt is a difficult one but Brazil, as a country which is itself a creditor to some other Third World countries and which also has considerable income from export of arms, motor cars and other industrial products, could not be included, for any except ecological reasons, on any credible list for remission. By all means let NGOs and people of good will in other countries as well as in Brazil itself do all they can to relieve the sufferings of pockets of severe deprivation in Brazil, as in the case of the indigenous tribes or in that of the street children of the cities of Rio de Janiero and Sao Paulo, but radical Jubilee remission of Brazil's sovereign debt, on economic grounds, is not a practical possibility. However, there is an urgent need for large loans to stabilise Brazil's economy in the present crisis.

Remission on Ecological Grounds Outside the Main Parameters of Jubilee 2000

If we consider possibilities of remission for Brazil on ecological grounds we find that the criteria of economic and ecological measurement work strongly in opposite directions. Clearly we are unable to grant remission on economic grounds, but it may well be possible to do so on ecological grounds through some kind of 'debt for nature' agreement. Brazil has great ecological riches of huge global value. She has 55,000 separate species of higher plants (native vascular species), the highest number of any country in the world. She also has 5,611,000 sq. km. of forest area, second only to the Russian Federation. The annual deforestation in Brazil is 36,700 km, 0.6% of the whole, and the highest in the world.[3] It is very much in the interest of mankind as a whole to preserve these great lungs of the world, and therefore we should seek for the remission of a substantial proportion of the $16 billion of bilateral debt, and possibly also the $9 billion multilateral debt in exchange for really effective guarantees of an end to deforestation. This would be a good bargain for mankind. Britain is owed about $1 billion by Brazil, and France just over $2 billion. This would be an excellent opportunity for an entente cordial between the two countries in creative debt remission. However, the bulk of Brazilian debt is owed to private creditors; therefore the scope for remission is somewhat limited.

So far, debt for nature agreements have been arranged by NGOs and have been on a relatively small scale and have chiefly related to specific nature reserve areas. The legal complications and delays involved in these schemes have been great.[4] If the cause of conservation and the cause of debt remission are to be made symbiotic, a simpler and bolder form of debt for nature swap is needed, and this will require action by creditor governments. In this kind of swap, stricter conditionalities would be needed than in debt remission based on economic grounds. Deforestation is relatively easily measurable from satellite data, and any remission could only occur after a suitable interval, where no deforestation occurs. Alternatively, suitable portions of Brazil's debt could be suspended in exchange for credible proof that the forests have remained intact.

Columbia, the Dominican Republic, Guinea-Bissau, Guatemala, Ecuador, Honduras, Paraguay, Thailand, Venezuela, Vietnam, Cambodia and Gabon have even higher percentage rates of deforestation, and their cases must be explored, but Brazil by reason of its size may be a good country in which to make a massive debt for nature swap in the first instance. Such swaps so far concluded have totalled less than $2 billion spread among a large number of different agreements. Politics is the art of the possible, and we must therefore concentrate upon an objective which is practicable and yet inspiring. Our main emphasis is total or near-total remission of the backlog of debt of the 51 poorest countries, but if we can add an ecological element this may strengthen the campaign.

Jubilee Remission on Grounds of Poverty

There are a number of measures of poverty. We could take the indicators in the World Bank and UNDP survey of world development. However, we soon find that these measures of life expectancy, health provision, provision of clean water, education provision and percentage of the population in absolute poverty correlate closely with measures of GNP per head. Countries at the bottom of the pile in one are at the bottom of the pile in the others. Therefore we have to adopt the standard measure of GNP per head based on currency equivalence as a working hypothesis, in spite of the fact that there are a number of other possible measurements.

There are, of course, two or three measures of GNP and all of them have their limitations. The standard measurement relies on currency equivalence. This is subject to variations as currencies appreciate or depreciate in relation to one another. Francophone Africa, for instance, showed a dramatic fall in the figures for GNP when France devalued the CFAO franc.

The figures for GNP per head show clearly that the vast majority of the countries in Africa South of the Sahara require total or near-total remission. 38 of the 47 countries in this region fall into this category, only Gabon, Mauritius, Seychelles, Botswana, South Africa, Lesotho, Djibouti, Cape Verde and Swaziland have a higher GNP per head. Eritrea and Namibia do not enter into the picture because having become independent a short time ago, they have no residue of past debt, and in fact both countries are at present unwilling to borrow from the World Bank. Neither Eritrea nor Namibia feature in the World Bank tables. Outside Africa South of the Sahara, there are it seems 13 countries eligible for 100% remission, on this criterion of GDP per head: in South America, Bolivia (which is on the list of eligible HIPC countries in the World Bank list), Honduras, Guyana, Nicaragua and Haiti; in Europe, only Albania should qualify; in Asia, Cambodia, Vietnam, Bangladesh, Laos, Sri Lanka, Nepal and the Yemen. In addition to these 13, a special case could perhaps be made for Romania, which suffered so much through its unwise decision to pay off all its debt from 1987 to 1989 and which now owes a further $8.3 billion. Romania is returned in most record books as a country with a GNP per head well over $1000. Myanmar is omitted since there is little prospect of removing its tyrannical government, (although it is in the World Bank list of 41 HIPC countries), but should the liberation from military tyranny occur, it would of course qualify. From this analysis we derive the figure of 51 countries in all who should be considered for total or near total remission (38 in Africa, South of the Sahara).

This list omits three large low-income countries with powerful economies - China, India and Pakistan. China is returned as low-income in World Bank tables and has an increasing level of debt, but it has also a very rapidly growing economy and has attracted a very high level of foreign direct investment from private sources. In any case, China's total debt of $129 billion (1996 figure) is only 16% of her GNP. India is a country which, at first, I included in my list, but my colleagues rightly persuaded me that it was not realistic to ask for Indian debt remission. Its debt, though high in absolute terms ($90 billion) is only about 26% of GNP, having reduced from 37% of GNP in 1993. The debt was reduced by $8 billion from 1994 to 1995 and by a further $5 billion from 1995 to 1996, one of the rare instances of reduction. Since the reforms of 1992, India has built up substantial currency reserves and she has a formidable export potential. The Indian government itself has never spoken in terms of its need for debt forgiveness, although some dedicated groups in India have shown their support for Jubilee 2000 for other less endowed countries. Pakistan falls into roughly the same category as India, and therefore we must leave it also out of our list. Both India and Pakistan have recently carried out nuclear tests, both incurring some economic sanctions from the West. Countries that can afford expenditure on nuclear weapons in order to achieve great power status do not need debt remission.

For countries with GNP between $765 per head and our cut-off point of $2000, we can only offer partial remission to pressing cases. The objective with these cases is not to reduce debt service payments to sustainable levels, but to provide a remission of the stock of past debt sufficient to leave the country concerned only with a sum which it can repay in the medium-term, without causing undue suffering to its people. Our aim in dealing with the debt of these middle-income countries must be the same as that in the policy for the low-income. We are looking for a goal of exit from debt, and not for one of reducing the debt to a 'sustainable' level, whatever that might mean.

A possible percentage remission could be 50%, or alternatively, a more elaborate formula of everything above 20% of a year's GNP, or 80% of a year's XGS (which ever is the least). This might be a suitable measure of the residue of debt which can be repaid by a country which is poor but not among the poorest. The countries which might reasonably be considered for partial remission include: Jamaica, Philippines, Papua New Guinea, Solomon Islands, Vanuatu, Algeria, Egypt, Morocco, Djibouti, Jordan, Ecuador,

Lesotho and Swaziland (and possibly also Peru, although her GNP per head is slightly above $2000). In this case, however, as in the decision on total or near-total remission for low-income countries, there will have to be a careful case-by-case analysis to see whether the country concerned can fall into the suggested category. The phrase 'case-by-case' has entered so deeply into the thought of International Financial Institutions and creditor governments, that we should not succeed in persuading them to adopt any debt remission programme that does not include it. The presumption, however, must be that unless there are very special reasons to the contrary, the country concerned will fit into the appropriate general category based on its GNP per head.

Above the $2000 per head cut-off point, only South Africa seems to qualify as an exceptional case, meriting partial remission (probably at the 50% level). As mentioned in Chapter 13, there may be developments after the year 2000 of a kind which enable us to do something for other countries, which are above $2000 GNP per head, but have special reasons to need our help. For the purposes of the Jubilee 2000 campaign itself, however, we must concentrate on the 51 poorest countries requiring total or near-total remission and the 14 or so countries in the list to be considered for partial remission. Without concentration, we shall not achieve the first stage of our objective.

The Special Case of South Africa

When I went to Westminster Abbey and heard Archbishop Desmond Tutu addressing the congregation on the 50th Anniversary of the foundation of the UN, I was delighted to hear him speak about Jubilee. I wrote to him to say that I had wanted to stand up in the pew and cheer, but that this seemed inappropriate in the Abbey! I explained that I was preparing a paper for the International Studies Conference in San Diego containing a list of countries recommended for various levels of remission, and asked what he thought I should recommend for South Africa. He replied that the external debts of South Africa (which now total about $23.59 billion, 1996) were incurred by the racist apartheid government; they should not be imposed on the new multi-racial, democratic state and should be forgiven in their entirety. South Africa itself has written off Namibia's debt to it, believing it effectively to be an odious debt incurred while Namibia was illegally occupied by the Apartheid Government.[5] It is surely only just to treat South African debt with the generosity equal to that which South Africa has shown to its own debtors!

During the Apartheid years, South Africa submitted no debt statistics to the World Bank. The earliest figures we have available from the World Bank debt tables show a long-term debt outstanding of $12,963 million in 1994 - the date of the installation of the new democratic government. All of this debt is owing to private creditors. It is reasonable to assume that nearly all this debt arose from the Apartheid years.

There is a fairly strong pressure group in South Africa suggesting that debts incurred during the Apartheid regime should be classed as 'odious' debts.[6] This is a category known to jurists and implies that the original debt transaction was flawed. In the South African case, international sanctions forbade the granting of new loans at that time. In that case, the odious debt would be declared invalid on the principle of 'ex turpe causa non est reum' (where the transaction itself is corrupt, no case arises). It might be argued that certain other debt transactions with non-democratic African governments such as that of Mobutu should likewise be classified as odious debt and thus cancelled. However, it seems to me that one could not accept a general principle that debts incurred by tyrannical governments are to be classified as odious, for this would invalidate a great deal of normal banking practice. It is hard for bankers to take account of the political merits and demerits of their official customers, for the Banks lack the necessary information and political judgement, but they can be expected to obey a UN or any other official ban on loans to particular governments.

It is noteworthy that South Africa has obtained its loans at a high rate of interest. As of 1996, it had not benefitted from any IDA funds. The average terms of new commitments in 1994 were 6.2% and in 1995, 5.4%, as contrasted with the average rates charged to sub-Saharan Africa as a whole - 4% in 1994 and 3.9% in 1995. It may be that in the last two years, South Africa has begun to be granted more favourable terms, but so far it would appear that the euphoric reception given by the international community to the establishment of democracy in South Africa has not extended to substantial concessions on debt. In 1996 for instance, South Africa paid $1,013 million in interest on its debts. The international community clearly has a duty to provide some adequate level of debt remission to South Africa and to arrange sources of finance on more favourable terms. If this is not done, it is going to be very hard for the South African economy to support the necessary levels of health, social and educational expenditure needed to make a reality of liberation from the woeful heritage of Apartheid.

South Africa is a fairly powerful economy despite the present devaluations of the rand. Its debts sell on the discount market for 90% of face value. The total South African external debt in 1996 was $23,590 million, of which only $13,907 million was long-term debt, with a total debt service charge equal to

11.1% of its XGS. According to the latest World Bank debt tables, the balance of $9,683 million consists of $8,800 million short-term debt and $884 million IMF credit. As of 1996, South Africa had no multilateral debt and no concessional debt. It owed its private creditors $10,348 million of long-term debt. South Africa had no debt to official creditors other than the IMF.

This is in marked contrast to the situation of almost all other low-income countries, whose debt owed to official creditors is considerably higher than that owed to private creditors. It is therefore not possible to solve South Africa's debt problem through the direct action of governments. Both the South African Government and the governments of relevant creditor countries can provide some inducement or other forms of persuasion for commercial banks to forgive 50% of the $10,348 million guaranteed debt owed by South Africa to private creditors in 1996 and 50% of the $3,559 million owed in private non-guaranteed debt. They may be able to do this partly through tax incentives offered to banks for debt remission. 100% remission of South African debt would involve a level of forgiveness by banks and other private creditors, and of cancellation of bonds higher than we are likely to be able to achieve. Therefore it would not be realistic to ask for 100% remission for South Africa; we should concentrate on obtaining a figure of 50% or thereabouts. This may be difficult but it is an important issue.

The difficulty of obtaining debt remission for South Africa is increased by the fact that her government has recently seen fit to incur further loans for the purpose of buying arms, only some of which are essential to her needs. This arms purchase is examined in detail on pages 96 and 97.

Notes

1   The World Bank dividing line between 'low-income' and 'middle-income'
countries has moved over the years. In 1992, it was at GNP per head of $500,
but has risen by progressive stages to $765 in 1997 (Global Development
Finance; Vol.1 1997 p.52). The change is largely due to changes in the value of
the dollar measured in terms of its purchasing power. The list of low-income
countries as designated by the World Bank has not changed very much. Some
of the Francophone countries in Africa, South of the Sahara, were not on the
list in 1992, but since the devaluation of the CFAO franc, all these
Francophone countries, except Gabon have been categorised as low-income.
Indonesia, which was in the low-income list in 1992, was re-categorised as
middle-income during its subsequent boom years, before the present disastrous
collapse of the economy and the currency. It may well now be properly

classified as low-income; the full effects of the present financial collapse have yet to be measured but they are very severe for poorer people in that country. There are, however, severe political obstacles to the implementation of any debt remission package for Indonesia. During the long period of rule of President Suharto, its human rights record has been appalling and it has over a long period continued to defy UN rulings on the need for a plebiscite on self-government for East Timor and Irian Jaya.

2   See classification of countries by income level in the *World Bank Annual Report and Accounts 1997*, p. 9.

3   *World Development Indicators 1997*, tables 3.1 and 3.2: Washington D.C., World Bank, pp. 94-98.

4   Correspondence of the author with a private bank official, who arranged a debt for nature swap for a fairly small sum after overcoming considerable legal difficulties and spending a great deal of time in the negotiation. He considered that the benefit was too small to justify any further debt for nature swap.

5   Keesing's Contemporary Archives December 1994 page 310. On 6 December 1994 President Mandela announced the remission of $190 million debt owed to South Africa by Namibia, saying that it would be immoral to finance South Africa's campaign for reconstruction with money owed by Namibia before it gained independence from South Africa in March 1990.

6   This term was first used over 100 years ago by the United States to describe a debt which was incurred not in the interests of the state but to strengthen a despotic regime, to repress the population that fights against it - Archbishop Njongonkulu Ndungane 'Seizing the New Millenium, Reshaping the World's Economy' in *Proclaiming Liberty*, p.29. There is a just symmetry in the two applications of the doctrine of odious debt: the debt owed to South Africa by Namibia incurred during the Apartheid regime should be remitted, while the larger debt owed by the new South African government to overseas private bankers, entered into during the same period, should also be forgiven.

7 Conditionalities for Remission

One of the most common criticisms made of Jubilee 2000 has been that it seeks to remove the burden of unpayable past debt from low-income countries, but fails to deal with the corruption and inefficiency on the part of their government and administrators that has often been one of the major causes of the debt. I have discovered that the overwhelming response of ordinary people to whom I have spoken in African countries is to say 'we welcome a Jubilee of debt remission, but how do we know that it will not be used by our rulers to enrich themselves yet more than they have done in the past?' Critics in creditor countries in the developed world also attack the concept of any debt remission, which is not accompanied by abandonment of corrupt practices, and suggest that to forgive the debts of corrupt governments is just to encourage further corruption in future.

In meeting these criticisms we have to show how Jubilee debt remission can be used as a uniquely powerful lever, to procure changes in the financial administration and government conduct in debtor countries, of a kind which will dramatically reduce the level of corruption and of waste through inefficient administration. We cannot seek to eliminate all corruption at once for at a certain level it has become part of the political culture, at the present, but this can be changed over time, given sufficient dedication and effort by the government and people of the country concerned. We can demand a dramatic reduction comparable to that which Britain achieved in the conduct of its own government and that of its Indian Empire between 1750 and 1850. Robert Clive, in 1773, having enriched himself by £250,000 through bribes and misappropriations during his period of rule in Madras and Bengal, declared that 'he stood amazed at his own moderation'. He spoke the truth, for other administrators of the East India Company were even more corrupt than he was. A hundred years later, however, after the profound changes effected by the Evangelical Revolution and by government reorganisation, such corruption became unthinkable. The age of the corrupt 'Nabobs' had given way to the incorruptible, even if at times arrogant, administration under the Indian Civil Service.

Meanwhile, a similar reformation had occurred in the governance of Britain itself. Early in the 18th Century, Walpole believed that 'everyone has his price'. Thirty years later, however, the corruption of Walpole's era had given way to the patriotic integrity of Chatham. In the nineteenth century

Gladstone typified a level of unquestioned honesty, where corruption was the exception rather than the rule.

Glaring instances of corruption occur in the government and institutions of the so-called developed world, as for instance in the case of the Swiss banks, who accepted Nazi gold extracted from the Jews. However, the level of corruption common in developed countries is much less than that in most of the developing world and its effect on public finance is less.

Third World countries such as Nigeria are perfectly capable of such a transformation to more honest public finance given the stimulus of Jubilee 2000 and of a continuing popular campaign.

There is an increasing number of younger educated people in Third World debtor countries who long for a new and more honest beginning. In Nigeria, for instance, the enlightened and dedicated members of various civil rights groups have been doing their utmost to educate ordinary Nigerians in the essentials of honest democracy. It is the task of those who negotiate Jubilee 2000 remission terms to insist on the structural and procedural changes in administration, which will give an opportunity for this vigorous reforming sector to create a new style of public life. These conditionalities must be firmly insisted upon from the creditor side, but at the same time the whole package must be developed by both debtor and creditor working together. The final agreement must embody a reform package, which a large number of people in the country whose debts are forgiven, accept as their own.

In dealing with countries whose claim upon Jubilee debt remission is high because of their low income, but whose governments are corrupt, we have to refrain from rejecting their case out of hand. At the same time, however, we must make it quite clear that certain reforms in better audit, in recovery of stolen funds from former rulers, in better financial management and in the establishment of democratic government and the rule of law must be made before any debt remission can be granted. Furthermore, there must be evidence that the sums released by the remission will actually be spent for the benefit of the poor and the maintenance of the essential services of the state. This distinction is not a pedantic one. We have to show to the people of the country concerned that we care for their plight and we have to give them hope, while at the same time insisting firmly on financial discipline in the future.

In order to ensure that sums released by debt remission are properly spent, we need some form of 'ringfencing' to separate these sums from general expenditure and to ensure that their control is vested in particularly reliable financial authorities in the country concerned. The expenditure must be subject to rigorous audit and must be accountable to the legislature and to the people of the country. Economists have often raised the objection against ringfencing that money is fungible; a specific undertaking to spend money in a particular way could be nullified by a reduction in the sums already allocated by the government of the country to the particular project, now being financed by a donor or by debt remission. Money is indeed fungible, but as a senior World Bank official in a recent presentation at the Overseas Development Institute put it, 'contracts are not'. There remains a very difficult task of ensuring that the contracts entered into as part of the remission package are, in fact, honoured. Some have suggested that this requires direct supervision by external organisations or, alternatively, a period of probation before final debt remission. I find these alternatives smack too much of neo-colonialism, and suggest that if the remission is properly negotiated, the country relieved of its financial debt will assume a debt of honour to keep to these agreed conditions, in order to create a good reputation for themselves.

Hitherto, the IMF has imposed its own conditionalities and structural adjustment programmes attached to each tranche of financial assistance, even when that tranche was only the temporary expedient of a rescheduling of part of the debt. The suspicion has been aroused in the minds of many in the debtor countries that IMF terms have not been developed in the interest of the debtor country concerned, but rather in that of the creditors in the developed world. It is often assumed that the prime purpose of the compulsory changes imposed by the IMF is to safeguard the remaining debt owed to creditors. In the case of reforms accompanying Jubilee 2000 remission however, this suspicion will no longer be present for, in the case of low-income countries, all or almost all of the debt owed will be cancelled, thus leaving the creditor countries with no selfish interest in the debt. In the past, IMF conditionalities have aroused very great hostility in many debtor countries. They are seen as over rigid terms imposed as part of an ideologically inspired programme of monetarism. The IMF has been rightly criticised for relying on a single tool to deal with many different sorts of economic situations. Furthermore, this extreme free market emphasis has remained as a residue of the psychology of the cold war. In the fight against the dangers of communism, anything which smacked of socialism was an anathema to the financial administrators of World Bank and the IMF in Washington. Therefore conditionalities have placed a great deal of emphasis on privatisation. During the last decade many state enterprises have undergone various forms of privatisation in Third World countries as well as in the developed world. This has in many cases produced greater efficiency, but there are costs. The attempts of the IMF to impose a blanket privatisation strategy has, in consequence, met with considerable hostility in many debtor countries.[1]

This free market emphasis has also involved opposition to government subsidies, even where they are functional for increased agricultural production or the relief of poverty. It has also involved a rigid opposition to any form of exchange control or of protection of infant industries by import duties or quotas. Partly as a result of this policy local industry has been discouraged and the local currency has experienced a catastrophic level of devaluation. It seems paradoxical for the IMF to seek to remedy a cash crisis in debtor countries by insisting that their market should be thrown open to imports from all countries in the world. A person who has contracted a large overdraft, which he cannot service, is usually told by his bank manager to desist from ordering goods from expensive stores; the advice given to debtor countries by the IMF is the exact opposite. One can only conclude that this advice is given in the interest of exporters in the developed world. The forces of global capitalism and the unimpeded entry of the global market into the local economy have brought some advantages, but where all controls have been removed the costs in terms of human welfare have often been great. The most beneficial direction of IMF conditionality has been its attempts to produce proper audit and proper accountability of the actions of those who control government expenditure. This should have been the major emphasis of the IMF and World Bank, but often it has been overshadowed by the ideological emphasis on free market operations. It is in this direction that Jubilee 2000 conditionality will need to make its greatest emphasis.

A further emphasis of IMF conditionality has been on the reduction of government expenditure. It is true that in many Third World countries too much of the national income has been spent on bloated bureaucracies, though not all Third World administrations are parasitical. Furthermore, government employment is for many poorer people in towns the only way to avoid destitution. As Bill Peters has shown, IMF programmes have tended to be administered by young and inexperienced expatriates, who visit the country concerned for a relatively short period and produce these remedies in an arrogant manner, without consulting local people or taking account of local conditions. The rigidity of the IMF structural adjustment programmes has produced considerable hostility in many Third World countries to the whole concept of conditionality; it requires a long and detailed study to determine how far this criticism is justified.

It is essential to use the great opportunity of the negotiation of a near-total remission to pursuade the debtor government to adopt certain essential reforms for the benefit of their own country. If we do not do so, the country whose debts have been forgiven might fall back again into the well of debt, from which it has been rescued. Furthermore, we have to persuade taxpayers in creditor countries to make some sacrifice to obtain the remission. We cannot expect to do this, if they see the result of the Jubilee as being an opportunity for certain corrupt rulers in the Third World to make personal fortunes.

It follows, therefore, that the conditionalities on which we must insist should concern themselves less with free market dogma and reduction of essential government expenditure on social services, and more on proper audit and accountability, to prevent future waste of money. Many countries in Africa suffer from a disastrous lack of proper action to enforce financial accountability, and proper procedure to prevent stealing by high government officials. In Nigeria, for instance, Pius Okigbo, the elder statesman of Nigerian financial circles, was asked by the then Head of State, General Ibrahim Babangida, to report upon the Central Bank. In his report, Okigbo revealed that $8 billion of windfall profits from oil resulting from the Gulf War were paid into a special account controlled only by the Head of State and the Governor of the Bank. No accounts whatever were kept of this expenditure. This is typical of procedure in quite a number of poor debtor countries. [2]

In general, the problem is not one of lack of skilled auditors, but of obtaining effective action upon audit reports. The files of offices in Ministries of Finance in Africa are often full of ancient audit reports, ably written by local auditors, but never acted upon effectively by governments. We have therefore to obtain from the debtor government a credible guarantee that proper audit and enforcement of auditors recommendations will take place after the Jubilee and continue to be the practice. There is a need for some automatic administrative procedure in the governments of debtor countries, whose debts are forgiven, to ensure that the audit reports are brought up year by year to the attention of top administrators, to check on what action has been taken upon them. If no action has been taken, this may well be because some senior figure has been misappropriating government money and wishes to hide the fact. There needs to be some direct access of anti-corruption bodies and state prosecutors to the audit report each year. In this way, one might succeed in preventing the burying of uncomfortable audit revelations! Jubilee 2000 is a great benefit to the debtor country, but it is also a bracing call to better financial administration in future. The question arises as to whether a declaration of future sound financial practice will be sufficient, or whether some period of probation is required. My own inclinations are against probation, as it destroys the concept of Jubilee as liberation. We are, however, justified in seeking to ensure that the legal and financial structures are created for sound finance. The World Bank imposes a 6 year period of probation on HIPC countries before they qualify for remission, but this seems excessive.

There is, of course, a problem in ensuring that bodies, which look effective on paper, will function effectively in practice. Nigeria, for instance, has set up in its new draft Constitution a special body for the recovery of ill-gotten gains. This body is endowed in the Constitution with formidable powers, but has not yet begun to operate.[3] Under the Shagari regime (1979-83) the Constitution provided for a stringent Code of Conduct for all Government employees, but it was never enforced. This time the situation must be different. It is essential that as part of the process of Jubilee, there should be thorough consultations and agreements between the debtor government and the creditors, who are forgiving the debt. The agreements so reached will reinforce the determination of active citizens in these countries to seek a radical new beginning in financial matters.

The Jubilee must become a kind of second independence, and generate the energies necessary for a new beginning. I remember how, at the time of Nigerian independence in 1960, as I was touring around Tiv division making peace after the riots, one of the political representatives with me spoke with great eloquence. 'Now', he said, 'we are taking our destiny into our own hands from the Europeans. Hegen se tor uma uhe (now we take new life upon us)'. Alas, not all the expectations of independence were fulfilled; Jubilee however, gives a second chance. The Jubilee campaign has a dual nature; it seeks for a precisely defined remission of the debt of low-income countries incurred before 1996, at the same time, however, it seeks to kindle a flame of reforming energy among both debtor and creditor countries.

In the case of countries, whose rulers have acquired fortunes by embezzlement of government money or through bribes, we must seek to recover at least a part of this money. This can be done either through action in the country itself, or through legal proceedings to bring back to the government of the country concerned part of the corrupt fortunes of past or present political leaders.[4] A way has already been shown in the cases of President Mobutu, President Marcos and President Duvalier, and is likely to be shown in the case of the late President Abacha. The old rules of the total secrecy and inviolability of bank accounts in Switzerland and elsewhere have begun to be relaxed somewhat, as in the case of recovery Nazi gold taken from the Jews, to close these boltholes for corrupt holdings. Furthermore, for several years there has been a battle to combat the ill effects of money laundering in a number of states.

For psychological reasons, it is most important not to reject outright the case of a poor country with a corrupt government. We should acknowledge the moral case of the country for debt remission based upon need and, in some cases, such as Nigeria, on past common ties, but should qualify the acceptance in principle with a statement that no remission will be granted in practice until certain conditions have been met. In the Nigerian case and in that of the Democratic Republic of the Congo (formerly Zaire) this will also involve a return to civilian rule under a government chosen in a free and fair election. If Jubilee 2000 were to reject a low-income country out of hand and to indicate that it will never be considered for debt remission, we should be removing hope from that country, whereas if we accept it in principle, but declare that no debt remission will be implemented until certain specific conditionalities are met, we provide a powerful incentive for reform.

Notes

1   For a detailed analysis of privatisation schemes in various countries see section on 'progress on privatization' appendix 6 in Global Development Finance Vol. 1: Washington D.C., World Bank, 1997, p.115.

2   Following the death of General Sani Abacha the Head of the Nigerian Government in June 1999, a search of the office of his chief security advisor revealed a large cache of money, about $200 million (broadcast on BBC World Service 4.11.98). In addition, he was found to possess at least 30 houses in Nigeria. There have been a number of different reports of the sums of money misappropriated by General Abacha and his closest co-agutors. A source in the Nigerian High Commission in London informed me that the total of known misappropriation was about $600 million. We wait to see how effective will be the means used by the new Nigerian government to punish the culprits and recover the money.

3   Section 290 of the Nigerian Constitution drawn up for the return to civilian rule sets up a 'committee for the recovery of ill-gotten wealth' which is given effective powers to summon witnesses and examine documents as well as to recommend repayments of corruptly acquired finance.

4   The new government of General Abubakar Abdusalam in Nigeria has just ordered the family of the previous Head of State General Abacha to repay $750,000 (Britain-Nigeria Association Newsletter, October 1998). This is a good beginning, but only a beginning; it represents only a fraction of the money to be recovered from Abacha's family and associates. General

Abdulsalam Abubakar, the President elect, has first ordered that Nigeria needs strict moral standards in its public life. He has a high reputation as an honest administrator.

8 Benefits and Costs of the Remission

It is of the utmost importance to cost the proposed remission. The obvious question which is asked by almost all observers is, 'Who is going to pay for the forgiveness of the debts?' The face values of the debts of the 51 poorest countries for which we should seek total or near-total remission are as follows:

Table 5 Cost of debt remission

Country	face value of debt (US$ millions 1996)	net present value[1] (US$ millions)
Albania	925	?
Angola	10612	10859
Bangladesh	16083	9153
Benin	1594	920
Bhutan	86	
Bolivia	5174	3199
Burkina Faso	1294	646
Burundi	1127	523
Cambodia	2111	1436
Cameroon	9515	7482
Central African Republic	928	504
Chad	997	442
Comoros	206	?
Congo, Democratic Republic of (Kinshasa)	12826	11630
Congo Republic (Brazzaville)	5240	5357
Côte D'Ivoire	19713	16596
Equatorial Guinea	282	217
Ethiopia	10077	3435
Gambia	452	214
Ghana	6202	3776
Guinea	3240	2104
Guinea-Bissau	937	582
Guyana	1631	1583

Country	face value of debt (US$ millions 1996)	net present value (US$ millions)
Haiti	897	396
Honduras	4453	3707
Kenya	6893	5466
Lao PDR	2263	743
Liberia	2107	1963
Madagascar	4175	3189
Malawi	2312	1018
Mali	3020	1805
Mauritania	2363	1685
Mozambique	5842	4429
Nepal	2413	1180
Nicaragua	5929	?
Niger	1557	1016
Nigeria	31407	31000?
Rwanda	1034	480
Sao Tome & Principe	261	142
Senegal	3663	2510
Sierra Leone	1167	768
Somalia	2643	2213
Sri Lanka	8231	?
Sudan	16972	16206
Tanzania	7412	5389
Togo	1463	917
Uganda	3674	1868
Vietnam	26764	23319
Yemen	6356	5109
Zambia	7113	4963
Zimbabwe	5005	4016
TOTALS	269,219	202,596 (5 unknown)

Source: Face value figures from World Bank Debt Tables 1998. Net present value figures from Jubilee 2000 submission to House of Commons Select Committee Report on Debt, p.52, 5th May 1998. Note: Since 1998, the name of the World Bank Debt Tables has been changed to 'Global Development Finance'. The statistical contents are the same in the country by country analysis in Volume 2, but they are abbreviated in the summary tables in Volume 1.

This total figure for face value is, of course, much more than the actual cost of the remission. Most of the cost of Jubilee is a giving up of claims for future payment, rather than a payment of money now. Often the future claims are unrealistic, since the debtors are nearly bankrupt. They can no more be included in the assessment of the assets of the creditor than could a debt of 100,000 owed to Harrods by a person, who is now living on the Embankment and cannot afford even a cup of tea, be included in the assets of Harrods. In 1983, when we were celebrating the 150th Anniversary of the Bill abolishing slavery in the then British Empire, Sir John Biggs-Davison MP came to the lunch that my Buxton aunt and I had arranged. He catechised me on the meaning of this event: 'Dent, what we are celebrating is Jubilee, which means also the remission of debt. It comes in the Bible in Leviticus 25.' I replied, 'I know, Sir John.' He went on, 'We should forgive the debts of poorer nations because they will not pay anyway.' This seemed to me to be not only good morality, but also sound business sense, although it is not a full statement of the case. I concluded that if a commitment to Jubilee could be made by a Conservative MP, whose views on most subjects were well to the right of mine, I could put forward the Jubilee case, in which I already believed, without fear of being considered utopian in my generosity. (This was a one-off comment of Sir John, he did not start a campaign and when we met again a year later to celebrate the implementation of the Emancipation Act, he had thought better of his proposal and said that an economist should be consulted).

The discount value of the debts - i.e., what they would fetch on the market - can be obtained from the Cantrion internet website. It varies immensely from country to country. The debts of Malawi, Ghana, Philippines and Vietnam all have discount values of over 80%, while the debts of Sudan and Liberia have a value of about 5%.

Bilateral debt

The average discount value of the debts owed by low-income countries is given on the website as about 38%. A difficulty in using this measure of the cost of debt remission is that websites often give two separate figures for different sorts of debt owed by the same country, according to the conditions of the loan, the rate of interest and the date of redemption.

A more useful measure of the true value of official bilateral debts can be derived from an estimate of the debt servicing payments likely to be received in future. It is a fair assumption that, barring exceptional circumstances, these receipts will be about the same in the next (say) three years as they were in the last (say) three years.

If we seek to assess the cost to Britain of forgiving the bilateral debt owed to the British Government, we need to examine the accounts of the Export Credit Guarantee Department (ECGD). More than 95% of the bilateral debt now owed to Britain originates from ECGD. The residue of Overseas Development Administration (ODA) debt arising from loans made for aid purposes in the past, before a policy decision was taken some 20 years ago to make grants rather than loans for aid to poorer countries, has almost all been written off. Clare Short recently announced the write-off of a further £132 million and very little of this debt now remains; it is ECGD with which we now have to be concerned.

The Export Credit and Guarantee Department is not an aid agency and can only remit debt as part of a specific government policy decided upon by Ministers. ECGD have remitted relatively small amounts of debt in the past; in 1995 to 1996 their accounts show that £51.5 million was written off under the heading of 'recoveries abandoned'. This shows that there is no insuperable objection of principle to debt remission from ECGD; the problem is one of greatly increasing the amount of remission, where debts are unpayable. In their 1996-97 report ECGD comments on debt remission as follows, 'without this assistance debtor countries would never be capable of servicing their debt burdens for ECGD, this (i.e. remission) enhances the prospect of eventually receiving higher debt repayments and avoids having to maintain unrealistic expectations of recovery'. They go on to speak of the HIPC initiative as 'a fresh advance towards debt remission'.

There is clearly a profound difference of emphasis between the Jubilee 2000 position on remission of bilateral debt and that of ECGD, but in the final negotiations the two positions could perhaps be reconciled. ECGD are looking for a 'Laffer curve', where they can recover a greater proportion of their claims by asking for a lower percentage for recovery. Jubilee 2000 must in my view be looking for a radical remission and a new beginning for heavily indebted poor countries. The rate of remission for which we should seek, for low-income countries, should be 100%, or somewhere near 100%. In the final negotiations on remission it may well be necessary to bargain between these two positions. It is significant that in their bargaining session with overseas bankers, in 1992, the Nigerian Ministry of Finance achieved a rate of remission of about 80%. We should aim at a higher figure than this, perhaps 90 to 95%.

ECGD was set up in 1919 as a kind of government backed insurance agency for British exporters sending their goods to countries, where there is some element of risk or some difficulty in debt collection. The ECGD is responsible to the Board of Trade and carries out its financial transactions through the consolidated fund. It insures goods exported in exchange for a premium, usually about 1%, which has to be paid by the British exporter, but is usually added to the cost of the contract. As long as payments are being made by the recipient in hard currency the goods are classified as 'sums at risk' in the ECGD accounts and do not enter into the debt tables. On 31st March 1997, the total of these 'sums at risk' in ECGD accounts was £16,503 million. If, however, the recipient fails to pay for the goods, whether this is because he does not make the necessary payments in his own currency, or because the currency authority of the country concerned, having received payment in the local currency, fails to send the payment to ECGD in hard currency, the exporter in Britain has his bill paid within a few months by ECGD. This gives rise to an ECGD claim on the government of the country concerned. This claim is recorded as part of the bilateral debt owed to UK, and the ECGD representative sits in on the Paris Club of bilateral creditors, as part of the British delegation.

The total of the British ECGD claims outstanding against the 51 low-income countries for whom I have suggested remission is about £4 billion. Approximately half of this is owed by Nigeria. Britain is Nigeria's largest single creditor, to whom that country owes 23% of its bilateral debt of $15 billion. Nigeria, as we have seen, is way behind in its payments, and it seems unlikely that it will be able to catch up, in view of the pressing need for using its now quite modest oil revenue to meet the requirements of 100 million people.

The total receipts of Britain's ECGD by way of 'recovery of claims' on the low-income countries, including Nigeria, has been only about £40 million per year for the last three years. It seems to be a fairly safe bet that receipts on these claims in the next three years, even if there is no remission, will be no higher than they were in the last three. The annual cost, therefore, of the remission of the bilateral debt of poorer countries to the UK Government will be about £40 million per year. This could be covered by a mere 2% increase in our modest aid budget of some £2 billion per year. Such a remission would give the opportunity for Britain to give a lead to those bilateral creditors of the poorer nations, who are owed considerably more than we are,[2] as shown in tables 6 and 7.

Clare Short has complained that this proposed unilateral debt forgiveness would separate us from other creditors, and destroy our ability to influence them. This argument has force, but, however, it may well be that a practical demonstration of debt forgiveness by the United Kingdom government will carry more weight than any amount of good advice to foreign creditors from our Government, when we make the suggestion that they should join with us in a common act of debt remission.

There are two possible further objections to this remission. First, it is said that ECGD business has been privatised, when elements in the portfolio were handed over to the Dutch credit firm Nederland Credit Maatschappy (NCM). A study of the ECGD accounts reveals, however, that this does not interfere with the possibilities of debt remission. Second, that there is an agreement among the Export Credit and Guarantee Agencies of most creditor nations to conduct their enterprise in a way that balances the books and neither subsidises nor taxes exports. ECGD have achieved a rough balance over the past 20 years between the sums that they have paid into the consolidated fund and those that they have taken out of it. The argument that forgiveness of claims would upset this balance is surely invalid since relatively small sums have been recovered from claims in the last three years.

The good example which we would give by total or near-total remission of the ECGD claims on low-income countries is particularly important, because of the large totals of debt owed by the poorest countries to the four major creditors - Japan, France, United States and Germany. In 1994 these totals were as shown in Tables 6 and 7.

Table 6 Debts owed by low-income countries to major creditors

	African low-income Countries ($)	Non-African low-income Countries ($)	Total
Japan	7539	8225	15764
France	13283	995	14278
USA	4454	3128	7582
Germany	5941	1459	7400
UK	5258	482	5740
Italy	4193	594	4787
Spain	1333	439	1772
Canada	676	240	916

Table 7   Debts owed by all developing countries to major creditors

Japan	$121 billion
France	$43 billion
US	$40 billion
Germany	$54 billion
UK	$11 billion
Italy	$15 billion
Spain	$9 billion
Canada	$10 billion

Source: EURODAD World Credit Tables 1996

These totals include sums owed by some countries with GNP per head between $765 and $2,000, to whom it might be appropriate to grant partial remission. The largest of these are the Philippines, which owed a colossal total debt of $41 billion in 1996, of which $13 billion was owed to official bilateral creditors. $11 billion of this bilateral debt is owed to Japan and $1.27 billion to the USA. The case for considerable remission of Philippine debt by Japan is overwhelming. The sum owed is enormous and the moral debt of Japan to the Philippines is great. Japan has given considerable help to the Philippines through grants to enable the Philippines to repay debts. However, a more open and effective remission is needed.

Egypt, Morocco and Algeria are possible candidates for partial remission. Egypt has a GNP per head only just above our cut-off point for low-income countries of $765. In 1996, she owed total debt of $31,407 billion. In 1994, she owed: USA, $6,400 million; Germany, $4,900 million; France, $4,600 million; Japan, $4,400 million; Italy, $845 million; Spain, $733 million; UK, $577 million. These are large sums. Clearly the case of Egypt will need very careful examination to see what level (if any) of partial debt remission can be extended.

Morocco's GNP per head is just above our $765 cut-off line. It owes total debt of $21,767 million, $8,800 of this is bilateral debt; in 1994 she owed $3,928 million to France; $1,105 million to the US; $919 million to Germany; $869 million to Spain; $729 million to Japan; $467 million to Italy; $129 million to Canada and only $82 million to the UK. Morocco's case is also on the margin and needs careful examination to see what level of partial debt remission can be extended.

Algeria is in a roughly similar situation, having a GNP per head of about $1200. She suffers both from the catastrophic fall in oil price and from prolonged fundamentalist terrorism, partly due to poverty, which has now almost escalated to outright civil war. Algeria's total debt, in 1996, was $33,260 million and her bilateral debts totalled $13,767 million in 1996, having risen by $6 billion since 1994. Algeria's creditors were as follows (1994 figures): Japan, $1,439 million; France, $1,197 million; Spain, $1,105 million; USA, $760 million; Canada, $563 million; Italy, $555 million; UK, (only) $83 million.

The average yearly receipts (dollars millions) from countries for whom we should consider debt remission for the five years 1990 to 1994 inclusive are as follows:

Table 8   Yearly receipts of major creditors for period 1990 to 1994 from countries qualifying for debt remission

	inside Africa	outside Africa	total
Japan**	531	878	1409
France	477	53	530
Germany	520	66	588
UK*	306	61	367
USA	442	350	792
Italy	122	33	155
Spain	248	53	301
Canada	295	29	324

Source: EURODAD World Credit Tables 1996

*   The figures for the UK are greatly skewed in that $607 million was received in 1990, $507 million in 1991 and only $309 million in all for the three years 1992-94. The variation has been largely due to the irregularity of Nigerian payments.[3]
** Of the $878 average receipts of Japan from low-income and near low-income countries outside Africa, $565 represents debt payments made by the Philippines.

Nigeria paid $921 million out of the $1565 million received by Britain in the five years to 1994. The Nigerian payments have been sporadic rather than regular; in view of the present parlous state of Nigeria's finances and the urgent need of the population, it seems unlikely that their rate of repayments will ever recover to the original level.

The forgiveness of the unpayable residue of the debt of poorer countries will, of course, demand some sacrifice from creditors. We are embarked upon an enterprise of audacious global altruism; we cannot achieve any major improvement in the lot of poorer nations without some cost to ourselves, but the cost is far from being an excessive one. What we need is only the degree of self-sacrifice involved in the quality, which Chaucer described and praised as 'Gentilesse', that is to say, the degree of sacrifice and compassion one could reasonably expect from an honourable person, which does not imply the excessive destruction of his own interests. It is as though we were Dives, the rich man in the Biblical parable, at whose gate Lazarus the destitute beggar was lying. Because he failed to meet the basic needs of Lazarus when he had the chance, Dives was condemned to fires of punishment after death. He could, however, during his lifetime have met those needs by sacrificing only a little of the sumptuous food, which we are told he ate every day, or by selling off just a proportion of his 'fine raiment'. What was required of him in the parable was not heroic self-sacrifice, but decent behaviour.

We are in a similar situation with respect to poorer countries and we must not fail to make the necessary provision to meet their basic needs, including debt remission. The exercise will in no way involve the collapse of our own economy or of the international system. The Chancellor of the Exchequer, Gordon Brown, has promised an increase in our overseas aid budget from 0.25% of Britain's GNP to 0.3%. This figure is still small, though welcome; it leaves a great deal of room for improvement, and a lot of spare capacity for financing the giving up of the relatively small annual payments of debt service, which are extracted from the governments of low-income countries. The annual receipts of debt service payment have averaged £40 million over the last three years for which statistics are available to me. If we assume that debt service payments will remain roughly the same in the next three years has they have in the last three years, Jubilee remission would cost £40 million per year; this could be covered by a mere increase of 2% in our annual aid budget bringing it up from 0.3% of GNP to 0.304%.

Multilateral Debt

The total of World Bank debt to be remitted, from the window at commercial rates of interest (referred to in the World Bank Debt Tables as IBRD debt), is now greatly reduced, since so much of this low-income debt has been converted into IDA concessional loans. This represents a considerable achievement for the benefit of low-income countries, which is to the credit of the World Bank President, but it still leaves the burden of the eventual repayment of principal. The 1998 World Bank debt tables (p.172) give a figure for Africa South of the Sahara of only $6.4 billion for IBRD debt, as opposed to $29.5 billion for IDA debt for 1996. Surely, therefore, the World Bank should be able to finance the relatively small remission of IBRD debt of low-income countries, from its own resources. In his speech to the (Anglican) Lambeth Conference, in August 1998, James Wolfensohn, the World Bank President, said that the Bank's reserves were only $23 billion; this is surely a very considerable sum for a bank that has none of the risk elements which necessitate a 14% reserve for private banks. The vast bulk of the $105 billion owed to the bank by developing countries which are not amongst the poorest will be outside the scope of Jubilee 2000. The remission proposed would involve some loss of control by World Bank and IMF, changing their role for some countries to one of expert consultant, rather than authority which has power to dictate.

IDA debt is on generous terms of 0.75% interest (generally referred to as an administration charge). It carries the benefit of a 10 year grace period before any repayment of principal is due. This 10 year period is succeeded by a further 10 years where principal repayments are at the rate of 1% per year, and then by 30 years where repayments per year are at a rate of 3%, thus extinguishing the whole debt. These terms have undoubtedly brought considerable benefit to most low-income countries. They have been made possible by the regular replenishments made by richer countries from their aid budgets, when appealed to by the President of the World Bank. This is praiseworthy, but as I have pointed out, the richer countries must be prepared to go the second mile and to cancel outright some or all of the IDA liabilities of low-income countries, thus giving up the considerable repayments of principal and interest due in the final 30 years of each agreement. The cost of this will have to be borne by the major aid givers, who made the original contributions to the fund. However, since the repayments at the rate of 3% per year are unlikely to be made in any case by many of the low-income debtors, even if there is no debt remission the actual cost will be lower than the face value of the remission. Replenishments will, however, continue to be needed after the Jubilee, in order to provide the all-important capital for future development of poorer countries.

IMF Debt

The remission of IMF debt presents a difficult problem. The total for sub-Saharan Africa has risen sharply over the last 15 years, from $3 billion to $8.7 billion. The IMF generally acts in concert with the World Bank. It is not a bank and does not lend money; it provides temporary financial assistance by selling a member's Special Drawing Rights (SDR) or other members' currencies in exchange for the member's own currency. This is intended as temporary balance of payments assistance. A number of low-income debtor countries, such as Nigeria, have not been able to draw on IMF credits. Others such as Senegal have had IMF credits of a little less than 10% of their total debt stock, but have been able to reduce the total. The IMF was supplied with a reserve of $40 billion worth of gold when it was set up. Kenneth Clarke, the British Chancellor of the Exchequer, proposed that 10% of this reserve should be sold to cover the costs of debt remission. Clearly, the IMF could, if necessary, sell a higher proportion than 10%, since it is fully guaranteed by world governments, but the German government rejected even this modest proposal for a 10% sale. However, the statement made by Gordon Brown the UK Chancellor of the Exchequer to which reference has been made in the introduction by the two authors of this work indicates that the new German government has reversed this decision. Given the political will this plan can be revived and even extended, although the price of gold has since fallen by about a third. Recently, to our surprise Michel Camdessus announced the remission of 90% of a $100 million debt owed by Nicaragua and Honduras, which were devastated by Hurricane Mitch.

Benefits of the Remission

As Susan George has pointed out in her excellent book The Debt Boomerang, there are certain spin-off effects, which the developed world could expect to enjoy from the remission of the debts of poorer countries.[4] The countries of the world are, to a great extent, interdependent. Poverty or bankruptcy in one country often involves a fall in demand for the export goods from another. Exports to Africa South of the Sahara, for instance, have decreased markedly over the last 10 years. An effective debt remission for poorer countries would reverse this trend and make for an increase in mutually beneficial trade. It would also open the way for greatly increased investment, for the economy will no longer be bankrupt. Given proper conditions and the necessary controls, this investment could be of great benefit to both investors and recipients. The benefits of the remission to debtor countries will also be great, if the Jubilee is rightly presented and negotiated. It will present an opportunity for a new beginning.

In addition to this advantage, the country will be spared the necessity of finding money for debt servicing year by year. The interest on debt paid by the countries of sub-Saharan Africa has been at an annual rate of about $6 billion, while the low-income countries outside Africa have paid $1,149 billion. Principal repayments have been roughly the same, although the latter figure is somewhat obscured by the new loans received by debtor countries. This sum will not be overwhelming, but it could be extremely advantageous for development. It is, of course, essential that debt remission should not be an occasion for the ending of grants or of new loans on favourable terms. If that were to be the case, the last situation might be worse than the first. However, given the continuation or expansion of low-interest loans and grants, the use of funds saved from debt servicing could have a dramatic effect upon the condition of the people.

The sums so saved could be added to the existing budget or preferably they could be paid into a special trust fund ringfenced for essential needs and for the benefit especially of the poor. One is encouraged to see that even in Nigeria, whose general level of financial probity in government has been low, it has been possible to create an honest and effective Petroleum Trust Fund (its operation is described on page 79) of about $1 billion dollars per year from the proceeds of the special tax levied on petrol at the pump.

The psychological advantage of debt remission will be enormous. It will give new hope and energy to the populations of many low-income countries, hitherto pressed down by the burdens of unpayable debt.

Future Credit-worthiness

Much of the analysis presented by the World Bank and the IMF starts from the wrong premise. It assumes that the ultimate goal of low-income countries is to recover credit-worthiness, rather than to establish a decent standard of living for their inhabitants and a reasonable level of prosperity for the national finances. There is a suspicion that the World Bank is applying the yardstick common among American businessmen, where the ultimate disaster is to lose your credit status and your credit cards. It is not clear whether this unfocused viewpoint springs from a genuine error in assessing the interests of poorer countries, or whether it is a mere rationalisation of the creditor interest. It is however extraordinary how deeply this myopic vision has affected the language of the World Bank. It assumes, for instance, that the ultimate salvation of low-income countries burdened with debt is to attract larger private capital flows. This aspect features prominently, for instance, in successive volumes of the World Bank Debt Tables, which are entitled, 'External Finance for Developing Countries' and 'Global Development Finance'. They seem to assume that the removal of the burden of past unpayable debt is only important if it attracts new private investment.

It is undeniable that such investment may indeed produce spin-off effects beneficial to the country concerned, but the prime object of private financial investment is to make profit for the investor. Only through carefully constructed terms and suitable partnerships, with internal capital whether private or governmental, can the relation be made symbiotic.

It would be foolish indeed to attack debt as a whole or to seek a 'debt-free' 2000. Capital is one of the four essentials of production (the other three being land, labour and entrepreneurship-management). Where adequate capital is not available in the low income country itself, it has to be borrowed from outside. This is an elementary aspect of successful development. Debt only becomes injurious, when the positions of debtor and creditor are too unequal and the inequality in the power relation has been used to enforce unjust terms for the loan, which bear too harshly on the poor, or where old debt has become 'inert' instead of productive. Where the debt has not been used to create productive resources to finance repayment or where the total economy in the debtor country is near to bankruptcy, the debt has become a dead weight which must be removed before new economic progress can be made.

There is also a false assumption that debt remission will mean the cessation of future loans. It is not the objective of the Jubilee debt remission programme to put an end to new loans, but rather, in so far as they are beneficial, to increase the flow of loans for productive purposes. This is analogous to the action of a gardener, who prunes away the old unproductive growth and the dead wood in order to make room for new and fruitful shoots to grow. If one shifts the analogy to the human digestive system, it is as though food has stuck in the digestive channel and to prevent it poisoning the whole body, it has to be removed by surgical or other drastic means. The end of the process, however, is not the end of eating but rather a situation where food can be normally eaten and normally digested.

The bankers make much of the assumption that no one will lend to a country whose debt has been forgiven. This is contrary to most of the evidence. The very substantial partial remission of debt balances offered in the Brady Plan has, in the South American case, resulted in a higher and not a lower level of investment. Disbursements to Latin American between 1990-1996, the period of the implementation of the Brady deals, have risen from $34,000 million to $101,000 million, while foreign direct investment rose from $8,188 million to $41,982 million and portfolio equity flows from $1,599 million to $15,500 million. The Philippines, another beneficiary from a Brady-type deal which produced considerable debt stock remission between 1990 and 1992, received an increase in loan disbursement between 1990 and 1996 from $2,516 million to $4,762 million and foreign direct investment rose from $530 million to $1,408 million and porfolio equity flows from zero to $1,330 million. In Africa South of the Sahara, Nigeria has been much the biggest beneficiary from a Brady-type remission of debt owed to private banks (1992), and in that case there has been a fall off in the total disbursements of new official loans from $927 million in 1990 to $308 million in 1996, but there are special reasons for lack of investment in Nigeria. In the private sector, however, foreign direct investment, which fell from a peak of $1,882 million in 1989 to $588 million in 1990, rose again to $2,201 million in 1995 and $1,391 million in 1996. Portfolio equity flows have not been significant throughout this period.

We can surely conclude therefore, that Brady-type deals involving substantial debt reduction have not effected the level of future investments. What is true of the consequences of Brady-type reduction of debt has been equally true of the consequences of outright debt remission granted for political purposes. If we look at Egypt, which received debt forgiveness of over $11,000 million in 1990 from the US as a reward for joining the coalition against Saddam Hussein, the country has experienced falls in foreign direct investment in some years during the period 1990-96, and increases in others. The net pattern has been one of little overall change. In 1990, Foreign Direct Investment was $734 million and in 1996 $636 million. However, portfolio equity flows rose from nothing in 1990 to $1,233 million in 1996.

Poland, the spearhead of the revolution to throw off communist rule, has, as a reward from the US, experienced an extraordinarily high level of debt rescheduling, debt reduction and debt forgiveness. Reschedulings between 1989 and 1994 totalled $67,400 million, and debt forgiveness totalled $5,685 million, and debt reduction $7,869 million on a total debt stock of just under $50,000 million. (The total rescheduling exceeds the total debt in the Polish case because the same debt has been rescheduled more than once). The official loan disbursements to Poland increased from $1,025 million in 1990 to $1,475 in 1996, while Foreign Direct Investment rose dramatically from $89 million in 1990 to $4,498 million in 1996, while portfolio equity flows rose from zero to $722 million in 1996. The first jump in Direct Foreign Investment came after the end of the communist regime in 1990, but that investment has continued to rise year by year thereafter, indicating that the substantial debt remission granted to Poland has not dampened the enthusiasm of private investors.

It should also be noted that, as David Woodward said in his evidence to the International Development Committee investigation of debt relief, 'Debt cancellation will only affect creditworthiness to the extent that creditors expect it to happen again. Now that is a major part of the rationale behind the Jubilee 2000 campaign which is to associate the debt reduction explicitly with the Millenium.' Whether or not debt remission should be repeated at 50-year intervals in the literal pattern proclaimed in Leviticus 25 is a moot point. It is probably enough to seek for a radical one-off remission that will not be repeated (if at all) for a long time. Such an exceptional remission could not be a disincentive to future investment.

In the light of this convincing evidence, one can only conclude that private bankers, the IMF, the World Bank and the creditor governments have invented this scare of disincentive to future private investment merely in order to protect their own loans. It is indeed common sense to conclude that bankers and governments would not wish to lend to a bankrupt government, though they might be willing to do so to one which has been restored to solvency through debt forgiveness, combined with strict conditionalities to ensure proper financial management in future. Gresham's Law tells us that bad currency drives out good; it is equally true to say that the continued existence of bad debts, which have not been forgiven, drive out good loans.

For a number of years, Africa South of the Sahara has been a virtually 'unbankable' area. It has received almost no loans from private sources, with the exception of a few countries in very recent times. The average yearly level of net foreign investment to Latin America between 1990-1996 was about $23,000 million, and the figure for portfolio equity flows was $11,000 million. Compared to this, Africa South of the Sahara received a yearly average of only $2,400 million Foreign Direct Investment and portfolio equity flows of $1,200 million, and of the total figure for Africa South of the Sahara, a substantial proportion since 1994 was due to foreign direct investment and portfolio equity flows to South Africa. In 1995, for instance, South Africa received $4,571 million in portfolio equity flows and in 1996 $1,759 million. This was the majority of the portfolio equity flows into sub-Saharan Africa for these years. The conclusion to be reached is quite clear. Africa South of the Sahara received very little debt forgiveness during this period, it continued to owe far more in unpayable past debt than it could possibly pay, and it received very little foreign direct investment or portfolio equity flow.

The benefits of Jubilee-type debt remission will only be felt if the country concerned whose debts have been forgiven is able to borrow money for proper purposes in future, on terms which are not exploitative. Capital is one of the four essential elements of production, and if internal capital is not available, producers must be able to obtain their capital from external sources. If, however, the types and conditions of the loans are not to be such as to bring the country, whose debts have been cancelled into new unpayable debt, the rate of interest must be moderate and the period of repayment fairly long. Furthermore, the project or programme financed must be one which will itself generate income, and the extent of the loan must not be beyond the capacity of the country to repay. Alternatively, the inward investment must be on an equity basis, where the external lender shares both the risk and the profit, and where if the project fails he loses his stake and no continuing debt liability is created.

There is a strong case for replacing all loans made by governments for aid purposes with grants. The British government made this change some twenty years ago and is now in the process of converting all past loans into grants. A large part of the imbalance has arisen in the past from aid to budget loans. Some of these are necessary for temporary financial crises and are usually given by the IMF with the aid of a consortium. This is clearly a necessary function of the IMF, but the occasional medicine must not become the regular diet.

Countries whose debts have been cancelled will need to be very careful not to incur large loans for armaments, which are never productive resources. It is sad, for instance, to see South Africa incurring large new debts for the purchase of armaments, some of which are superfluous to her real defence needs. It appears that South Africa has been contemplating the purchase of various types of weapons including battle tanks, submarines and helicopters. The helicopters are certainly necessary in order to enable South African peace-keeping forces to prevent large-scale loss of life in any future situation in the continent like that which occurred so tragically in Rwanda in 1994. South Africa has so far been reluctant to develop a peace-keeping role under international auspices in Africa. It is to be hoped that this reluctance will be speedily overcome so that South Africa, like Nigeria, can project military power in a humanitarian role.

Battle tanks would seem to be less necessary - against whom could the new South Africa be contemplating a tank battle? Armoured cars are, however, admirable weapons for security purposes and action against armed bandits. Submarines are a totally unnecessary weapon. South Africa's interest is solely to preserve the peace and freedom of the seas for the commerce of all nations. Frigates could be invaluable in order to sweep smugglers and pirates from the seas and to preserve fish stocks, but vessels designed for superpower confrontation should have no place in South Africa's armament. South Africa has been rightly critical of the imposition of the burden of loans incurred during the apartheid period. It may be possible to win partial remission for these debts, but this becomes more difficult if the debt burden is to be again increased for reasons of military prestige.

As has been explained in Chapter 7, IDA funds have been extremely useful to poorer countries; they have provided low-income finance with a relatively long grace period. They will increasingly constitute a burden to those countries as the ten year grace period elapses and is replaced by ten years of repayment at 1% of principal and then by thirty years of repayment of 3% of principal p.a.

The Jubilee package of debt remission should therefore include these IDA funds, which were in any case originally designed in the 1960s as a kind of substitute for aid payments. It is most important that after the Jubilee remission, the flow of IDA funds should not stop, but each payment from the fund will be of a kind which finances the creation of resources, with which to make the 0.75% administration/interest payment and in due course the 1% and later 3% repayment of principal. IDA funds come from replenishments made by the governments of richer nations, and therefore all that is required is the political will. Normally, the President of the World Bank makes the periodic appeal to donor governments for a replenishment. It is essential that this should continue and increase.

After the Jubilee remission, we should be looking for regular and adequate inflow of foreign direct investment and portfolio funds. The poorer nations do not need either a flood or a drought. The vast investment in Mexico (where net foreign direct investment plus portfolio equity flows totalled $18,700 million in the year 1993) was followed by the currency and debt crisis of late 1994, when the Mexican economy had to be rescued by the inflow of large funds from the US, the IMF and other bodies. The present flood of foreign direct investment in China, which totalled $27,500 million in 1993, $33,800 million in 1994, $35,800 million in 1995 and $40,200 million in 1996, has helped to transform the economic life of certain regions, but already it is reported that almost none of the investing companies are making a profit, and one suspects that in about ten years time there may be a crisis and a failure of China to keep up the necessary repayments.

If a huge flood of investment could be dangerous (particularly in the form of loans), a drought is equally bad for any country that does not have adequate locally generated capital. There is no way of guaranteeing such a regular flow, but the general optimism and sense of economic self-reliance likely to be created by the debt remission should make poorer countries a better field for the making of loans, whether private or official. The services of such bodies as the ECGD will continue to be of crucial importance. Since the Jubilee is a one-off remission not to be repeated for a considerable number of years if at all, the fact that it has happened should increase rather than decrease the security of future ECGD guarantees from Britain and from other countries, since in future it will involve fewer defaults of payment and fewer claims on sovereign states. This in turn will help to ensure adequate loans and supply of imported capital goods.

Notes

1   'Net present value is the value now of a sum or sums of money arising in the future. A given sum of money is worth more now, than at a later date, both because of uncertainty and because it could be invested now to produce a greater sum in the future. The present value of money in the future is calculated by discounting the future stream of money by a rate of interest equivalent to the rate it obtain if invested' (report of House of Commons International Development Committee on Debt Relief, May 5th 1998, p. XXVII-Annex). The discount rate is generally taken to be 5% p.a. The net present value measurement seems at first sight to be a more exact and suitable measure, than the face value. However, debts that are often rescheduled change their net present value, which is based on the original repayment schedule. On the whole, I find it more convenient and useful to use three measurements:- the face value, the current value on the discount market and the value in terms of estimated future return, based on debt service payments made in the immediate past, (unless the terms of the loan provide some specific repayment holiday).

2   Figures taken from *EURODAD World Credit Table*, (ed.) Nicholas P., Brussels, 1996, and from *ECED Annual Accounts*.

3   The figures for the UK receipts are greatly skewed in that $607 million was received in 1990, $507 in 1991 and only $309 million in the 3 years 1992 to 1994. The large sums received by Japan in debt service have been balanced by very considerable sums paid out in grants.

4   Susan George, *'The Debt Boomerang'*: London, Penguin, 1989.

9 Some Individual Case Studies

The problem of unpayable debt is a general one, affecting especially some 51 of the world's poorest nations, and some 12 who are poor, but not among the poorest. The solutions which we offer must be general ones in terms of remission, though, of course, the conditionalities will vary from case to case and any special factors will need a special analysis. The cases of Nigeria, Malawi and Nicaragua illustrate the problems in a concrete manner.

Nigeria has moved from being one of the richest countries in Africa to becoming one of the poorest. This has been due to two factors: the fall in the oil price and misgovernment. Oil was discovered in Nigeria in commercial quantities in 1956, but it was not until after the Civil War that it began to come on stream in large volume, reaching a level of 2.3 million gallons per day soon after the conclusion of the Civil War.

With the dramatic oil price rise in 1973 and again in 1977, Nigeria reached a situation of comparative affluence. Yakubu Gowon, the then head of the military government, somewhat rashly stated that finance was no longer a problem for Nigeria's development. An ambitious 5-year plan was launched involving expenditure of some $32 billion naira (at that time, worth some 20 billion). The projects which were implemented through the plan were, on the whole, sound ones which left lasting benefits to Nigeria. However, the rate of expenditure involved could only be met without external borrowing, if the oil boom lasted. A host of contracts were awarded, some on inflated prices involving considerable corrupt payments from contractors to government officials and ministers. Nigeria's debt had remained low throughout the exigencies of the Civil War, 1967 to 1970. This was, in part, due to the prudent financial management of Chief Obafemi Awolowo, the Minister of Finance, and his Permanent Secretary, Alhaji Atta under General Gowon. During the temporary fall in oil prices under General Olusegun Obasanjo, Nigeria began to run into debt. Nigeria went into elected civilian rule in 1979, under Alhaji Shehu Shagari with debts of some $9 billion. At the end of four years of civilian rule, the total was $20 billion. It continued to rise throughout the next seven years of military rule, from 1983 to 1990, when the debt totalled $33 billion. The debt has oscillated around that figure for the last 9 years.

Throughout the last 25 years, Nigeria has been treated much more harshly than the rest of Africa South of the Sahara in the terms of its loans. Nigeria has paid an average rate of interest, on loans taken out between 1985 and 1991, of 7.8%, whereas the rest of Africa South of the Sahara had to pay only 4.3% in this period. Recently, most governments South of the Sahara have had their multilateral loans transferred into IDA on concessional terms, whereas Nigeria has only benefited from $348 million of IDA funds as against $2,762 million IBRD debts (1996 figures). During the period 1985-1992, Nigeria paid $8,165 million in interest on all its debts and received only $1,627 million in grants - a position in stark contrast to the rest of Africa South of the Sahara, whose grants have considerably exceeded interest payments. Furthermore, Nigeria's present debt balance of $30 billion contains $9.2 billion of principal arrears and $5 billion of interest arrears (1996). [1]

The reason for this harsh treatment of Nigeria has been the false assumption that Nigeria is now a rich country because of its oil production. In fact, oil prices have fallen to about $12 per barrel and Nigeria's population is about 100 million. The net oil revenue of some $9 billion per year is not enough to provide both for Nigeria's essential needs and for the colossal rate of debt repayment that Nigeria was making prior to 1992, therefore Nigeria has recently fallen far behind in its debt payments.

This affects the British government, since although Britain is in general a much smaller creditor to low-income countries than Japan, USA, Germany or France, in the Nigerian case, the UK is owed 23% of Nigeria's total bilateral debt. The United Kingdom is easily Nigeria's largest single creditor, being owed nearly $4 billion, which is about half of the total of bilateral debt owed to Britain by low-income countries. In the five years from 1990 to 1994, Nigeria paid Britain $921 million dollars, in debt service, out of a total payment to Britain of $1,370 million paid by the 51 low-income countries, for whom we are seeking a 100% remission. [2] We can see from this the very large share of ECGD income of the UK which derives from Nigeria. During the last two years, however, Nigeria has been unable to keep up its repayments and this has resulted in the very low figure of $40 million dollars per year received by ECGD from low-income debtors in 1996. One hopes that the failure of the United Kingdom Government to give the same support to Nigeria in its dealings with the World Bank-IMF, as has been given by France to Côte D'Ivoire, is not due to reluctance to forego Nigeria's debt servicing payments, and that with the new democratic government under General Obasanjo Britain will give full support to Nigeria.

The economic situation in Nigeria is a very depressing one. Tens of thousands of employees of government have been laid off on IMF advice. The level of business has dramatically declined, and most Nigerian manufacturers are working at a small percentage of their capacity. This general fall in economic activity has also been reflected in drastic reductions in government expenditure, causing great hardship. In a number of cases, government staff pay is several months in arrears. The hospitals are mostly in very bad shape, schools badly provided for and roads in increasingly poor repair. Very many Nigerians have left their country to go abroad seeking better opportunities. I have found that among the Tiv people, in Benue State in Nigeria, whom I visit frequently as an honorary Chief, there has been an increasing level of violence due to land disputes between clans. Poverty is a great aggravator of violent strife; however, we have now made effective peace.

Government in Nigeria has acquired a reputation for a high level of corruption. It is not easy to quantify this phenomenon, but it is certainly a significant factor in Nigeria's economic difficulties. During the regime of General Babangida, enormous sums were removed from government funds and used as 'gifts' to key military officers to ensure their support. A particularly glaring example of this kind of financial mismanagement was brought to light by Dr Pius Okigbo, the much respected financial administrator, when he examined the accounts of the Nigerian Central Bank. Some $9 billion of windfall oil profits, arising from the Gulf War were paid into the Central Bank. They were put straight into a special account, whose authorising officers were the Governor of the Central Bank and the Head of State, General Babangida. No accounts were ever kept of how the money was spent! Any credible plan for Jubilee remission will have to impose conditions on debtor countries that would ensure that this sort of thing cannot happen again. The government of General Sani Abacha which succeeded that of Babangida, proved equally corrupt. After the death of Abacha in June 1998, a search of the office of his Chief Security Advisor revealed a very large sum in dollar notes. Abacha was succeeded by General Abdulsalam Abubakar, the former Chief of Staff, who seems to have made a genuine effort to remedy the disastrous situation which he has inherited. He ordered the family of Abacha to repay three-quarters of a million dollars from their fortune.

A hopeful example of a corruption-free fund that has been spent for the benefit of ordinary people through essential government services has been the Petroleum Trust Fund. When the Nigerian military government of General Abacha raised the low pump price of petrol, the revenue so raised was put into a special fund of some $1 billion per year, ringfenced for the purposes of providing essential services and help to the poor. This has been administered with remarkable honesty and efficiency by a team headed by General Buhari, which is separate from the ordinary business of government. Buhari was the ultra-strict head of Nigeria's military government from January 1984 to August 1985, when he was overthrown because his regime was considered to be too stringent for ordinary people. For the purposes of running this fund, however, Buhari and his team have proved admirable trustees. This sort of special fund, ringfenced from general government expenditure and administered under some strict trusteeship control, could well be a model to follow in ensuring the proper use of monies released in debtor countries through the Jubilee.

A further significant fact from Nigeria's debt relations has been the generosity with which private banks have treated Nigeria. Whereas Nigeria has not benefited from any remission from creditor governments or from International Financial Institutions, it obtained an 80% Brady-type deal from the private banks after a long session of negotiation with Alhaji Abubakar Alhaji, the Minister of Finance, exchanging some $6 billion of principal debt owing to banks, plus a further $2 billion in overdue interest, for $2 billion in bonds, which the Nigerian government promised to service punctually. Nigeria has regarded this as a debt of honour, and has kept up the payments due on the bonds, with only one rescheduling.[3]

Recently, the Jubilee 2000 office gave me a most disturbing paper prepared by the staffs of the World Bank and the International Monetary Fund entitled 'The Initiative for Heavily Indebted Poor Countries: Review and Outlook' (August, 1998). In footnote 7 on page 7, it states 'Nigeria has since been 'excluded' (from the list of 41 HIPC countries potentially eligible for debt remission) as it is not IDA only; a prerequisite under the initiative'. The point is made again in footnote 2 on page 29, 'excluding Nigeria (which is not IDA only) from the 41 original HIPCs'. The decision to exclude Nigeria, from concessional finance, was made by the IDA, which is administered by the same staff as the Bank. James Wolfensohn, the President of the Bank, is also the President of the IDA. The World Bank bases its decision to exclude Nigeria on a decision of IDA for which it is itself primarily responsible. This is a manufactured reason and leaves one to suspect that the World Bank President is using one of his decisions as authority for another. It is not clear whether or not the exclusion of Nigeria from the debt remission list has anything to do with the fact that it is Britain's largest debtor! The decision is particularly unfortunate because the present Nigerian government is in the process of repairing the errors of its two predecessors. Since about one-fifth of the black race resides in Nigeria this is a matter of more than local significance. It is a 'double-whammy'; first

Nigeria was excluded from IDA concessional finance, then as a consequence, it has been excluded from consideration for debt remission as an HIPC.

Nigeria is not alone among HIPC countries in being financed by IBRD as well as by IDA. Côte D'Ivoire, the darling of France, had in 1996, IBRD loans of $1,304 million as against $1,019 million of IDA loans. Côte D'Ivoire, however, has remained on the HIPC list while Nigeria has, for the moment at least, been excluded. One cause of this may be that Côte D'Ivoire has a powerful 'fairy Godmother' in France, while Nigeria enjoys no such backing from Britain. I was, however, very pleased to hear from a senior official at the World Bank press conference, that Nigeria's exclusion is not irrevocable and that discussions are going on in Washington between the World Bank and Nigeria's representatives.

Recently, General Abubakar Abdulsalam stated that Nigeria would sell off some of its parastatals in order to pay its debts. If this is done the Nigerian government should ensure that it gets a reduction, by way of remission, at least equal to the 80% granted by private banks in 1992, and preferably at a 90 to 95% level. If Nigeria can be treated so favourably by ordinary commercial bankers, who have no moral obligation to the country, surely she should be treated with at least equal generosity by the British government, which has a 'family responsibility' from the long colonial and post-colonial period. Nigeria has held a succession of elections culminating in the poll for the choice of President on 27th February 1999. The winner, General Obasanjo, will assume office on May 29th. The expectations aroused by the return to democracy and civic culture will need to be buttressed both by the economic effort of Nigerians and by the remission of all or nearly all of Nigeria's $30 billion debt.

Our second case history is that of **Malawi**. Malawi's economic and geographical situation is, in many ways, very different from that of Nigeria, but it suffers from the same acute problem of having to service a totally unpayable level of debt, which is unmatched by productive resources. Malawi, which became independent on 6th July 1964, is a relatively small country (118,000 square km) with few natural resources, but a population of about 10 million people. They are predominantly engaged in agriculture, creating considerable pressure on the land. Malawi's income per head is the seventh lowest in Africa. Its income from XGS in 1996 was only $476 million, while imports in 1994 cost $961 million (no figure given for 1995-6). This huge deficit was partly due to debt service payments of $89 million, leaving the country excessively dependent upon grants and new loans.

The remission of the whole of Malawi's long-term debt of $2,092 million in 1996, if achieved, will have a considerable effect in releasing sums currently paid for debt servicing, but desperately required for health, education, roads and other services needed by the mass of its population. At present, medicines are hardly available in the hospitals. The schools and universities are under considerable pressure and although girls have just been exempted from secondary school fees, the level of fees for boys is higher than most parents can afford. Malawi's debt repayment of $89 million in 1996 was greater than her total budget for health and education in that year. Besides all this, Malawi's total debt is 486% of the 1996 XGS and 107% of the GNP in that year. It has gone up in every one of the last eight years and is now $2,312 million (1996) including short-term debt. This sum could not conceivably be repaid, and this situation has had a depressing effect on Malawi's self-confidence. The robust political culture of self-reliance in the years immediately after independence has given way to a new dependency culture, where the answer to every economic problem has been seen by many as the need to search for foreign donors.

The extravagance of the former Life President, Dr Kamuzu Banda, who delighted in building palaces that the country could not afford, exacerbated the financial situation. With the removal of Dr Banda through the Presidential election of 1994, and his replacement by the regime of President Bakili Muluzi, the wasteful prestige projects came to an end, but an increase in indiscipline spread to many levels of administration. There is a proverb in Chichewa: 'Walira mvula, walira matope - if you are crying for rain, you are also crying for mud'. The liberation from a strict authoritarian rule conferred great benefits in terms of human rights, but it was not surprisingly accompanied by increased criminality and by corruption at lower levels of government.

Malawi needs both the remission of its debt and a further increase in the $260 million level of grants, which it received in 1995. It also desperately needs to be able to produce marketable products to supplement its present income from tobacco and tea. Numerous appeals have been made for debt remission on Malawi's behalf by a number of people, including the Bishop of Birmingham, but for a long time this was without effect, and Malawi remained off the list of the 41 HIPC countries, whom the World Bank was considering for debt remission. This was said to be because the ratio of the debt service which she has paid each year, to export of goods and services, was below the 20% level which the World bank has set for admission to HIPC status. In fact the average ratio of total debt service (TDS) to export of goods and services since 1989, has been 25%. I was at a loss to understand why Malawi was excluded. Malawi's debt service ratio is high enough to cause acute suffering; the reason it is not higher is because the majority of Malawi's debt has been transferred to IDA concessional terms which, as explained in Chapter 5, have produced a beneficial reduction in debt service liabilities in the short-run, but will impose a considerably greater debt service burden, when the ten year grace period expires and repayments at the rate of 3% per year fall due.

When I sent a detailed study of Malawi's debt to the World Bank representative in London, he replied that he had sent the study on to the World Bank Country Group and stated that Malawi was potentially eligible for debt remission.[4] However, representations made to the World Bank by the Bishop of Birmingham elicited the response that Malawi was not on the list of 41 HIPC countries; the list quoted in the confidential World Bank/IMF report on 'the Initiative for Heavily Indebted Poor Countries: Review and Outlook', August 24th 1998 gave a list of 31 HIPC countries, which did not include Malawi. This is a further example of the lack of transparency in the World Bank consideration of countries eligible for debt remission. It was clearly essential that creditors should correct the glaring omission of Malawi from the list of countries to whom debt remission can be made. I was therefore delighted to receive from the Jubilee 2000 office a copy of the latest IMF website of March 3rd 1999 which reported that the IMF and the World Bank have begun a process of consultation on debt relief and the Heavily Indebted Poor Countries initiative. On page 3 of this report there is a list of countries within this initiative. Malawi (at last!) is included (although Nigeria is still excluded). It is gratifying to see that the World Bank and IMF are not deaf to an unanswerable case if it is put to them with perseverance. Claire Short, the Governor of the World Bank, appointed by Britain, helped in the correction of the injustice previously done to Malawi.

Nicaragua, like Haiti and Guyana, is one of the three poorest countries in South and Central America. Its GNP per head is only $380, whereas the great majority of states in these areas have a GNP per head of over $2000. Nicaragua's history has been a turbulent one. From the time of the Spanish conquest in the 16th century onwards, there was a considerable cleavage between the more privileged classes, who owned most of the land and the poorer farmers. There has also been a long record of United States' armed interference and of resistance to that intrusion by guerilla campaigns. The most famous of these was that led by Augusto Sandino against the US Marines in the 1920s and 1930s. Although Nicaragua only has a population of 4.5 million (1994 UN estimate), it is proud of its strong and self-confident popular culture. Though Nicaragua has one of the lowest measures of GNP per head, it prides itself on having one of the highest concentrations of poets per capita!

In 1933, a coup established the dictatorship of the Somoza dynasty, which was only overthrown in the popular insurrection of 1979, led by Daniel Ortega and the FSLN (the Sandanista National Liberation Front). Ortega's Marxist regime produced a great deal of social development, especially in health and education, but the economy soon came under severe pressure. Nicaragua acquired a formidable arsenal of Soviet weaponry and was thought by some of its neighbours to present a military threat. This in turn provoked very severe sanctions from the Reagan regime, which also encouraged and financed armed incursions by the Contra rebels. These armed groups caused a great deal of military and economic dislocation, including the destruction of 20% of the health clinics in the war areas. In 1990, the disastrous war between the Sandanista and the Contras came to an end, largely through the mediation of President Arias and of Cardinal Orbando, the senior Bishop of the Catholic Church in Nicaragua.

In the election which followed, the conservative coalition of UNO defeated the FSLN and Violeta de Chamorro defeated Ortega in the Presidential election by a margin of 10%. Considerable restraint was exercised by both sides, and to the surprise of many people, Nicaragua has now largely escaped from the destructive confrontation of left and right. Economic policy has now become progressively more liberal, but there has been no victimisation of the losers. The economic situation inherited by de Chamorro and by her successor Arnoldo Alleman has been a desperate one, and to add to her difficulties, Nicaragua, after the civil war, was left with a debt burden of some $10,707 million and debt service payments totalling $528 million, of which $200 million was due to interest. This enormous burden was clearly making it impossible for Nicaragua to recover from the ravages of the Civil War, the difficulties were, of course, increased a thousand-fold by hurricane Mitch and the resultant floods of October 1998.

Even before the hurricane, the international community had responded to Nicaragua's needs with a degree of generosity greater than it has shown to most other low-income countries, and had reduced the total debt outstanding to below $6 billion, but this is still a very heavy burden. A special committee of the IMF and the World Bank was set up to review ways to help Nicaragua, but the level of aid and debt remission was still far from enough to allow a real new beginning for the economy. The United States, for instance, expended far more energy in seeking to overthrow the Sandanista regime than it has subsequently shown in helping that of Chamorro. Nicaragua enjoyed debt forgiveness of $1,641 million in 1995 and $3,088 million in 1996. The reunified German government forgave Nicaragua 80% of the debt it owed to the former East Germany, totalling $714 million; [5] this very considerable sum reflects great credit on the German government and contrasts with the rather meagre remission so far granted by most other creditors to their debtors. The Russian Federation has taken over the debts formerly owed to the USSR and has, on the whole, sought to deal with them in a commercial rather than an ideological manner. After a good deal of bargaining, Russia agreed to reduce the value of the rouble in which the debts were denominated to more nearly its present level. This involved a remission of some $1.4 billion.

Nicaragua is still in a desperately difficult economic situation and is greatly dependent on grants. It received $622 million in 1996. Imports of goods and services in 1996 totalled $1,610 million, while exports totalled only $913 million. Clearly, Nicaragua needs extensive aid and advice on how to increase its export income, but it also needs further remission of its debt, which still totals 650% of XGS and 355% of GNP(1996 figures). The 1996 level of debt service payments is $221 million (World Debt Tables), which is 24% of XGS; in 1995 the figure was 39.7% and in 1994 42.4%, giving an average for the three years of 35.4%. The saving of this sum through a total or near-total remission of the backlog of unpayable debt would help greatly to close the gap, but Nicaragua will still need other help as well on a massive scale.

At the end of October 1998, Nicaragua, Honduras, Guatemala and El Salvador were struck by the disastrously severe impact of hurricane Mitch and attendant floods causing thousands of deaths and hundreds of thousands of displaced persons and destruction of all their property. The Nicaraguan authorities and those of Honduras reckon that it will take some 20 years for the country fully to recover from this disaster, and to catch up with the loss of development potential. The immediate urgency is clearly to save lives, restore essential services and care for those displaced by the hurricane. However, in the longer run there will be an equally important task of recovery and this will require total or near-total forgiveness of debt. This is the only decent thing that we can do in these tragic circumstances.

Clare Short, the British Minister for International Development, however, in her initial comments on the disaster, dismissed the call for debt remission as an irrelevance and declared that the Nicaraguan Ambassador to Britain, who together with many NGOs in Britain, had made the call for debt remission, did not know what was best for Nicaragua. It is the most elementary common sense that immediately after a disaster one should concentrate on providing the necessary emergency aid, but it is equally clear to those endowed with fellow feeling for the community that has suffered, that we should seize this opportunity to make a really generous debt remission. Clare Short reversed her position within 24 hours and the British, French and other governments have asked for special debt remission for these disaster areas. Even the IMF, an authority not generally noted for generosity, announced the remission of 80% of a debt of $100 million owed by Nicaragua. This declaration of principle will be of value only if it is implemented swiftly and in a radical manner.

Gordon Brown, the Chancellor of the Exchequer, asked for a moratorium on debt servicing; this would be a partial remedy, but we need the final forgiveness of all, or almost all, of Nicaragua's debt. The likely scenario following a moratorium could well be that the debtor country having been forgiven payments of interest and principal for a number of years, would fail to resume payments at the end of the moratorium period. This might produce a kind of remission by default, but the psychological impact of such a remission would be one of conflict rather than consensus. It would remove the generosity of the Jubilee 2000 remission and take away the sense of a new beginning. Clare Short declared that the remission would be made as part of the World Bank's HIPC initiative, which as we have seen, is mean and inadequate, for it would leave the debtor country with a total of debt equal to 80% of a year's gross national product and a debt service requirement equal to 20% of a year's income from export of goods and services. Thus, Nicaragua which pays about 38% [6] of its income on debt servicing, would still be left having to pay 20%. Something much more generous than this is required! In a recent interview on television a Minister of the government of Honduras stated that for the purposes of long-term recovery, the forgiveness of debt is even more important than the provision of financial aid.

Notes

1   I was recently informed by Clare short, Secretary of State for International Development, that Britain has given the Nigerian Government the services of a British expert, to help determine exactly how much is owed by the Nigerian Government to overseas creditors.

2   These figures for Nigeria's debt to the United Kingdom and for debt service payments are drawn from the EURODAD World Credit Tables, Brussels, 1996

and from the ECGD Accounts. See also argument in 'International Development Committee', evidence of Ann Pettifor, where the figure is given as $60 million (£40 million). *International Development Committee of House of Commons Third Report*, 5th May, 1998.

3 When Bill Peters and I had the opportunity of a lunch meeting in Paris with Monsieur Jerome Haas, the Secretary of the Paris Club, he complained that Nigeria had kept up its payments to banks, but had paid almost nothing to the governments represented in the Paris Club. I replied that he could find the reason for this in a famous passage in the Bible, 'He to whom much is forgiven loves much: he to whom little is forgiven loves little', and if I could be allowed a gloss, 'He to whom nothing is forgiven does not love at all, and does not even keep up his regular payments'. The private banks had given Nigeria generous remission, whereas creditor governments and the World Bank had given none at all.

4 For a more detailed study of the Malawi case see *'Malawi Debt Cause of Great Suffering and Impediment to Development: Means of Removing the Burden'*, by M. J. Dent, and also postscript personal note by W. Peters, British High Commissioner in Malawi 1980 to 1983, *Society of Malawi Journal*, Vol. 50, No.2, 1998, pp. 1-16.

5 Keesing's *'Contemporary Archives'*, November 1995, p.40818.

6 The figure of 38% of XGS was given by the Nicaraguan Ambassador (see the Times, November 9th, 1998, page 24). As explained in this text, the World Bank Debt Tables give a figure that has varied widely for different years since 1990.

10 Non-economic Benefits from Cancellation, for Creditor as well as for Debtor Countries

BILL PETERS

These case studies illustrate in detail how a varied selection of HIPCs have been affected by their debt burdens and the procedures already in place for mitigating those effects. It is clear that the institutions set up by the creditor countries and the International Financial Institutions to 'temper the wind to the shorn lamb,' while probably well-intentioned, are insufficient. Twenty six million children under the age of five will die before the year 2000 because of deprivation of adequate food and health care, while the number of illiterate people in HIPCs will be increased by then by 90 million girls and women for whom schooling is not available. How many more deaths are needed before unsustainability is recognised and treated? Is a programme either humane or economically sound which in current conditions requires HIPCs to adopt economic policies, prescribed by the IMF and World Bank for six years, before alleviating measures begin to operate?

The IMF and World Bank are optimistic. They point out that the country data collected in the World Development Reports 1997 and 1998 (which replace the annual World Bank Debt Tables, cataloguing the fine detail of each country' debt situation) show that year by year social indicators such as infant mortality, life-expectancy, availability of health services and education are steadily improving; unfortunately, the general improvement is evident only where the statistics for all countries are taken together; when the figures for HIPCs are taken separately, they paint a very different picture.

The same institutional optimism has affected the judgment of the IFIs in other ways. For example, for several years, when they were estimating the HIPCs' incomes from exports, as a base for their ability to meet service charges, they consistently exaggerated their calculations as proved by the actual outcomes.

The IFIs failed to take account of the ill-effects over the years of their own prescriptions, which involved sharp cutbacks in budgets for social support, particularly health and education.

Economists, a majority of the staff of the IFIs, naturally prefer to conduct economic discussion in economic terms; thus, they are reluctant to give weight to the thought that if HIPCs are able to return to their pre-crisis levels of trade with more developed economies, the problem of unemployment worldwide will be reduced, a change which will also reduce stringencies now felt in world trade in general. Globalisation is already bringing far-reaching changes in the world economy; analysts everywhere peer into the future, adding up the pluses and minuses; no doubt the debt situation will be pulled in several directions by this factor. One conclusion seems unavoidable - that a fully functioning global economy will be more fruitful for humanity taken together, than one in which two-fifths of the whole does not function at all.

A further economic benefit which could result from generous cancellation would be the reopening of large areas of the globe to investment. The greater part of investment flow at present is directed towards the demographic giants, China and India, the Caucasus, the Middle East and Latin America. The Pacific 'Tiger Economies' also, until the end of 1997, received large investment flows. Following the recent crisis, investment is now taking the form of acquiring equity in established industries in countries such as South Korea and Taiwan - a somewhat problematic adjustment in ownership rather than productive investment, which could lead to future friction. As long as HIPCs carry a large debt burden, no investment in them can be contemplated for the simple reason that it is difficult to insulate funds transferred to such countries from the debt recovery process. After debt burdens are removed, openings for investment would once again appear in these countries, thus enabling more evenly distributed and rational investment programmes to be effected worldwide.

In the field of world order and maintenance of the rule of law, the debt problem has major consequences, including violent conflict. What Frank Kitson called 'low intensity operations' in his book of the same name (1998, London: Faber) are all too familiar in large areas of the Third World. Nothing contributes more readily to the disorder than acute poverty in the population. Poverty ensures a ready supply of young men, who in their teens face a cultural challenge to prove their manhood to earn the right to marry and have a family. It was this challenge which in earlier times drove large numbers to work in the minefields of South Africa or Zaire or Sierra Leone. The same impulse is now fuelling the conflicts in Rwanda and Burundi and the

Democratic Republic of Congo. An ambitious soldier or politician can very easily gather round him a force of young men who respond to his offers of adventure and profit. This dangerous possibility is increased when debt obligations not only reduce the availability of daily necessities, but also through pressure on domestic budgets, remove food subsidies and health and education provisions. The cost to the developed countries of such conflict is increasing. UN peacekeeping forces are very expensive, with the cost increasing as more sophisticated methods of conducting low intensity operations develop. When disagreements occur about methods of paying for the Forces, there is added tension in the UN and among the capitals of the countries supplying, equipping and transporting them.

Another source of friction and recrimination on the contemporary scene is economic migration, which often merges with movements of political refugees. Without the burden of debt repayments, poor people in indebted countries would have fewer reasons to migrate in search of a better standard of living. As recent tragedies in the Eastern Mediterranean and the Adriatic have shown, migrants often face extreme danger and perilous conditions. Who can doubt that they would not face these and the trauma of uprooting themselves from familiar surroundings and a settled way of life if their living conditions in their original abodes had not become intolerable? At the receiving end, grave difficulties arise also for the countries of resettlement. For certain elements in their populations, the migrants are highly unwelcome, creating a target for aggression and social disruption. Despite the historical record of refugee communities which have greatly added to the richness of the cultures of their adopted countries, their first years of resettlement appear inescapably to be marked by violence and hostility. Compassion in debt management could be a cheap way for most creditor countries to avoid these problems.

Frank Judd used to paint an alarmist picture of a future situation in which the people of Europe would awake one morning to hear that the straits of Gibraltar were choked with a mass of humanity, fleeing a continent where conditions of life were no longer tolerable. Such a scenario about the same time caused alarm when it appeared in a television programme broadcast by the BBC. Perhaps scenarios like this are overdrawn, but they draw attention aptly to a current danger, which offers benefit for no-one and could cause immense and unwelcome complications for populations which are still relatively settled and peaceable.

A further blot on the contemporary world scene is the drug trade and the drug cultures which develop from it. They destroy many lives and families, in prosperous countries as well as poor. Why are farmers in HIPCs turning to cannabis, poppy or khif rather than crops like cocoa, coffee or tea? The answer is that the steady decline in price to the grower of standard, mainly tropical, commodities results in those growers being unable to support their families in present conditions. Naturally, the high price they can get for drug-related products is very attractive to them. When the pressure of prices is allied to unstable political conditions, the drug trade, at source, all too often flourishes. No doubt some drugs originate in countries which are not heavily indebted, e.g., Thailand and Colombia. But there can be little doubt that the possibility of weaning farmers away from growing plants from which drugs can be manufactured would be much greater if their governments, unburdened by debt, were able to support them in a better standard of living than they now suffer.

As the rainforests in Brazil, Indonesia, Malaysia and Papua New Guinea continue to shrink, we hear more urgent warnings about global warming, something which will harm the prosperous countries no less than the poor. The forests are disappearing partly because, with the need for fresh sources of hard currency income in debtor countries, valuable tropical hardwoods are extracted beyond the limits which allow regeneration of the forests. The other heavy use of the forests and surrounding selvage is to provide fuel for domestic heating and cooking. In the 60s and 70s, many villagers in HIPCs were persuaded to convert their stoves to use alternative cooking fuels such as kerosene or butane. With the stringencies on family income resulting from the debt burden, they are no longer able to afford such fuel; their women once more go out to collect the daily supply of firewood, ranging further and further afield to collect their requirements. In some countries like Malawi, areas of former forest are now almost totally denuded. In India, by contrast, a vigorous programme of planting fast-growing trees around villages to meet foreseen needs is making headway. This example gives some hope for the future but is outweighed by examples of huge forest destruction which have occurred recently, for example, in Indonesia, Papua New Guinea and on the Himalayan slopes of Tibet. The two cases cited of over-exploitation of valuable timbers and pressure on bush and low forest from domestic needs are examples of environmental damage on a world-harming scale resulting in part from debt pressures. Environmentalists should be close supporters of campaigns for debt cancellation. Debt reduction would bring good for the populations of rich as well as of poor countries.

Despite the reluctance of economists to quantify and bring into their calculations any recommendations for political action they may make, such factors as have been described above in both the economic and political spheres, taken together, amount to a considerable package; one, moreover, relating directly to widely-held concerns about potential violent conflict and global instability. It is neither naive nor unrealistic to envisage the World Bank and IMF, in their role of the world's bankers within the global economy, as the equivalent of the high street banker who lends to local businesses and individuals. If he is equal to the importance of his job (not, as so many now are, merely the purveyor of financial packages), he takes into account the economic well-being of the community he serves.

The overarching global economy interacts daily to changes in the different regions. Adverse conditions in one will, in time, affect conditions elsewhere. Against this background and at the level of government, given that there is no international insolvency law, while it is important that discipline be maintained between state debtors and creditors, surely there are circumstances in which to pursue a debtor government a l'outrance is unwise. Leaving aside any moral or humanitarian consideration, such a policy would have highly unpalatable consequences for the creditors, arising, among others, from the factors described, whether singly or in a variety of combinations.

The most dangerous possible consequence is that a gulf will be opened at state level between the haves and have-nots of the world. That it already exists, anyone would know who has lived in Third World countries, as opposed to visiting on holiday or missions, such as IFI personnel undertake. Those who operate in Western capitals or at IFI headquarters may not have registered the deeply-held resentments, which are apparent at levels below the elite groups which generally control affairs in Third World capitals. Such groups have interests and attitudes which differ widely from those of lower levels in the population. Cancellation of food subsidies or the withdrawal of social services do not seriously hurt most of them, whereas in the villages and the suburbs they can be crucial, even to survival.

For this reason, senior officials dealing with economic policy quite often question the need for debt cancellation because, 'there is no demand for it from Third World representatives at the gatherings where we meet.' The case of India, a powerful voice, is worth spelling out. In discussions about debt cancellation, one of the main objections put by many Indian officials is that if substantial funds are used to permit cancellation of debt, the cost of routine Indian borrowings from the World Bank and IMF will increase. This is possibly true, although the World Bank has cumulative accrued profits of $16 billion as part of the total reserve of $23 billion with which to write off its own IBRD debt, and the remission of IDA debts will fall on the aid budgets of richer countries, not the World Bank. There are compassionate Indian officials, nevertheless, who concede the need for debt cancellation. It is from the disadvantaged in India that the strongest support for Jubilee 2000 has been shown.

Intelligent, hard-working business people trying to make a living for themselves as citizens of Third World countries complain not only about the stringencies they face because of the debt overhang, the near-impossibility of obtaining investment capital from abroad, the scarcity of domestic savings, the slowness of their external trade, the ever-increasing cost of imported goods and the collapse of the prices of their own products; they also complain that the obstacles to starting up fresh enterprises are well-nigh insuperable. In addition to problems relating to the transfer of technology, they are attempting to compete with established producers following a well-worn trail where they are breaking what for them is new ground. Despair and resignation are the frequent outcome, with loss of the will to persevere. The psychological burden of the debt overhang suppresses inventiveness, energy and hope.

Several efforts have been made to bridge definitively the gulf between the haves and have-nots, notably at Calcun in 1977. These have all failed. Too little was offered and the conditions were too harsh. Generous cancellation of debts at the end of the second millenium A.D. is perhaps the last opportunity for a reconciliation to become available for the foreseeable future, in which globalisation, environmental protection and the explosion of information technology will change the landscape. How wonderful it would be if Jubilee 2000, like the great Jubilees of the past, could be celebrated by all with universal rejoicing at a fresh, bold demonstration of the solidarity of mankind; it could be the start of a new relationship between the First and Third Worlds.

Much could be wiped off the slate in the process. The case-by-case agreements which need to be drawn up for the debt cancellations of individual debtor countries, could be a major vehicle for readjustment and reform, towards which some African leaders are already taking a positive direction, e.g., President Yoweri Museveni of Uganda; President Julius Nyerere also says he is conscious of a new ethical approach abroad among his colleagues. With support from them, the clinching of generous debt cancellation might be reciprocated by the adoption by African leaders of a new financial self-disciplining code, perhaps even cleared through the OAU.

The creditors, including the IFIs, also have much to offer in a major resettlement. For example, richer creditor nations might rededicate themselves to the UN Resolution in which they pledged 0.7% of GNP for aid. They might set some rules for lending, e.g., that major loans in future will be limited to projects that contain a revenue-earning component from which interest costs may be paid. Following the British proposal for a register of arms sales, they might begin to regulate world arms sales and production. They might encourage the World Bank and IMF to abandon some of the institutional optimism, which leads them to overestimate HIPC's export capacity and to underestimate the incremental effect of their economic prescriptions for HIPCs, both on the social fabric of their countries and their competitiveness in world trade.

A denouement along these lines could open the way for consideration of more far-reaching structural changes. At present, HIPCs suffer from a regulatory system in which they appear as petitioners before a board of their creditors and the IFIs. Moreover, the IFIs act as arbiters as well as policing the loans and economic conditions. There is no appeal from their decisions; non-compliance leads to very grave consequences. A body such as a Security Council for Social and Economic Affairs (as proposed by Christian Aid) might be more impartial and representative, doing for the World Bank and IMF in the economic and social field what the existing Security Council does for the UNGA in the political field.

Parallel with this could be consideration of an International Law on Insolvency and some oversight of banks' deposit policy with the attendant problem of secrecy conflicting with public interest. An Economic/Social Affairs Security Council would also hold a brief for guiding lenders and borrowers in such matters as dedicating a proportion of major new loans to education and health (the UNICEF 20x20 proposal). HIPCs have already learned much from the present loan situation; it is encouraging that some recently independent countries like Namibia (also the Czech Republic and Bulgaria) and post-apartheid South Africa are eschewing all unnecessary loans from IFIs. Few of the players on the debt scene have any doubt that future lending must be regulated in a way which avoids the situation which called for the existence and campaign of Jubilee 2000. It is no less clear that the tensions and animosities aroused by the debt situation need to be faced squarely.

11 Parallel of the Anti-Slavery Movement in the 19th Century

MARTIN DENT

As already pointed out, there is a close parallel between the campaign in the last century to liberate people of African descent from the burdens of slavery, of a legal and coercive kind, and our campaign to free the 51 poorest countries of the world from the economic burden of debt slavery. The weight of suffering caused by physical slavery was no doubt greater, but the root injustice is the same in both cases. The people concerned suffer from an irremovable burden and do not own themselves. The two campaigns also have considerable similarities, and at crucial points face the same decisions as to the interconnection between principle and tactics. The campaign had a most vigorous presence both in Parliament and in public opinion in the country as a whole. The parliamentary leadership prior to 1823 rested with William Wilberforce, the great prophet of the anti-slavery movement. After his retirement from active leadership, on grounds of old age and ill health in 1823, he passed the mantle to my great-great-great grandfather Thomas Fowell Buxton, who was, in the words of Reginald Coupland a historian of the anti-slavery movement, 'the Joshua to Wilberforce's Moses'. It was under Buxton's parliamentary leadership that the Whig government of 1833 was forced to introduce the great Emancipation Bill, which freed 800,000 people of African descent, in the West Indies and elsewhere.

There are four precise lessons to be learnt from the Holy Cause[1] of the campaign, first to abolish the slave trade (1807) and then slavery itself in the British Empire (1834):

1. The first lesson relates to the all important role of public opinion. The victory was achieved only after a colossal mobilisation of opinion. The Anti-Slavery Reporter, a newspaper of those days, described public opinion as 'the steam which will enable Parliament to extinguish slavery with one majestic stroke.'

1.4 million signatures were submitted to the House of Commons committee on slavery. The women of England, Scotland Wales and Ireland submitted 187,000 signatures in one month. These were taken up to the Speaker's chair by Thomas Fowell Buxton, the member for Weymouth, accompanied by three other strong supporters of the cause.[2] The government of the day was hesitant to incur the hostility of West Indian slave owners, but was pushed from one position to another by the leaders of the campaign, until it agreed to introduce the final Emancipation Bill, which passed in 1833 and took effect on the 1st August, 1834. Amendment after amendment was enforced on the government by Buxton and his supporters in committee.

The triumph of the anti-slavery campaign in the great act of 1833 was truly described by de Tocqueville as, 'The act of the nation and not of its rulers'.[3] The mobilisation of public opinion was the result of the combined efforts of a number of groups. The original Anti-Slavery movement was initially somewhat more cautious and limited in its objectives, but it responded to pressures from the vast and active popular movement and switched its objective from amelioration and gradual extinction of slavery to outright abolition. In this the campaign was influenced and aided by the principled activism of Joseph Sturge and the Agency Committee, which professionalised the campaign by employing paid lecturers and carrying out intensive lobbying of all candidates for parliamentary election. The Agency Committee represented the radical end of the anti-slavery spectrum. It appealed to considerations of abstract justice and of religious duty, whereas Mr. Buxton and the official leaders of the Anti-Slavery Society of which the agency committee was a formal part until 1832, though no less firm on the the essential point of principle - the need for emancipation - were also influenced by considerations of practicality and the need to build a broad coalition for emancipation. The relation between the two bodies is recorded in detail in Howard Temperley's book, 'British Anti-Slavery 1833 to 1870' (Longman, 1972). When the government finally agreed to introduce the Bill abolishing slavery in the British Empire, Stanley, the Colonial Secretary, described the irresistible force of public opinion which had induced the government to cease to procrastinate:

> There is throughout the country from one end of it to the other a determination, a determination the more absolute and irresistible, because it is founded in that deep religious feeling, on that solemn conviction of principle, which admits of no palliative or compromise, and which has declared itself in a voice to which no minister can be deaf, and which no man who watches the signs of the times can misunderstand.[4]

When the emancipation came on the ever-glorious 1st August 1834, 800,000 people of African descent passed from slavery to freedom. When they woke up the next day, they had no more money in their pockets or food in their larders, but they were free men and all the great subsequent achievements of Caribbean culture were made possible by this liberation. May it be the same in Africa after the achievement of Jubilee 2000! It is interesting to relate that when Buxton died, in 1845, a considerable part of the money needed to create his monument in Westminster Abbey was subscribed by black people who had benefited 11 years before, from the ending of slavery. This is recorded on the plinth of the monument in the North Aisle of the Abbey.

2. A second parallel points to important lessons for the Jubilee 2000 campaign. Buxton's letters, as recorded in the life written in 1846 by his son Charles, show that he was acutely aware of the danger of a slave revolt if the Emancipation Bill was delayed. For this reason, he was prepared to go along with the Government bill, imperfect though it was - providing for an 8 year period (amended in committee to 6 years) of compulsory apprenticeship to follow the abolition of slavery and for compensation of 20 million from the Treasury for the slave owners, but nothing for the slaves. Buxton knew that if he introduced his own bill, the process would take longer. Buxton warned of an approaching storm if nothing was done:

> A breach deadly and imminent lay between them (the planter and the slave) and already had some mutterings been heard of the storm which would surely burst with terrific fury if steps were not quickly taken to turn its wrath aside.

Charles Buxton, Thomas Fowell Buxton's son and biographer wrote, 'This idea of a general revolt of the negroes was a source of genuine distress to Mr Buxton; 'the gun is cocked and on the shoulder', he said with great emphasis, when speaking of the subject to one of his great friends.[5] He was acutely aware of the disastrous example of Saint Domingue (later named Haiti). In 1791 a slave revolt put an end to the harsh oppression of the slave owners. For a brief and glorious period, Saint Domingue prospered under the inspired leadership of Toussaint L'Ouverture. General Vincent, a contemporary French commentator, who served under Toussaint, remarked on how, during his rule, 'races melt beneath his hands'.[6] Black, white and coloured were united in their service of Toussaint and the new state. Unfortunately, the pride and greed of Napoleon could not stomach the rule of a black King in a former

French colony. He sent an expedition of 30,000 men to Haiti, forced Toussaint to make peace and then broke the terms of the peace agreement by taking away Toussaint as a prisoner to a cold castle in the Alps, where he died from hunger and cold. After the death of Toussaint, almost all the Frenchmen in Haiti were massacred by his successor Dessalines, and the country suffered from a long succession of periods of anarchy and of tyranny. Furthermore, Buxton was also aware that both the British and the French had lost upwards of 30,000 soldiers in their respective disastrous campaigns in Haiti and other West Indian islands, partly from battle but especially from fever.

The abortive and partial slave revolt in Jamaica of 1832, which was put down by the government with some ease and great severity, served as a warning that the government of Britain could not indefinitely put off the emancipation. The Whig government of 1833 was, in theory, committed to the abolition of slavery, but omitted all reference to it in the legislative programme announced in the King's Speech. Mr. Buxton informed the leaders of Earl Grey's government that if they did not introduce a bill abolishing slavery, he would do so as a back bencher, whereupon the government gave way and introduced their own Emancipation Bill.

The abolition of slavery in the West Indies and the rest of the British Empire came about as a result of the Act of Parliament and not of a successful revolt, but the real possibility that such a revolt might occur concentrated the minds of both the anti-slavery campaign and the government, and added to their humanitarian concern to achieve abolition quickly. We are faced with a similar situation in that although our motive in working for Jubilee must be that of our sense of justice and of love of the human race, we should also be aware that if debt remission is not granted in an ordered way with proper conditionalities and clear boundaries, it might occur as a result of reneging by debtors, resulting in an embittered quarrel between creditors in the richer part of the human family and debtors in the poorer part. Such a situation would do no good to either side, but its possibility must be a spur to induce us to work for a full Jubilee remission to be achieved by the end of the year 2000 or very soon afterwards.

The full analysis contained in Edouard Dommen's article in UNCTAD Review Vol.1, No.1, 1989, on 'Lightening the Debt Burden - Some Sidelights from History' shows that repudiation of debt and failure to pay debt obligations have been very common phenomena in many countries over a long period of time. The earliest default by an official borrower seems to have been the failure of a number of Greek municipalities belonging to the Attic

Maritime Association to pay their debts, which they had contracted with the Delos temple. Philip II of Spain, in 1596, repudiated his debts by simply destroying all documents containing evidence of them. The Soviet Government after the Revolution published a decree stating that all state loans concluded by the 'governments of the Russian landlord and Russian bourgeoisie numerated in a special list are hereby repudiated. All foreign loans without exception are absolutely repudiated'.

The ability of governments to repudiate loans depends to a considerable extent on the relative strength and weakness of the borrowers and creditors. Germany's debts arising from reparations for the 1914-18 War were dealt with in the Dawes Plan, they were systematised and further reduced in the Young Plan, but agitation against this plan was a considerable element in the German bitterness which helped Hitler to rise to power;[7] when in power Hitler repudiated the debts altogether. After the Second World War in 1952, Germany received a further dramatic remission of the debts which it owed at that time. This remission was based on the assumption that the reduction should be to a level where Germany would not have to pay more than 5% of its annual earnings in debt service. As Germany grew richer, the debts were extinguished. It was therefore surprising that until the advent of the present Schröder government, Germany did not support the campaign for a similar concession to indebted low-income countries in Africa south of the Sahara. These examples are but a few among many instances where debts have been formally forgiven, openly repudiated or just made to lapse through prolonged non-payment.

Dommen concludes:

> It can be argued that the debt problem of the 1980s is the result of the rigid view now taken of debt obligations. If they are fixed, something else has to give. There is little choice other than to press the debtor government to oppress the poor in its own country, or to encourage the debtor country to grow out of debt. The first solution is inhuman and the second has its own absurdities and contradictions, such as the oversupply of commodities on the world market.

There are a number of countries whose situation is such that it would be strongly against their interest to renege openly on their debts. This would result not only in the ending of all aid receipts, but also in their inability to get new loans. As already pointed out, all the countries in Africa South of the Sahara, except for Nigeria and South Africa, received more in grants plus new loans than they pay out in repayment of principal on loans and payment of interest on loans. Nigeria, on the other hand, paid an average of 3.5% higher rate of interest than the average for the rest of the countries South of the Sahara, and has paid in all $8.165 billion in interest between 1985 and 1992[8] and from 1993 to 1996 it has paid a further $4.076 billion, giving a total for the 12 years (1985-96) of $12.241 billion, an average of just over $1 billion per year. Grants received have averaged only $70 million p.a. This is so great a burden that the Nigerian government has fallen a long way behind in its interest payments.

Of the countries north of the Sahara, Algeria has experienced an unfavourable net transfer on debt (after deduction of grants) of $13 billion from 1987 to 1994 inclusive. Morocco experienced an unfavourable net transfer on debt of $5.3 billion in the same period. If one were to measure the direct financial consequences only, it would clearly be in the interests of Nigeria, Algeria and Morocco to renege on their debts. The reason that they do not do so is the desire to remain within the world financial community based upon trust and also a feeling of moral obligation. If, however, there is a moral obligation to pay debts, there is also an equally strong one to forgive debts that cannot be repaid. Both the New Testament and the Holy Koran[9] enjoin this duty of forgiveness of unpayable debt and it also corresponds to the sense of most people as to what is right. One cannot rely on this sense of the moral duty to seek to pay unpayable debts to continue indefinitely to counterbalance the natural desire of countries to be free of those debts, by renouncing them if other channels are not open.

If one looks at South America, one finds more countries whose equation of transfers on debt less grants received is unfavourable to the country concerned. In the 10 years from 1987 to 1996, Brazil has experienced an unfavourable net transfer of debt (after deduction of grants) of $27 billion. In addition to this massive unfavourable movement, Brazil has also suffered a rise in its total debt stock over the ten year period 1987-1996 of $57 billion (a 46% increase). Mexico has experienced an unfavourable net transfer of debt of $18.3 billion. This huge unfavourable balance has occurred at a time when Mexico's total debt has risen from $109 billion to $157 billion, a rise of $48 billion or just over 44%. This situation is surely unstable unless radical action is taken to reduce the debt overhang. In the case of Argentina, there have been very large interest payments. From 1987 to 1996 these payments total almost $40 billion, but these have been counterbalanced by large disbursements of new debt, resulting in an increase in Argentina's debt from $62 billion in 1990 to $93 billion in 1996, a rise of 50%. Clearly, the international financial community cannot continue indefinitely to stave off unfavourable figures for transfer on debt by making new disbursements and increasing the debt by almost 50% in seven years. At some time, there will almost certainly have to be massive debt reduction on a scale greater than the Brady Plan.

These South American examples do not fall within the list of countries for whom the Jubilee 2000 campaign can seek debt remission, but at some time in the fairly near future appropriate action will have to be taken. In the case of these countries, it is especially the element of interest which has been chiefly responsible for the burden. Only a few South American countries benefit from any concessional finance. Most countries in the region receive almost no IDA, and those who do receive it do not include the larger debtors. In Asia, Indonesia is the most outstanding example of the rise in total debt stocks. In 1987, the total debt was $52 billion; in 1996 it had risen to $129 billion, a rise of $77 billion or nearly 150%. It is clear, therefore, that we are in a position analogous to that described by Buxton in the anti-slavery campaign. If we do not take adequate action ourselves within carefully defined limits, equilibrium which has just been upset by a cash crisis, will probably be restored through unilateral reneging of debt. This repudiation could take the form of an outright abnegation or of a concerted failure to pay. It is our task to head off this threat by a prompt and adequate remission of the stock of debt, carrying with it reduction of yearly debt payments.

3. The third lesson from the anti-slavery campaign is the need for a radical and simple goal rather than a complicated half measure. For 10 years from its inception in 1822, the anti-slavery campaigners in the British Parliament (who then numbered only about nine and were vastly outweighed by the West Indian slave interest) worked within the parameters set by the government's policy of 'ameliorating' slavery and working for its 'gradual extinction'. Buxton and his supporters presented the most powerful evidence against slavery, especially in the remarkable pamphlet on the intolerable conditions on a slave estate, written by Mr Whiteley, a former official on an estate in the West Indies. In their stated goal, however, they had still kept to the government's guidelines of amelioration and gradual extinction.

Indeed in 1823, when a number of abolitionists including Wilberforce took up the cause of abolishing slavery itself, they established the Society for Mitigating and Gradually Abolishing the State of Slavery Throughout the British Dominions. From this over-cautious beginning, the impetus of the campaign itself and of its many new supporters moved to a more radical goal.

The women members of the anti-slavery movement were particularly vigorous in attacking the compromises of the 'ameliorationists'. Mrs Elizabeth Heyricke, for instance, produced a pamphlet of which Wilberforce seems to have disapproved, entitled 'Immediate and not Gradual Abolition'. It contains the ringing challenge:

> Men may propose only gradually to abolish the worst of crimes and only to mitigate the most evil bondage. I trust that no ladies' association will ever be found with such words attached to it.[10]

Finally, at a great meeting in Exeter Hall in 1832, a certain Mr Postlethwaite (of whom we otherwise know rather little) got up and declared that the anti-slavery campaigners were fed up with waiting for the promise of government that always was delayed. He proposed immediate, total abolition of slavery. The cheers that greeted this liberative plan nearly took the roof off the hall. Buxton was in the chair and told the delegates that he would go to parliament and propose their plan of immediate abolition. His proposal was met by the government with an amendment to the effect that abolition should be according to their previous plan of amelioration. Buxton, despite the requests of many members of his own Whig party to desist from opposing the government, stuck to this proposal and rejected the government's amendment. He was defeated by 130 votes to 90, but throughout the year 1832, the campaign was carried into every town and hamlet in the country and eventually resulted in the government giving way and introducing their own Emancipation Bill in 1832, which passed in 1833 and took effect on 1st August, 1834. We see from this that a simple, radical proposal providing for a full answer is a far more effective mobilising agency than a complicated half-measure. This is why Jubilee 2000 must work for total or near-total remission of past, unpayable debt and not just for rescheduling or an easement in the terms of debt servicing.

Throughout the anti-slavery battle, the cause of immediate abolition was opposed by those who put forward a supposed need for the slaves to become worthy of freedom through a long probation of bondage. Such a position failed to realise that freedom is a birthright and not a reward, only to be granted to those whom the masters considered worthy. As Rousseau put it, 'Those who are made slaves against nature become by nature slaves'. The opposition to emancipation was vociferous and strong. The West Indian slave owners resisted every attempt at the amelioration of slavery. They considered the instructions which they received from the Colonial Office in London as unwarranted interference in their own institution. Even among ministers and other decision-makers in Britain, there was a false idea that one could not grant freedom from slavery because the beneficiaries were somehow considered to be unworthy of it. Stanley said in his speech introducing the Emancipation Bill that, 'the slaves at the present moment are unfit for the joys of freedom...Sir, it is slavery which debars them from acquiring industrious habits.' There is a striking parallel between this language of the opponents of the emancipation of slaves and the warnings of the World Bank, the IMF and some conservative financial decision-makers. They do not ever dare to trust the governments and peoples of low-income countries to manage their own affairs in a proper way. The experience of the years since independence has in many cases been a sad one characterised in some cases by dictatorship and financial corruption. However, if these countries now fallen into the well of unpayable debt can be rescued by remission accompanied by strict conditionalities relating to audit and accountability, as well as to wise policies encouraging the free enterprise of their people, energies will be released sufficient in most cases to ensure financial prudence and achieve prosperity.

4. The fourth lesson relates to the decisive achievement of emancipation, but also to the continuing requirement to correct abuses and to create a civil society in the West Indies embracing all races. The leaders of the Agency Committee carried on an unrelenting campaign against the continuing abuses of the compulsory apprenticeship which followed the abolition of slavery. In 1838 the governments of the West Indian Islands themselves agreed to put an end to this system of forced labour and to rely on the incentive of wages. The apprenticeship system, which was originally proposed by the government to last 8 years, was amended in committee and incorporated in the Emancipation Act of 1834 to last for six years. In fact, it was subsequently abolished by consent after four. As Buxton pointed out, the system was flawed in that it failed to provide a proper incentive for work. The use of the whip was abolished, but the incentive of wages and free contract was not present under the apprenticeship system.

The volume of the production of sugar rose[11] in some colonies but fell in others, especially Jamaica. In the West Indies as a whole, sugar production declined slowly over the next 20 years, but this was due to a number of cases of which emancipation was only one. This was counter-balanced by the growth of sturdy and self-reliant small farmers and by other sources of income. The most important achievement of the West Indies following emancipation was the growth of self-confidence, expressing itself in a whole host of black institutions, from thriving and self-governing church congregations to co-operative enterprises. The stability of marriages increased and the decline of the population was reversed.

Contrary to the foreboding of the prophets of doom, the abolition was affected with a degree of peace and orderly conduct which belied all the dire prognostications of the enemies of abolition. On the night of 1st August 1834, most of the 800,000 slaves of African descent in the West Indies were in their chapels and churches waiting for the hour of emancipation. They celebrated their freedom joyously but with no disorder or rancour against their former masters. Shortly after the emancipation, an old opponent in Parliament went up to Mr Buxton and congratulated him, saying, 'You West Indian fanatics were right after all'.

Abolition of slavery had come with no disorder and no threat to the state. Some twelve years after the abolition of slavery the prosperity of the West Indies suffered a severe blow, not from the effects of emancipation, but from the conversion of the government to a rigid policy of free trade. After a long debate, 1841 to 1851,[12] the protection in the British market hitherto granted to West Indian sugar was rescinded and slave grown sugar, from Cuba, Brazil and elsewhere, was admitted to the British market on the same terms as the more expensively cultivated free sugar of the British West Indies. The climate of opinion in Britain had changed; Manchester doctrines of free trade prevailed with government over those of Exeter Hall. The anti-slavery movement opposed the abolition of duties on sugar from countries which retained slavery, but their views were over ridden by government.

We learn from this that, in the latter years of the campaign, the abolitionists established the fact that it was safe to abolish slavery. Buxton, for instance, having told his fellow MPs that it was immoral to drive people to work with the whip, went on to say that, in any case, it was not as effective as wages. When a particular opponent said to him, 'There is a great deal of unpleasant and demanding work to do in the islands. If there are no slaves, how will it be done?' Buxton, who as a brewer was a practical businessman, replied, 'Today is Thursday and if you declared emancipation today the slaves would take the day off and also Friday and the weekend. But on Monday, if you paid them properly, they would come back to work'. This is essentially what happened.

The Jubilee 2000 movement has the same need to convince governments and parliaments that it is not only moral, but also economically sound to abolish the backlog of the unpayable debt of the governments of poorer countries. When the battle of ethics has been won, it is still necessary to triumph in the battle of economics.

Notes

1   This was the name used by those who took part in the campaigns against the slave trade and later against slavery itself in the then British Empire. The leaders of the campaign were overwhelmingly people of strong religious persuasion.

2   Charles Buxton (ed.), *'Memoirs of Sir Thomas Fowell Buxton'*, second edition, London: John Murray, 1849. Gives an interesting first hand account of the increase of public feeling in 1833 which pushed the government into taking action. See pages 313 to 315.

3   Robin Blackburn, *'The Overthrow of Colonial Slavery 1776 to 1848'*: London, Verso, 1988, p. 458.

4   Buxton op. cit., 1849, p. 331.

5   Op. cit. p. 317.

6   Wenda Parkinson, *'This Gilded African'*, London: Quartet Books, 1980, p. 149. This book gives a graphic account of the life and career of Toussaint L'Ouverture. The title is a quotation from the racist comment of Napoleon, that he would get rid of 'this gilded African' and would 'tear the epaulettes from every negro in the colonies', (p. 155). At the end of his life, when he was in St. Helena, Napoleon regretted that he had fought Toussaint instead of allying with him. By this time the repentance was far too late; he had extinguished the best hope for independent Haiti by murdering its most admirable and revered leader. No other ruler emerged in Haiti of anything like the quality of Toussaint.

7   Ian Kershaw, *'Hitler: 1889 to 1936'*: London, Penguin Press, 1998, p. 310 et.seq.

8   M. J. Dent, 'Jubilee 2000 and Lessons of the World Debt Tables', 1994, p. 15 (booklet printed and circulated, but not published).

9   Op. cit., p.27. Chapter 2 Bakara verse 279)

10   Blackburn, op. cit., 1988, p. 423.

11   See Howard Temperley, *'British Anti-Slavery'*: London, Longman, 1972, pp. 114-121, for a detailed analysis.

12   Op. cit., pp. 153-167.

12 Tactical Considerations and Means of Implementing the Jubilee

We have not only to demonstrate the justice and need for a Jubilee-type remission. We need also to sketch out the detail in terms of what countries should be given what level of remission and on what terms and conditionalities, sufficient to open the way to a new beginning; I have attempted this task in Chapters 6 and 7. We have also to take account of the opposition to Jubilee remission and to see in what respects we can challenge it head on, and in what respects we can adjust our policy to make the Jubilee more acceptable to creditors. In this, we need to assure them that debt remission is not an incremental and open-ended phenomenon that would undermine the whole sanctity of debt.

The Case For and Against an International Bankruptcy Procedure

This is a groundless fear; the Jubilee remission is to be carefully defined within the boundaries that we have outlined, it is to apply only to sovereign debt and not to that owed by individuals or corporations. Debts within a country can in any case be enforced by ordinary law. In these individual cases the ultimate safeguard of a bankruptcy procedure provides a way in which individual debtors or company debtors can have their debts extinguished. This, however, involves a certain level of stigma when the debtor is declared bankrupt. At the end of the process, neither the debtor himself nor his heirs or dependents is lumbered with the debt. In legal terms, it is effectively extinguished.

Many commentators, including Professor Kunibert Raffer, Archishop Ndungane of Cape Town and Professor Sir Hans Singer have asked for an equivalent to this bankruptcy procedure for sovereign debt. This could conceivably be a useful stepping stone towards a Jubilee type debt remission. Professor Singer has called for 'a new contract in which debtors and creditors join forces in an effort to overcome the debt crisis. There should be more scope for HIPCs, creditor countries and multilaterals to work as partners towards a solution which is sustainable financially, as well as in the sense of providing a suitable basis for comprehensive development'. Professor Kunibert Raffer has coupled his recommendation for an equivalent to the bankruptcy procedure, with the idea for a precise implementation procedure conducted by an independent body, with a neutral chairman, on which debtor and creditor would be equally represented. He has suggested a considerable number of separate committees to consider the debts of each country, whereas Archbishop Ndungane, in his chapter on 'Seizing the Millenium, Reshaping the World Economy' in 'Proclaim Liberty'[1] has put forward the proposal of a single Mediation Council, whose responsibility will be to negotiate the remission of debts of developing countries. Such a Council, in his view, should consist of four parties - an independent international body, a similar regional body, the IMF and the country concerned. It is not clear whether the country concerned is the debtor or the bilateral creditor; both would surely have the right to be in such a Mediation Council. The Archbishop's suggested Council seems to be a sovereign body dealing with all instances of remission of debts of developing countries.

Kunibert Raffer's proposal is based on the procedure used in the United States for dealing with the unpayable debts to the US Government of bodies controlling lesser parastatal organisations. Both suggestions involve an equal participation of debtors and creditors, with some form of neutral chairman or outside body to mediate between the opposite interests. This procedure offers an attractive means for allowing debtors and creditors to reach an acceptable solution through the casting vote of the outside mediators. But there are considerable difficulties in using this kind of procedure to effect the Jubilee 2000 remission.

What criteria could be taken in evidence to prove that the debt is too onerous to be honoured? Would these criteria relate only to the financial circumstances of the debtor country, or would they also involve any actions of creditors as a whole, which have worsened the economic situation? Would the examination also involve a thorough investigation of any possible corrupt actions of the debtor government, such as misappropriation of funds by members of that government or their associates? Finally, one must ask whether there would be any equivalent of the transfer of assets from bankrupt debtor to creditor, which characterises bankruptcy proceedings for individuals or companies in domestic law. The application of such a transfer to the unpayable debts of governments would be unjust, like the situation described by the Prophet Nathan in his rebuke to King David over the murder of Uriah the Hittite and David's subsequent marriage to Bathseba,[2] his widow. Nathan told the king of an imaginary situation where a certain rich man with a huge herd took away the sole pet lamb of his neighbour, who had cherished it with so much love and care. Transfer of productive assets in an international bankruptcy procedure would be a case of countries, possessing very large productive resources taking away the small resource possessed by the poor debtor country. Would unjust creditors seek to exchange the forgiveness of Nigeria's $30 billion sovereign debt for the transfer of Lagos? The thought is ridiculous.

An additional tactical objection is that of the length of time which the procedure is likely to take. We do not want the urgency of the campaign for remission of debts by the year 2000 to give way to a long negotiating procedure lasting for several years. Furthermore, it would be unwise to ask the International Financial Institutions (IFIs) to make two profound changes in procedure at the same time. It will be difficult enough to persuade them to make a massive remission of the stock of debt. The World Bank, as we have seen, accepted the principle of debt remission in 1996 in the HIPC initiative and the Paris Club has done the same in the Naples Agreement. We are asking for an extension of the terms and percentages of the remission and of the number of countries to be made eligible. This is a fairly radical change. If, at the same time, we are seeking to remove the control of creditor governments and IFIs over the remission of debts owed to them, through a profound change in procedure, we may find this to be too big a mouthful for them to swallow in one gulp. Therefore, in my view, the change in procedure for dealing with unpayable debt in the future may have to follow the remission rather than precede it. The Kunibert Raffer procedure, or that Archbishop Ndungane, or Sir Hans Singer, could be used, after the initial Jubilee 2000 remission to deal with any other exceptional cases that have not been addressed.

The goal of Jubilee 2000 must be a radical remission of debt to be followed by a new beginning. If the Raffer pattern of a separate negotiating committee for each country helps to achieve the Jubilee goal, it should be proposed. It may well be that, faced with such a radical challenge to their own role in debt negotiations, the IFIs and the Paris Club may decide the make the necessary radical remissions themselves, in order not to lose control.

A certain degree of flexibility will be needed in the timing of the implementation of the remission. It is possible that the total or near-total remission of debts of low-income countries which Jubilee 2000 seeks to associate with that year may well not be complete by that time. It took the British Government from 1984 to 1990 to enunciate the Trinidad Terms, and then it took the G7 another seven years to reach the Naples Agreement on roughly the same terms. The conversion of the World Bank to the principle of debt remission only occurred in 1996 after some fourteen years of acute debt crisis. Much as we would wish to see the whole remission tied up and agreed by December 2000, it is possible that we should have to make do with a somewhat slower procedure in some cases. Gordon Brown, in the Mauritius Mandate, has praised the NGOs who have drawn attention to the year 2000 as a good occasion for pressing the cause of debt remission. He has also promised to set in motion the remission of the debts of two-thirds of low-income those countries owing money to the British Government by the year 2000. This is a great help to the urgency of the campaign. We must, however, realise that an unalterable commitment to total or near-total debt remission may be the most that we may achieve in the case of several countries. Provided that that commitment is made in an irreversible way and with a realistic timetable attached to achieve rapid remission, we must, I think in these cases, accept this deviation from the strict letter of Jubilee 2000, and continue to campaign for implementation of the promise as soon as possible.

A further objection to the Kunibert Raffer procedure, is that it opens the possibility for very different outcomes to arise from the consideration by separate bodies, of the debts of countries which are essentially in the same financial position. Justice is seen by most people as involving an essential element of symmetry. Similar cases must be dealt with in the same way. The vagaries of different committee chairmen, or of different levels of eloquence by creditors and debtors in several separate committees, might produce a result which appeared to be manifestly unfair and inconsistent. If the Jubilee case is in any way deficient in manifest justice, it will not prevail. We need some objective criteria by which to judge the eligibility of countries for debt remission, and thus to produce some consistency in the outcome.

The initial opposition to be overcome is that of the instinctive rejection of debt forgiveness as a principle. This is not so strong among private banking institutions as it has been in the World Bank and the IMF. Ordinary private banks regularly write off debts from quite a number of customers, whom they know will never be able to repay. The evidence of this is freely available in annual reports and accounts submitted to shareholders meetings. Furthermore, they sometimes make substantial partial remissions in exchange for getting the rest of the debt put into some form of secure bond. This was the case in the very substantial round of Brady remissions of the debts of quite a large number of lower-middle income countries, especially in South America and in East Asia. The remarkable Nigerian remission, to which reference has already been made, was an outstanding example of a Brady-type remission; $6 billion principal and $2 billion overdue interest was forgiven by the bankers in exchange for the creation of some $2 billion worth of bonds which the Nigerian government promised to honour. This constituted an 80% remission.

The World Bank, on the other hand, as we have seen, has come only recently to accept the principle that some of the stock of debt owing to it should be forgiven, in the HIPC initiative. It is interesting to note, however, that the World Bank contribution to the Trust Fund to pay for this debt forgiveness comes largely from their yearly retained profit. According to the 1998 World Bank Report showing the accounts as audited by Price Waterhouse, the total of these retained earnings was at that time just over $16 billion. Every year for a considerable period, up to 1996, the World Bank accounts have shown a profit of just over $1 billion. After deducting the relatively small funds which it has donated to various aid projects such as IDA funds and funds to help the new Palestinian Authority in Gaza, a residue of about $500 million has been added to the cumulative total of retained profits.

The World Bank's position is extremely secure. It has triple 'A'status on the American money market; it has a status of creditor of first resort for all sovereign debtors; it is backed by nearly all of the richest countries, and at the same time as its members made their original subscription payments to the bank, they agreed to provide a considerable sum as an amount subject to call if the World Bank ever had difficulty in meeting its obligations, a situation that has in fact never arisen and seems unlikely to do so. The total of amounts paid in at that time was $10 billion, while that of amounts subject to call is several times greater. This is a colossal cushion for emergencies, so big as to make the holding of so large a sum as the $23 billion reserve superfluous protection. We therefore need an investigation to show us what has happened to the huge total of retained profit, and whether there is any reason why most of it should not be available for the remission of the large debts owed by poorer sovereign countries to the World Bank. In addition to this requirement, we need to set the HIPC initiative in its true light. It is not a case of the World Bank, in its generosity, giving $500 million a year to the Trust Fund to implement the HIPC initiative. This $500 million comes from the profits of World Bank activities. The Bank lends at a rate some 0.5% higher than that at which it borrows, and it does not have to pay any interest on the initial capital paid up by members. If the World Bank is, as Dr Kamel, one of its senior officials explained to me on my visit in 1996, 'A co-operative enterprise for poorer nations', then any profits made, after providing the essential minimum reserve, should automatically be spent for their benefit.

The World Bank, like private bankers, has an interest in ensuring that the debts owing to it are not so high as to make the likelihood of regular repayment remote. In debt management, as in taxation policy, there is a Laffer Curve. If the rate of tax is fixed too high, the yield goes down. Similarly, if the face value of debts owing is too great, the yearly return to the creditor is likely to be less than it would be if the rate were lower. A vast and totally unpayable debt total puts off the debtor and results in a lower yield. This principle, which is well known to economists, has recently been described by Benjamin Cohen, quoting Paul Krugman, as '(creditor) countries on the wrong side of the debt relief Laffer curve.' Krugman uses this argument to show that in certain circumstances and at a certain level, debt relief is in everyone's interest.[3] This principle can be incorporated into the Jubilee 2000 argument, for those cases of countries which are poor but not among the poorest, for whom we seek for partial remission. Such a remission might indeed actually increase the debt recovery payments made to creditors by these countries.

Can a High Level of Partial Remission Ever be Accepted as a Substitute for Total Remission?

For all low-income countries for whom I have suggested 100% remission, the dilemma remains that creditors, primarily acting through their ECGD departments, may well be willing to grant substantial remission if they know that the residue will be put into bonds or other safe instruments. The rationale and the Biblical paradigm of Jubilee remission point to a total forgiveness of past debt, full and free, to be followed by a genuine 'amendment' of financial practice on the part of debtors and creditors. If we retain some of the debt, we reduce the psychological impact of the act of liberation and make it more difficult to inspire in debtor countries the sense of new beginning that comes from a total forgiveness. Furthermore, the complications and costs of rescheduling smaller debts if the need for further rescheduling should arise, could be as great as those for rescheduling the larger amounts.

This is an apparent contradiction of aim which can only be resolved in detailed negotiation. Our correspondence and interview with the ECGD at their headquarters in Harbour Tower (Bill Peters and Martin Dent) have led me to the conclusion that the British ECGD would probably welcome debt remission deals, if they resulted in a sufficient residue of unforgiven debt that would actually be paid. It may be that for tactical reasons, Jubilee 2000 should ask for total remission but be prepared to accept a near-total remission ratio of perhaps 90 to 95%. A Keele University colleague, arguing from his experience of individuals, suggested to me that it is often better to associate debtors with the process of their own delivery from debt, by requiring them to pay a small proportion of the debt that they owe since this may make them value freedom from debt all the more, for they themselves will have done something to achieve it. The acceptance of a formula for partial remission, of the debts of the low-income countries, may be a necessary tactical compromise, provided that the proportion of debt remaining for the debtor to repay is low enough for them to be assured of a smooth and swift exit from debt, at a cost which will not involve intolerable suffering for their people. This exit must be one that can be made in the short-medium term - say, six years. Any repayment schedule which involves a longer period is not part of the gospel of Jubilee and should not be negotiated. Poorer countries in Africa and elsewhere need good news in the existential now, not just in the long-run, for, as Keynes put it, 'In the long run, we are all dead'.

Mobilisation for Jubilee

We have seen from the example of the successful Anti-Slavery movement in Britain in the 1820s and 1830s, that public opinion was 'the steam which will enable Parliament to extinguish slavery with one majestic stroke' and it is same for our campaign. It is of the utmost importance, however, to examine the means by which that steam is generated and the mechanism by which it is fed into the machinery of government. There is a contrast between the language of mobilisation, which needs to be stark and uncompromising, and that of dialogue with decision-makers, which requires us to add to the strong principled case, a careful measurement of the difficulties and the details of the procedure. It is also necessary to show the beneficial spin-offs that may come from the achievement of Jubilee, while continuing to emphasise the need to preserve singleness of purpose. We have to keep our eyes on the ball to ensure that the remission occurs and that it is of proper dimensions. If, at the same time, we can achieve greater transparency, that will be an additional advantage, but it is not our prime purpose.

The same applies to the question of how far we can achieve a bottom-up as opposed to a top-down approach. It is important that large numbers of ordinary people in debtor countries see the Jubilee remission as a new beginning. Unless these people feel that they share in the battle for Jubilee, it will not achieve its full effect. On the other hand, in the final analysis, Jubilee is likely to be implemented through negotiations between governments, debtor and creditor, and International Financial Institutions. There is a particularly important role for the United Nations whose Secretary General and Under Secretary General for Economic and Social Affairs have already expressed support to us for the goal of debt remission.

It seems to have been part of the original idea underlying the creation of both the United Nations and the Bretton Woods institutions that there should be a close connection between the two. The Economic and Social Council is the body that could best achieve this goal, but so far it has failed to develop its potential. Articles 57 and 63.2 state that it 'may Co-ordinate', but they do not expressly command it to do so. The Administrative Committee on Co-ordination chaired by the Secretary General of the UN with membership of the heads of all specialised agencies, including the World Bank and IMF, was set up in 1946. It has obvious potential to produce beneficial change, but unfortunately attendance does not seem to have been regular and meetings are at fairly rare intervals. The members tend to regard the committee as a forum to put forward their own interests rather than as a body to co-ordinate policy.[4] It will be both a help to our campaign on debt, and a beneficial spin-off from it, if the Economic and Social Council of the United Nations can establish some powerful influence in the affairs of the international financial institutions.

It is essential for us to involve the governments as well as the people in the debtor countries in the campaign. It is also important to gain support from continental and supra-national organisations such as the Organisation of African Unity. If we do not involve governments of debtor countries in the campaign, it may be hard to bring them into the negotiating process. It is interesting that, although the Anti-Slavery movement involved mass mobilisation and a host of semi-autonomous local committees, a great deal of the attention of the leaders was devoted to negotiation with the Government. In the end, under the strong pressure of the movement in the country, the Government itself introduced the Bill and accepted the necessary amendments in committee.

In the Jubilee 2000 campaign the roles of government decisions and popular pressure are likely to follow the same pattern. Finally, it will be governments and International Financial Institutions who will approve the remission package, but intense popular pressure, like that of the anti-slavery movement in 1832-3 will be needed to help to induce them to do so.

In a successful movement, there is room for the activities of different people with different talents. Procrustes would not be a good commander of such a movement for, although we require suitable co-ordination, we do not require enforced uniformity of method and detail. There is a role both for inspired publicists and for careful thinkers, who present the all important detail in a measured form.

There is a lesson to learn from the process of Italian unification. The methods of Mazzini, Garibaldi and Cavour were widely different, but the end result was successful, and all three of them contributed to that success. Mazzini was the prophet figure, who based his argument upon principle and sought for his support from the people. Garibaldi was a soldier of ardent conviction and magnificent courage, who challenged and overcame much greater forces. At the end of his victorious campaign, he was humble enough to accept the leadership of Cavour and the King of Piedmont. Cavour was a realistic statesman, who knew how to move in the fields of international diplomacy to achieve the desired result. A similar multiplicity of skills is necessary in the peaceful campaign for Jubilee 2000.

The energies of the campaign need to be directed to a number of channels. The true heroes of the campaign are the very large body of ordinary people who devote so much skill and energy to its propagation; their contribution is even greater than that of the originators and present leaders. Public opinion itself in many countries has to be aroused by autonomous Jubilee 2000 committees, both at national and at local level. A meeting of Jubilee 2000 organisations of 40 separate countries was called in Rome in mid-November, 1998. There has to be some co-ordination and this role is at present being most effectively fulfilled by Ann Pettifor and her staff and by the coalition committee in Britain.

Legislators in relevant countries must be continuously lobbied and brought into dialogue. The World Bank has at times been helpful to the case of debt remission and at others it has been a considerable hindrance. Where specific policies of the Bank and the IMF are wrong, they must be attacked with vigour, but there is also room for praise for those policies which are right, and consultation and dialogue, for our professed goal of the elimination of poverty is the same as theirs. It is our task to ensure that the International Financial Institutions make a reality of this professed goal, and adopt policies on debt remission radical enough to remove the impediment of the debt overhang. We have to move the World Bank from its fallacious idea of reducing debt to a sustainable level, to one of achieving a once and for all remission of unpayable past debt, which is inert and is not counterbalanced by productive resources. We have to campaign for the development of the initiatives which it has so far launched to make them far more extensive. The IMF, which has at times acted as a brake upon debt remission, needs to be addressed directly. The United Nations must be brought into the fora where decisions on debt are made.

The churches, which have given such splendid leadership in the campaign, need to maintain the momentum which they were able to develop in the Birmingham gathering of May 1998 to break the chains of unpayable debt, and in subsequent meetings and seminars like that held in Lichfield on 17th July 1998. This involves both action at parish or circuit level and leadership from Bishops and clergy. In our campaign, as in that of the Anti-Slavery movement, the influence of a petition with over a million signatures can be great. Whereas that campaign presented 1.4 million signatures, the Jubilee 2000 campaign has so far achieved 3.0 million signatures (February 1999). The gathering of Jubilee 2000 supporters in Cologne in June 1999 to repeat the pattern of the Birmingham meeting by making a chain of people holding hands around the meeting of the G8 will be of crucial importance. We must greatly exceed the number of 70,000 people who came to Birmingham.

There is scope for a number of different emphases contributing to the combined thrust. We have to arouse the sense of justice and of compassion of ordinary people, who increasingly realise that the continuance of a situation of the unpayable debt of poor countries to rich creditors is not tolerable. At the same time, we have to appeal to the realism of decision-makers. It has to be demonstrated (as is indeed the case) that the debt remission, which we seek will not produce catastrophic consequences for the economy and that indeed it will also have beneficial side-effects for mutually beneficial trade, resulting in improved employment in exporting industries. Among people in the debtor countries, we have to make it clear that debt remission is the beginning and not the end of the process of development, and that its benefits must not be allowed to be misappropriated by those in power, if they happen to be corrupt. Very many good consequences can flow from the achievement of debt remission. It is part of a general campaign for the eradication of poverty and not a substitute for it.

Clare Short and her Ministry have launched an admirable campaign aimed at the eradication of poverty by the year 2015, but there has been an unfortunate tendency on Clare Short's part to imply that the two causes of debt remission and the eradication of poverty are somehow in conflict with one another. This, of course, is not the case. Help to poorer people in poorer countries is the major cause, and this implies action in many fields, though many of them are dependent on finance, which in turn is continually threatened by the need to make large debt servicing payments. The cause of debt remission is part of the general campaign for the eradication of poverty which was put forward in the White Paper of the Department For International Development. It is not a sufficient cause for poverty eradication, but it is an essential cause. Clare Short emphasises again and again that debt remission is not to be sought purely for its own sake. This should be sufficiently obvious. The Jubilee year in scripture is defined as a great Sabbath, and Sabbaths are made for man (and woman!) and not men for the Sabbath. All aspects of the campaign to eradicate poverty should therefore go forward together without mutual recrimination.

Furthermore, the Jubilee campaign is in line with the many initiatives directed to the cause of human solidarity in rich and poor countries. The search for peace, the ecological cause, the campaign for the elimination of hard drugs and the efforts to establish viable democracy in Africa and other countries will all be helped by the elimination of debt. We must never allow one good cause to be played off against another, for we can advance together on all these fronts and the consciousness of this will add strength to our campaign.

This is reflected in the fact that the management of the campaign has now been vested in a coalition of NGOs, most of whom cover a fairly wide field in their areas of interest. Each of them has its own particular point of emphasis. But they unite in a common campaign despite occasional arguments. There are some inevitable tensions in this sort of organisation, but so far it has worked effectively, and has great potential to mobilise the efforts of the very many people who support to these NGOs.

Notes

1 Professor Sir Hans Singer, 'Debt Relief for the Heavily Indebted Poor Countries' in *'Proclaim Liberty'*, Eldred Willey and Janet Banks (eds.): London. Christian Aid, 1998, p.44.
2 II Samuel Ch.12v.4
3 Benjamin J. Cohen, 'Developing Country Debt: a Middle Way', in *'Essays in International Finance'* No. 173: Princeton University, May 1989.
4 Douglas Williams, *'The Specialised Agencies and the United Nations'*: London, Hurst, 1987, pp. 106-110.

13 Beyond the Year 2000

Jubilee 2000, like the campaign for the abolition of slavery, has a specific goal, but it also looks to a wider future. Those who fought for the abolition of slavery in the British Dominions did not rest when it was attained on the ever memorable 1st August, 1834. Sturge and others went to the West Indies after emancipation and lobbied successfully for the ending of the period of compulsory apprenticeship. The act provided for a period of six years, but after four years the legislatures of the islands themselves agreed to put an end to the compulsory system and rely upon the incentive of wages. The anti-slavery movement continued to lobby and exercise the considerable diplomatic influence of Britain in order to make the abolition of the slave trade effective, and also to persuade more countries to abolish slavery itself within their dominions. In the United States, the latter goal was only achieved during and after the Civil War, which caused such appalling bloodshed and which Lincoln, in the first part of his second inaugural address, saw as a fitting punishment for the sin of slavery.

With regard to slavery in South and Central America, the campaign lobbied the Pope and others to persuade the governments of France, Spain and Portugal to abolish slavery in their remaining colonies. Buxton, for instance, seized the opportunity of his visit to Rome in 1840 not only to inspect the prisons in the Papal domain to suggest improvements, but also to congratulate the Pope on his decision to issue a Bull condemning the continuing slave trade in Portuguese and Spanish colonies and the maltreatment of the Aborigines. The Pope also condemned slavery itself. Emancipation of slaves was effected by different countries at different times throughout the 19th century, the last two to achieve the end of slavery were Brazil, in the 'Golden Law' of 1888 and Cuba (still under Spanish rule). It is interesting to note that when Souaryez de Silva, the Brazilian Foreign Minister spoke to the chamber of deputies in Brazil to introduce a law abolishing the slave trade in 1850, he said 'can we resist the torrent? I think not. We cannot resist the pressure of the ideas of the age in which we live'.[1]

The idea of the inadmissability of using people as slaves had grown from its small beginnings with the Quaker Anthony Benezet in New England in the 1760s and with the early Clapham sect in England, within a 100 years, to become generally accepted doctrine. We too, in a shorter period must change the climate of opinion so that it is seen as no longer acceptable to hold low-income countries in the chains of unpayable debt.

As regards the condition of the population of the West Indies after emancipation, Buxton and his fellow leaders of the campaign were well aware that this was only the beginning of the long march to the full development of Caribbean culture and prosperity. In a peaceful campaign for a great cause, as in a battle, one has to pick on a particular key point to attack. This is essential because only through concentration of forces can a smaller army defeat a larger one. Having seized this position, however, the way is clear to a more general advance on the whole front. Having freed the 51 poorest nations from the burden of the backlog of unpayable debt by the year 2000, we have to go on to other objectives. We must devise and implement the means to ensure a growing prosperity. This implies, as the World Bank has so often pointed out, the creation of a favourable policy environment in the country concerned. It also requires increasing and not decreasing aid, better terms of trade and a free and fruitful sharing of technology. This is all part of the campaign to abolish poverty by the year 2015 in which the British Department For International Development has taken a leading part so far.

Beyond this, it also involves expansion of the liberative principle into other fields not covered by the strict original Jubilee 2000 campaign. Among the Tiv people in Nigeria, it is common when indicating the height of a child to hold out one's hand with the fingers pointing upward rather than flat, for the child is a living creature that will grow. It is the same with Jubilee 2000. The campaign starts as a specific way to deal with the unpayable backlog of the debts of poorer countries, but it will in time generate new life in many areas and extend into many fields.

As we have already explained in Chapter 12, we may be able to achieve a juster and more open procedure for dealing with sovereign debt in the future through a case-by-case analysis and an arbitrating committee, where the debtors are equally represented alongside the creditors, with a neutral chairman. This procedure would not, in my view, be suitable, except in the long run, for the debts of a country which has already been granted Jubilee remission. It could, however, be used to meet the case of a poor or nearly poor country, which has somehow not been involved in the Jubilee remission and whose debt has been found to be particularly onerous.

A further area of development of the Jubilee principle after the year 2000 might be a practical means of correcting the disastrous 'magic of compound interest'[2] (as Keynes described it), whereby the burden of interest payments can come to exceed those of the repayment of the principal of the loan itself. Nigeria, for instance, has paid a very large sum over the years in interest on its debt. Between 1980 and 1996, Nigeria has paid over $20 billion of interest and has still been left with a debt of $31 billion. Furthermore, a substantial part of this $31 billion is composed of interest arrears capitalised into the debt stock.

South America presents an even more disastrous picture of the evil cumulative effects of interest payments. Between 1985 and 1992, Latin America and the Caribbean paid $204 billion in interest to commercial banks, and on their debt to all creditors, private and public, they paid $242.6 billion on a debt which now totals $677.9 billion, a certain proportion of which is composed of capitalised interest arrears. This drain of between $20 and $30 billion per year has continued since before 1980. This is surely an intolerable situation. South America as a whole has a considerably higher GNP per head than Africa South of the Sahara, but it is still at a level well below that of most middle-income countries, and there are large areas of acute poverty in most South American countries. Partly this is the fault of the governments themselves, who have allowed a very unequal distribution of income. Partly, however, it is a product of South America's disadvantageous position, through this enormous burden of interest payments on past debts.

It has been a common characteristic of the three Abrahamic faiths to condemn interest payments. The Old Testament is explicit on this subject. The Muslim community has, in its doctrine, roundly condemned all payment of interest as opposed to profit-sharing on loans. There are many verses in the Holy Koran expressly referring to this. The Christian Church, for the first fifteen or sixteen centuries of its existence, preached a firm condemnation of interest payments. R.H. Tawney, in his 'Religion and the Rise of Capitalism', relates how this has been gradually softened to meet the needs of modern capitalism. The Jews, the Muslims and the Christians have often demanded and accepted interest on loans, but all three faiths have felt somewhat unhappy with this situation. Various ingenious devices have been produced to ensure the lender some return on his capital, while not breaching the formal prohibition.

It is not the purpose of this study to pronounce on the validity or otherwise of these procedures, but rather to indicate that there is a strong religious as well as practical case for suspicion of the magic of compound interest as applied to loans to poorer groups and to limit the level of interest payments. The practical answer most appropriate to our needs may be to devise a simple formula to limit the cumulative total of interest that may be levied on any particular loan. The exact percentages would probably require a great deal of analysis and negotiation to determine, but a rough approximation might be to declare that after half of the principal of the original loan has been matched by interest payments made, every subsequent payment of interest should count, in part at least, as a repayment of principal. Perhaps this formula could be stated as follows:

> Wherever the cumulative total of interest paid (on a sovereign loan) exceeds 50% of the original sum lent, every subsequent payment of interest shall count, to the extent of 50% or more, as a repayment of principal.

The second area for further development might concern the partial merging of action to remove the burden of past debt of countries, which are not rich, with the campaign to preserve the ecological heritage of mankind. There will, of course, be a spin-off for preservation of the environment from the Jubilee remission of the debt of low-income countries. As they are freed from the need to increase their export of cash crops or of timber, there will be less pressure on existing forests. The land will no longer be needed to expand production of crops destined for markets in the developed world. We must, however, in the long run go beyond this and use debt remission as a lever for ecological improvement.

Low-income countries which qualify on economic grounds for debt remission could be asked as part of their conditionalities to undertake effective preservation of their ecology. Furthermore, several countries which are not low-income, but which are in the lower bracket of the middle-income countries, possess irreplaceable treasures of forests, mammals, birds and higher plants which are under great pressure in many cases. We could use the offer of substantial debt remission as a lever to ensure their preservation. In Brazil, as we have already pointed out, the disastrous destruction of 36,700 sq. km. of rainforest per year could perhaps be reduced or even prevented should a sensible package of remission of bilateral debt be put together. In the Brazilian case, however, a good deal of the debt is beyond the power of governments to forgive. Brazil's bilateral debt to other governments totals $17 billion, while Brazilian short-term debt totals $35 billion, private creditors are owed $68 billion, and private non-guaranteed creditors a further $49 billion. World Bank debt totals only $5.88 billion. It would require great ingenuity to devise adequate remission of these debts, though the success of the Brady Plan tends to show that in a proper environment, commercial creditors are willing to accept some debt reductions as part of a general package giving greater security of the remainder of the debt.

Other countries with substantial riches of biodiversity may offer an easier field for debt/nature swaps. So far, these swaps have been on a small scale.[3]

Epilogue

We have traced the progress of this remarkable Jubilee 2000 campaign from its first beginnings to its subsequent growth as a great and liberative movement. We have seen how two streams of action join together when Bill Peters and Martin Dent joined together after the Tirley Garth Conference of 1993. One of them had campaigned personally and vigorously on an international level since he wrote his valedictory address as a retiring High Commissioner in 1983, the other aided by friends and colleagues had started a small, but effective, campaign under the name of Jubilee 2000 from Keele University from 1990 onwards. We have seen how their effectiveness increased immensely after they joined together when Bill Peters became a Co-Chairman of Jubilee 2000. With the help of the churches and other dedicated people, we have seen how its true strength resides in the enthusiasm and determination of the thousands of supporters in a number of lands, who are determined to see an end the injustice of the unpayable debt of poorer countries and have set their minds on the great year 2000 as the time for decisive victory. We have seen how under its present governance with a board from NGOs, an able Director and dedicated staff, a Chairman of the Board, a President and two Vice-Presidents, it has spread throughout Britain with the help of the churches and other committed people. We have seen how the campaign is having an increasing influence upon decision-makers. We have seen the birth of similar Jubilee 2000 organisations in 40 different countries. Meanwhile, the body of thought on the details of Jubilee 2000 has developed and been refined into practicality. This is a truly remarkable phenomenon for which we can only be grateful - the religious to God and the secular to the spirit that has inspired this expression of global altruism.

It remains to describe what we can expect to follow at the end of the great year 2000, which is the 'Kairos' year, when we can hope to lift the financial relations between rich and poor countries to a new and more just balance. When we set up Jubilee 2000 in Keele, we set ourselves a finite time span and a precise goal. We cannot ignore this limited aim, but at the same time we must realise that the Jubilee 2000 campaign has released a flood of creative energy, which will be seeking for new directions of achievement to help eliminate poverty and to banish the debt trap forever.

It would be a pity if the team that has been set up, and the support that has been generated, were to disperse without trace on January the first 2001, leaving behind the less than total level of finalised debt remission, that we are likely to have achieved by that time. We have therefore to set ourselves two goals. Those countries which are deserving of debt remission, but to whom it has not yet been promised by the end of the year 2000, must go on to achieve a firm commitment from the international community, and those promises must be held before decision makers to make sure that they are implemented. The same necessity will apply to the countries, who by the end of the year 2000 have received promises of remission which have not yet been implemented. Gordon Brown spoke at the Mauritius Conference of the need to ensure that at least two-thirds of eligible low-income countries will have entered on a process of debt remission by the year 2000. We wish to see all low-income countries who are suitable actually attain their remission by December 31st 2000, but if they have not done so a continuing Jubilee campaign must keep on putting their case.

Besides these clearly defined practical goals of debt remission for specific countries there is a wider task that will carry us well into the next millennium. My Jewish friends tell me that the great concept of 'Tikkun Olam' (repairing the world) implies more than just to make it as it was before it was damaged; the world has to actually to become greater than it was before. St. Augustine in the Christian tradition writes of the fall of Adam as:

> Felix culpa quae tantem et talem meruit redemptorem (blessed fault producing so great a redemption of such a kind).

The meaning of this is that the final redeemed state is better than that before the original sin is committed. Applying this paradigm to the debt trap, we seek a situation where the creative energies of the Jubilee 2000 debt remission process will have produced a better situation for low-income countries, than that in which they were before the debts were incurred; it will be not just a reversal but an extra achievement.

This is part of a living process. Those who follow us in this task must have not just a specific legacy of debt forgiven, but also a living legacy of a heightened consciousness among many people in the world of the need to close the gap between rich and poor, in order to ensure a fairer distribution of the world's resources among the human family and to establish grants, loans and investments of a kind which will help and not hinder the development of poorer nations. We are faced with a crossroads. One route, that advocated by the World Bank and the IMF, would lead only to the remission of past debt to a so-called sustainable level, leaving a crippling balance. It would mean that the outcome of our vast Jubilee 2000 Campaign would be disappointing.

The other route, that of the original vision of Jubilee 2000, with which I set out in 1990, provides for liberation from this backlog of past debt, to be followed by proper financial management, where future debt is productive and kept to sustainable levels. The liberation from past debt can be achieved through total or near-total remission of the debt of low income countries, where what is left unremitted is only a sum which can be paid off in the short term by the debtor country without undue social cost.

Since writing this text, two important events have occurred: just before his death on 17 June 1999, Cardinal Hume asked especially for the lifting of the burden of debt from the governments of poorer countries. Our Prime Minister, who attended Cardinal Hume's funeral, cannot ignore this request. Secondly, the World Bank 1999 Global Development Finance Volumes have been issued. These show for 1997 a general increase in debt owed by all income groups and all areas except the Low Income Group and Africa South of the Sahara, where debt levels have flattened out. The debts of half of these countries have gone up and half have gone down. Also, in 1998 the export income of low income countries fell considerably. Total debt remission for 1997 was $7.9 billion, whereas the total we need is $280 billion. These trends will not produce adequate debt reduction without massive remission from creditors. The increased debt forgiveness offered by the G8 at Cologne was from $50 billion to $70 billion. This $20 billion was the balance of ODA debt, where aid was given by loans instead of grants.

Notes

1   Hue Thomas *'The Slave Trade'*: London, Picador, 1997, p.742
2   I am indebted to Ann Pettifor's address at the launching of the Jubilee 2000 Africa Campaign in Ghana, 1998, for this reference to Keynes.
3   The World Bank Debt Tables Volume 1 for 1996 has a section on 'Debt for Nature Swaps', p. 89. The external debt stock of participating developing countries was reduced by $178m and 'in recent years debt for nature swaps in recent years have slowed to a trickle' Only the intervention of governments in proposing massive debt for nature swaps could make this particular route for debt remission productive of significant results.

14 The Origin and Development of the Campaign for Debt Relief/Cancellation and the Critique of the IFIs, 1983-93

In the first quarter of 1983 the earliest signs of the impending debt crisis in the Third World began to appear. I was at that time British High Commissioner in Malawi with diplomatic oversight of the Southern African Development Division, the ODA's regional organisation with responsibility for all British aid for countries in Central and Southern Africa between Dar-es-Salaam and the Cape. In the previous few months I had witnessed and, to some extent, been involved in, a World Bank mission to Malawi and had been asked to help one of the British commercial banks in placing a minor loan with the Government of Malawi. The unusual circumstances of the latter event should have set me on the alert - normally the initiative for borrowing came from the borrower. Had I been sufficiently alert I should probably have avoided involvement in the loan, despite my general duty as a British diplomat to help British companies and other organisations with their business in the country where I was accredited. To his credit, David Edelman, who was leading the WB team at that time, did query the transaction. Malawi's economic situation, after a run of above average harvests and with tobacco prices high, was reasonably sound, with a growth rate of around 7% maintained for several years under President Banda's policy of strict financial control (except when his own enterprises were involved), contrasting with neighbouring countries such as Zambia; but Malawi was being propped up by donor countries and the IFIs, pleased to encounter relative financial probity: her debt, consisting of a large proportion of soft loans, was 'sustainable' but clearly needed cautious management without stimulation from eager lenders. Multinational corporations such as Unilever, Bookers, BAT, Imperial Tobacco, Lonrho and Coca Cola continued to regard her as a sound location for investment.

But, from 1983, the foreign investment flows into Malawi, as into the whole of the region, had begun to fall off, a situation which was to continue with increasing intensity for the next 15 years, (and continues today). Involved not only in British aid, but also aid from the European Community (now European Union), I witnessed this across a range of donor countries; the World Bank tables confirmed the diminutions provided one was prepared to separate out from their generally optimistic picture the details for the least developed countries (as they were then known). At this juncture an International Monetary Fund team came to Malawi on a routine visit, part of the process of vetting the use of past loans and determining the response to requests for new ones or rescheduling. Although its members did not go out of their way to make contact with resident diplomats, rather the reverse, it was clear that the majority of them were comparatively recent recruits to the IMF cadre, having emerged from their Universities, mainly Western, in the late 'seventies, well instructed in the disciplines and procedures of their employer. It was also clear that almost none of them had experience of the fragilities of a developing economy based primarily on tropical agriculture, serving domestic needs and a limited export market. Through friends in the Malawian Ministries mainly concerned with the team - Finance, Development, Health, Agriculture, Works, Education - it was possible to piece together an outline of the proposals they were putting to the Malawi Government; a structural adjustment programme (SAP). This was a shock. To the main recommendations, devaluation and a switch from production for the domestic and neighbouring markets to production for hard currency export markets, were added injunctions to reduce subsidies, cut back on public service expenditure and prune budgets to concentrate resources on essential infrastructure or direct revenue-earning activities. Although targets for budget reduction were not specified in detail, to those with experience of the country, it seemed obvious that the provision of services like health and education would inevitably come under pressure. My concern about this dubious menu was such that, having been given no opportunity to voice it to members of the team, I felt obliged to tell my own Government my fears about the likely consequences of the SAP, with a recommendation that future teams should be encouraged from the Washington end of IMF to engage at least in minimum dialogue with well-intentioned local diplomats representing governments which had executive directors on their governing boards.

In April 1983 my service in the British diplomatic service ended as I reached age 60. My uneasiness about the prospects for Malawi was confirmed by a round of visits I made in my last few weeks to some of the more remote areas of the country. The British charity 'Lepra' had suggested to me that after retirement I might consider joining them with a prospect of becoming Chairman when a foreseen vacancy occurred. To improve my knowledge against that possibility - it was also useful for my regular duties as High Commissioner - I obtained clearance to accompany some of their Leprosy Assistants in their rounds. (When roads allowed they quite welcomed travelling by air-conditioned Range Rover rather than their normal bicycles or, at best, motor bikes.) What I saw horrified me. I knew that the Malawi health service was thinly stretched but these Leprosy Assistants, by the nature of their jobs and the disease they tended, were getting to places the health service didn't reach. The squalor and deprivation in some villages was very bad. I even came across villagers in bark clothing which I had believed had been totally displaced by textiles many years earlier. Ruined houses and broken down village granaries (nkokwe) were commonplace, and, of course, the roads were appalling. Against 100 in 1975 Malawi's terms of trade had fallen to 32 by 1982. Even though the remoter villages were cushioned against this it was evident that returns on agriculture were becoming insufficient to maintain even minimal nutrition. Leprosy was being held in check, even reduced because of a vigorous campaign, but other diseases such as malaria and poliomyelitis were creeping back, a view the Leprosy Assistants were able to confirm.

Post-retirement, occupation as adviser to a major construction conglomerate, as Chairman of Lepra and as a member of a British Rotary Club starting up a water supply project in a village near Lilongwe called 'place of dryness', took me back to Malawi in January 1985, less than two years after I had left. The change was striking. The signs of increasing impoverishment were everywhere to be seen outside the main towns and cities. In the villages along main roads unroofed houses were common together with some unrepaired public buildings such as schools; the village granaries were often equally broken down and it was rumoured that even the enormous modern grain silos, the main national reserve, outside Lilongwe, were almost empty. Roads had deteriorated. Distressing signs of malnutrition, the protuberant bellies of young children, skeletal figures among older ones, streaming, fly-plagued eyes were to be seen beside busy roads. Parents were beginning to choose which of their children could be schooled, whether the bright, older ones could be kept at university. As I talked with some of the humbler members of the church congregation to which I had belonged in Lilongwe it was all too obvious what had happened. The drive to produce more export crops had not brought advantage to the ordinary farmer. The price he was getting for his crops, stripped of subsidies, had steadily diminished as had that for farmers producing for the export market, filleted by gluts as several countries at the same time increased production of the same narrow range of crops. The prices of essential, imported goods such as fertiliser, boosted by devaluation, was rising steadily. A farmer who needed to produce six bags of maize to afford a bag of fertiliser in 1983 needed to produce twelve by 1985 and the upward trend continued. Moreover, as pressure to adjust budgets continued the state support for education and health services was gradually stripped away. As Vice-Chairman and later Chairman of the United Society for the Propagation of the Gospel (USPG) I became all too aware of the punishing overstretch on the Society's resources for maintaining our schools, hospitals and clinics as government support withdrew.

In April 1983 I had alerted the British Government to the likely consequences of IMF prescriptions for structural adjustment in some developing countries. Details of the follow-up to this opening gambit will appear later. Meanwhile my peripatetic post-retirement occupation as an adviser in international finance gave me opportunities to observe what was occurring, financially and economically, in other parts of the Third World. (This term is used merely as a familiar pointer without any implication of priority; the term 'two-thirds world' is probably preferable and more 'P.C') The International Moral Re-Armament Organisation based in Caux also drew me into a series of conferences and mediation efforts in troubled countries in South and Central Americas, South Asia and Africa while my growing responsibilities in the USPG opened the way to the global spread of countries where they are active in the post-missionary business of encounter and exchange within the Anglican Communion. Moreover, engaged over Tibet since 1944 during war service with the Gurkhas, my growing friendship with the Dalai Lama brought me other overseas initiatives as did my membership of the South Atlantic Council which developed from my service as Ambassador in Uruguay, 1977-80.

Taking first the wider issue of financial and economic changes affecting Third World and other countries, between October 1983 and July 1998, I was able to make observations on over 25 overseas journeys, six to various parts of Africa, six to Iraq, southern Asia, Hong Kong and Japan, five to central Asia, four to North America and four to Central and Latin America. The purposes of these journeys, as already indicated, were various. With an overriding interest in the debt issue, and as a trained diplomatic commentator latterly much involved with economic issues, I was able to register trends and assess needs. The countries visited in Africa ranged from the comparatively prosperous, such as Gabon (Dec 1983), Botswana (March 1992), Namibia (March 1992 and Feb 1994), South Africa (Feb 1994) and

Côte d'Ivoire (Dec 1983 and Feb 1994) to the heavily indebted, low income such as Tanzania (Jan 1988 and March 1992), Zambia (March 1992), Malawi (Jan 1985 and Feb 1992). In the latter group it was clear that poverty was increasing; my early concern about the effect of IMF policies was confirmed. Special conditions prevailed in some of the countries. For example the North/South conflict in Sudan over-rode all others in Government and rebel policy-making; it also ensured that the long term issue of exploitation of the oil reserves in the centre of the country remained on the shelf. Egypt, visited in Jan 1990 and Dec/Jan 1991/2, was another special case with large subsidies flowing in for political reasons. In Zimbabwe the prosperity gap between the better off, mainly white, and the poor, mainly black, loomed as a problem still to be worked through politically as well as economically, a picture repeated in South Africa but somehow less starkly in the genial presence of Nelson Mandela and a conscious drive for reconciliation. It was heartening too to learn that South Africa in 1992 had forgiven its apartheid-era debts due from Namibia, and, while itself practising the same initially, was warning 'this small, newly independent neighbour' to eschew borrowing as far as possible, particularly from the International Financial Institutions (IFIs). This advice, tellingly, was also being given in 1992 to Namibian ministers by all accredited African representatives in Windhoek.

Guinea Ecuatorial in 1983 was at the crossroads, with newly discovered oil deposits readying for exploitation, a strong Chinese presence displacing the Russian but the French influence thrusting for dominance, about to absorb the country into the CFA zone. This thrust was evident in other Francophone countries such as Gabon, Côte d'Ivoire, Cameroon (where francophones and anglophones were contesting for political and cultural pre-eminence); economic interest from non-French sources was often stifled by French advisers and coopérants but could be circumvented by direct approaches to local Ministers and some senior level officials, who were keen to loosen the French grip and vary sources of investment. In Tanzania the sidelining of Nyerere by western governments who on neo-classical grounds believed his Ujema (socialist) policies were inimical to his country's 'true' interests was healthily countered by Scandinavian governments, while the major enterprise of the Tazara Railway, connecting Dar to the Zambian and Southern African railway networks, ensured growing, though unobtrusive and unaggressive Chinese influence. On 2 October 1987 Julius Nyerere had inaugurated in Geneva the South Commission to strengthen co-operation among LDCs, a sensible counter to his isolation. Later I heard more of the work of this Commission in Dar, notably from its and Nyerere's formidable, devoted Secretary, Joan Wickham; in a personal encounter in London Nyerere discussed with me the effects of the debt burden on the Tanzanian poor; he said, as famously repeated on several public occasions, 'Am I to let their children starve to meet the demands of rich creditors?' I recall we executed a little dance together, chanting 'Market rules are sacred and must be obeyed'. In all the African countries visited, not surprisingly I found ready listeners to what I had to say about debt cancellation, and promises of support.

In South Asia the countries visited were India (Oct 1984, Jan 1986, Aug 1989), Pakistan (Oct 1984, Jan & March 1986, Sept 1990), Sri Lanka (Jan 1986) plus Iraq (Nov 1989), Japan (April/May 1990), Hong Kong (April 1986, Oct 1987 and April 1989). India, Pakistan and Sri Lanka, middle income countries with, at the time of the visits, manageable debt obligations, nevertheless were conscious of the debt problem of less developed countries, in India's case reinforced by the government's leading position in the Non-Aligned Movement and aspirations for Security Council status. India and Pakistan were, as always, highly conscious of each others' policies and alignments; India was receiving substantial aid and technical know-how from the Soviet Union and Pakistan was similarly supported by China but with US support also because of its proximity to and clandestine involvement in Afghanistan. Indian Ministers and officials in particular, while protective of their own country's requirement to continue to obtain low interest loans from the World Bank (WB) and IMF, encouraged by the skilful management of Indian finances by a succession of highly intelligent Governors of the Central Bank, acknowledged the need, despite its likely effect on the pool of funds available to them from the IFIs, for generous cancellation of highly indebted poor countries' unpayable debt. I had the opportunity of discussing the topic briefly with the President of India, Dr Zail Singh, at Rashtrapathi Bhavan, in Delhi on 18 August 1989 and earlier, with an old friend, George Fernandez, then Minister for Railways, later Defence Minister. A noticeable feature in India, repeated mutatis mutandis to some extent in Pakistan, was the sympathy felt for the poor in LDCs by people who originated from or championed the cause of the 'untouchables' - the dalits, the scheduled castes, the adivasis. A leading spokesman from this group, a Professor of Theology and Anglican Priest, Dr J Aruldas of Madhurai Theological College, explained to me that frequently the official spokesmen of LDCs at international conferences and organisations failed to emphasise the burden of debt; such spokesmen in the main came from the elites of their countries who managed to maintain a comfortable life-style despite the debt and were not unduly exercised by the hardships suffered by their poor neighbours. It is from the dalit element in India that most of the organisations working for debt relief come and from them the signatures on our Jubilee 2000 Petition.

In Sri Lanka the overwhelming consideration was, and still is, the Tamil struggle. Most of my contacts were among Christian Singhala who had knowledge of the debt situation and sympathy for LDC poor. A theologian from Sri Lanka, the Revd Duleep de Chikera, currently teaching at the College of the Ascension (USPG) at Selly Oak is helping with Buddhist texts suitable for inspiring Buddhist believers to support debt cancellation. My Lepra responsibilities brought me into contact (literally) with some of the most deprived people in India, Pakistan and Sri Lanka; their need was all too patent. (It may be worth mentioning as a personal note that in October 1984 I was actually in Delhi pursuing a detail of research into leprosy (at the All India Institute of Medical Sciences) when Indira Gandhi was brought in after her assassination, for the final few moments of her life.)

Perhaps I may also mention a seminal point in the development of my own views on debt and poverty. On 3 May 1985 I gave a small private dinner at my house in London for the First President of Bangladesh, Judge Abu Syed Choudhury, and his wife Kurshed; he had been a personal friend from the time in 1960-63 when I served as First Secretary, and, for a time, Acting Deputy High Commissioner in Dhaka, then in East Pakistan. At that time one of my neighbours had been Sheikh Mujibur Rahman, the 'Liberator of Bangladesh'. Among the guests in London was Charles O'Donnell, a close colleague of those days, when he was US Consul General; author of the standard history of the Bangladesh Independence Movement. Also present was the recently returned British Deputy High Commissioner in Dhaka, Roy Fox. Our conversation was on the economic future of Bangladesh. We asked Judge Choudhury about the extent of the economic resources to maintain a population, then of 123 million, in his country - jute, tea, sea produce, rice, cotton, indigo, timber (from the Chittagong Hill Tracts), handicrafts; as the list ran out he commented sadly 'and then we shall have to look to our friends for help ...' Happily the Bangladesh economy is now looking hopeful, as the current Prime Minister, Sheikh Wajid Hasina told me in Edinburgh on 24 October 1997; GNP is rising substantially and the country's main creditor, Japan, has found an ingenious method through compensated refinancing of easing the burden of her debt .

In Iraq in October 1989 shortly after the end of the Iran-Iraq War and with oil revenues moderately high I experienced a problematical high income country facing major social problems but with the clouds of the Gulf War only dimly discernible. The personality of Saddam Hussein was evident in the colossal photographs of him adorning all the main thoroughfares in Baghdad and the memorial to the fallen of the Iran-Iraq War, an enormous arch of two swords held by forearms modelled directly from the President himself. A visit to Kurdish territory at Arbil showed that the condition of that minority was fragile although their energy ensured moderate prosperity in time of peace. In Tokyo in May 1990 (for a Conference on Tibet) the other side of the debt picture showed clearly. Enormous activity, energy and skilled application; but a yearning to find a leading and peaceful role in the world which I believe is beginning to manifest itself in a more relaxed attitude to debt cancellation despite the very strong Japanese cultural and social rejection of debt failure in their own community. I was able to speak on Third World debt during this Tibet Conference and was surprised that such reaction as I could discern was not wholly unfavourable. The Conference also gave me access at the Imperial Temple in Tokyo to the chief Shinto Priest there, the Rev Daien Uchida, who ran the Conference, which I hope is resulting in high level help with the Japanese Jubilee 2000 campaign. My three visits to Hong Kong in 1986, 1987 and 1989 amply confirmed the extraordinary economic potential of this 'Asian Tiger', a prospect which remains after absorption into China and 'one country, two systems', and the S E Asian collapse.

My acquaintance with Central Asia developed from involvement in Tibet dating from 1944, and Chairmanship of the Tibet Society of the UK and Tibet Relief Fund from 1985 to 1993. I was in China, Mongolia and Siberia in April/May 1986, China including Xinjiang, Kazakstan, Tadjikistan, Kyrgyzia, Uzbekistan, Turkmenistan and Azerbaijan in Sept/Oct, 1987, Nepal, Tibet and China April 1989, Xinjiang again in Sept 1990 and Siberia/Altai Sept 1991. Central Asia is an area of the world which may appear remote from the problems of Third World Debt. This is not true - Nepal is certainly a highly indebted, low income country and Tibet, if viewed from the point of view of its indigenous population, is far down the scale of deprivation, while Mongolia is on the lower limit of middle income countries. China, on the other hand, with its enormous Western province of Xinjiang, in some respects, (eg GNP per head), is a Third World Country, obscured by the very high rate of economic growth in its maritime provinces, its physical size and 1.3 billion population. Xinjiang and Inner Mongolia are on a political faultline. Among their minorities are Manchus, Mongols, Tadjiks, Kyrgyz, Azeris, Uzbeks, Turkmen, Kazakhs and Uighurs. All these peoples apart from the Manchus are linked to segments of their own stock now in the newly independent republics of Kazakstan, Tadjikistan, Kyrgyzia, Turkemistan, Uzbekistan and Azerbaijan, and in Mongolia and

Afghanistan. The Uighurs are verging on rebellion within Xinjiang; they belong to an organisation of Central Asian peoples led by the Joint Committee of the Tibetan, Manchurian, Mongolian and Uighur Peoples. China is content at present to penetrate and influence the surrounding countries by trade but is watchful, alerted by violent outbreaks among the Uighurs in Xinjiang who see themselves being outnumbered and overwhelmed by Han immigrants, as do the Tibetans in Tibet and the Mongols in Inner Mongolia. In discussions with the Dalai Lama at a Conference in Panchgani, India, in January 1986, about his political prospects, I was able to sound him on the debt issue; he is publicly and privately sympathetic to HIPCs. In present circumstances, of course, this is insignificant, set against the enormous influence of China as a Third World leader. But the Dalai Lama is now a world figure despite his lack of a political base. It would be foolish to attempt to foresee directions for change in Central Asia if the faultline implodes. Suffice to say that there are many possibilities. The strength of China which I witnessed in three long journeys is impressive; particularly notable was a comment by a Chinese official in the Gobi desert where large oil reserves have been identified; he said 'Oh that .... we are reserving it for the middle of the next century.' Given the enormous oil production at Karamay not far to the North, such a comment inevitably had a strong, no doubt intended impact.

As a footnote to this Central Asian section, I was disturbed during related visits to Siberia in April 1986 and September 1991 to be made aware of the potential for disintegration of the former USSR and of Siberia which remains integrated with Russia. Having been present in Moscow on 22/3 August 1991 when the coup against the state failed, as Gorbachev returned from the Crimea, and Yeltsin jumped on his tank outside the White House, my mind was alert to a whole range of political possibilities; I watched on TV the proceedings in the Central Committee. The scene on 23 September round the overthrown statue of Dzerzhinsky in Lubianka Square as an 'excited' crowd yelled slogans such as 'Exile them (the plotters) to Chernobyl' and scrawled graffiti such as XYNTY NA XY (cuntu na cou), recalled 1917 all too easily. And in Gorno Altaisk on 14 September I heard leaders of the Altai people calling for 'national autonomy'; the Altai people number not much more than 30,000 and are not even a majority in their own oblast! That, together with evidence even then of exorbitant excesses in the switch to private enterprise were warning signs of the economic crisis which now faces Russia and presents the world financial and economic communities with a problem which deepens other related problems.

My journeys to Latin America and Central America touched more directly on the debt issue. I was in Uruguay and Argentina in March 1985, in El Salvador, Guatemala, Costa Rica and Nicaragua in November 1985, in Venezuela in September 1986, and in Colombia and, again, Guatemala in April 1987. On 1 March 1985 democratic government was restored in Uruguay after 14 years of military rule, the only such episode in the country's history, contrasting with almost every other state in Latin America. Since I had, as Ambassador from 1977 to 1980, shared the travails of democratic Uruguayans, I was very pleased to participate with them at the restoration. From 1 to 3 March I joined some of them in a Conference which dealt with current problems including the need for reconciliation, which allowed several participants who had taken an active role on the road back to democracy to recount their experiences. I got a ready hearing there for my views on debt relief, although an old friend, Ramon Dias, editor of 'Economista' (the Urugayan equivalent of the Economist) and a disciple of Milton Friedman, clearly had strong reservations.

The situation in the four Central American states visited in Nov 1985, El Salvador, Guatemala, Costa Rica and Nicaragua, was far from easy. The least disturbed of them, Costa Rica, had renounced military force several years previously and maintained a small police corps only to preserve order. It seemed like a good prescription. In El Salvador 45% of the national budget was still dedicated to the guerilla war. Death squads from the Frente Farabundo Marti para Liberacíon Nacionál appeared still to be active in the capital, San Salvador, and main cities. 25% of the population had been displaced by guerilla activity. Exports stood at $900m, loan repayments at $800m. In Guatemala the military were much in evidence, controlling the development programme and keeping a tight rein on the remoter parts of the country where Indians of Maya descent and from other races formed the major part of the population, more than 50% of the country's total. 50% were said to be in absolute poverty, 82% mainly in Indian areas in extreme poverty. The situation in Nicaragua was different because of the large Soviet presence, but no better. The continued political struggle with the Sandinistas (Frente Sandinista para Liberación Nacionál) confronted by the US-supported 'Contras' led by Edén Pastora. The State of Emergency, dropped when the Nueve Commandantes led by Daniel Ortega took over, had recently been re-imposed. But they were 'building a new society from the bottom up', sending young teams of enthusiasts to rebuild schools and health centres, targets of the 'Contras', in the rural areas. Soviet exports to Nicaragua rose from 42m roubles in 1985 to 138m in 1984 but large Russian items of equipment were everywhere to be seen abandoned for want of spare parts. Managua, still in ruins from the earthquake of 1970, struck me as the most wretched capital city I had ever seen.

On both visits to Guatemala I met President Vinicio Carezo, on the first occasion as he faced the final run-off confirming him in the Presidency. On both occasions I discussed the debt issue, of which he was well aware, on the second leaving a paper[1] I had prepared on the topic. He was at that stage much beset by demands for land distribution. In Costa Rica also I met the President, Dr Luis Alberto Monge Alvarez, whose Presidencia had joined with the Trade Union Institute of Education in a three-day Conference on social issues. I spoke on the debt and other Third World matters and the President accepted my paper. In Nicaragua I was unable to meet Sr Daniel Ortega, the charismatic leader of the Nueve Commandantes, but I subsequently met his brother, Fr Escoto Ortega in London where he had arrived as Nicaraguan Ambassador. He accepted my paper for transmission to his brother: Sra Violeta Chamoro, recently dropped from the Commandantes, but active and high profile in the Nicaraguan press, also received my paper and subsequently gave it good exposure in her principal newspaper. I also discussed debt and Third World issues in the University of Nicaragua with several academic staff including sympathetic US Professors.

In all four Central American states a deep seated Indian problem was evident, more prominent in Guatemala and Nicaragua where the population of Indians to total population is high - over 50%. As they are very low in the economic scale of their country the relevance of the debt problem to them is salient and cancellation a most pressing issue. At several gatherings where Indians predominated, notably in villages around Lake Panajachel; people from the Catchitel, Quiche and Sutui tribes speaking mainly the Quiche language derived from Mayan, showed particular concern for increasing autonomy for their villages where they now had their own mayors; not surprisingly they readily heard what I said on debt cancellation.

In Venezuela in September 1986 a recent fall in oil prices had damaged confidence, high since the bonanza of the second oil shock and the open field for sovereign leading which followed. Efforts by the government to recover some of the flight capital which left the country after the bonanza were meeting with little success but reserves gave two years import cover. The Brady and Baker Plans were still ahead. A number of large development projects including the Caracas metro and major construction around Maracaibo were under discussion. British conglomerates interested in starting up in Venezuela were being advised to buy into debt-ridden local companies (cf Korea, Taiwan etc 1997/8).

In Colombia in April 1987 I encountered the most stable at that time of the Latin American countries visited around the Caribbean, nevertheless disturbed by the recent massacre by guerillas of most of the country's senior judiciary at the Palacio de Justitia; drug links were emerging, an issue preoccupying the British Ambassador in Bogota, my former colleague Dick Nielson, who had been one of my First Secretaries in Canberra in the early 'seventies. Colombia was not heavily indebted; nevertheless I spoke on the subject at a three day Conference on reconciliation at Cali, getting a positive response and subsequent opportunities to pursue the topic in Bogota in Ministries and at the Central Bank.

From the point of view of its global position as a super-power, its influence within the G8 and in the UN and its close links and powerful levers in the IFIs, the United States is undoubtedly the most significant destination among my travels. Apart from attending an International Conference at Georgetown University in June 1985 (dealt with later) I made three visits to North America, 28 April - 2 May 1988, 15-31 April 1996 and 25 June - 9 July 1998. Their purpose was to inform myself of current policies and attitudes in Congress and the Senate, at the World Bank and IMF, at UN in New York and in cities outside the beltway such as Minneapolis, San Diego, Cincinatti, Atlanta and Chicago; to allow me to lobby on behalf of generous debt cancellation particularly with people of influence within Washington and New York, and to assist in the building up of self-propelled organisations in the US working along lines similar to Jubilee 2000 in the UK. I also developed a range of contacts in Canada, based on Vancouver, which proved very valuable in July 1998 when I was making preliminary contact with Canadian Anglican Bishops before the Lambeth Conference. One major event, the annual International Studies Association Conference for 1996 in San Diego, enabled Martin Dent and me to present substantial papers on debt cancellation which obtained wide circulation among a large group of influential opinion-formers. This was associated in my case with a dialogue with the Association of Christian Economists of the United States.[2] I continued extension into academic circles with speaking engagements, at the University and the Hubert Humphrey Institute in Minneapolis on several occasions, the University in Vancouver and the Carter Center at Atlanta. Among other institutions and organisations where I developed the Jubilee 2000 theme were the Institute for International Finance (Prof Chris Barrett), the International Institute for Economics (Fred Bergesten) , the Center for Concern (Fr Peter Henriot) and the Center for Strategic and International Studies (Doug Johnston), all in Washington. On 'the Hill' in April 1988 I made contact with Senator Bill Bradley through his Economic Adviser, David Apgar (Senator Bradley was in 1988 actively engaged with the development of the Baker Plan), Senator Mark Hatfield, Senator Paul S Sarbanes (an alumnus of my own Oxford College) and had the privilege of a meeting with Senator William J Fullbright who commented sympathetically on what I told him about the campaign, for gaining world support for generous debt cancellation.

From the US Treasury I met Mr David Jay of its International Finance Division at a WB Seminar as well as Mr Bloomingsteen. During my visit in 1996 I was able to meet Robert Rubin's Chief of Staff, who received my paper on debt cancellation with encouraging remarks. Mr Marshall Mays, President of the Overseas Private Investment Corporation, a State Department affiliate concerned with direct investment in the Third World, was pessimistic about the prospects for cancellation, but nevertheless said, in relation to my ideas for a future international conference on debt, 'Do what you plan'. At the World Bank in 1988 I had discussions with Joe Formoso and David Flannery of the International Finance and Debt Management Division and later joined a Seminar led by Diane Page on Debt for Nature Swaps. This was part of a wider discussion on a variety of debt swap devices being added to the many methods being elaborated for debtor governments and their creditors; Debt for Development became the most important of these. (But a personal effort to help Anglican churches in Southern Africa to devise debt swaps relating to USPG's annual subventions came to nothing because the amounts involved were too small.) At the UN in New York I had a substantial interview with Mr M Ripert, Director for Aid & Development, together with his colleague Mr J McIntyre; they received my paper on debt and took on board the plans for an international conference on debt (see Appendix 1) which I had canvassed in Washington also, particularly with Senator Fullbright. (It came to naught.) At the UN in 1996 I sought support from the Irish and Norwegian Permanent Representatives for an UN Resolution declaring a special date to recognise the need for solving the debt problem; and in 1998 canvassed the Botswanan, Australian and New Zealand Permanent Representatives about sponsoring an actual resolution. In Atlanta in April 1996 Judge Jack Etheridge was a knowledgeable ally, providing entrée to the Carter Center (where however President Carter's State Department Adviser, Gordon Streib, proved unenthusiastic) while the Afro-American journalist Portia Scott gave helpful introductions particularly to Mr Jimmy Young's circle.

In Washington and New York in 1996 I broached the subject of generous debt cancellation with the Presiding Bishop of the Episcopal Church of the USA (ECUSA, linked to USPG), the Most Rev Edmund Browning, and Bishop James Ottley, the Official ECUSA Observer at the United Nations, with pastoral responsibility for UN and WB Christian staff, renewing the latter contact in June 1998 just before Bishop Ottley and his fellow bishops in the USA departed for the ten yearly Lambeth Conference in Canterbury. The Presiding Bishop by then was the Most Rev Frank Griswold. Unfortunately these approaches to ECUSA proved to be of little value; the majority of ECUSA Bishops arriving for the Lambeth Conference were much more concerned about 'human sexual orientation' than Third World Debt, the topic all the other Anglican Bishops of the world had put at the head of their priority list.   I had the impression that ECUSA had been heavily influenced by the public relations drive of the IFIs begun by James Wolfensohn in November 1996 after launching the HIPC Initiative; they were possibly influenced also by considerations of US hegemonism and their friends in Wall Street.

Other Christian denominations in the US were more supportive. Very good relations developed with the Religious Working Group on the World Bank and IMF which brought together Catholic, Methodist, Quaker, United Reformed and Presbyterian leaders. In personal correspondence I gained promises of support from the American Baptists but not the Southern Baptists ('we have our own poor'). Among n.g.os. Bread for the World led by David Beckman, President, made a commitment during meetings in 1998, (working with Jubilee 2000 USA), to pursue debt cancellation as their main campaign target for 1999. Finally two important sources of support. American business obviously needs bringing into any campaign of our type if it is to succeed. In Minneapolis I was at the heart of the grain industry and obtained a sympathetic hearing from several large grain processors there notably the world giant, Cargill. To my surprise in both 1988 and 1996 I found that their Vice-President for Governmental Relations, Mr Robin Johnson, had no difficulty in wishing success for our campaign; Cargill's strategic objective of producing the maximum amount of safe food for the maximum number of people worldwide at the lowest possible price did not in any way collide with cancellation of unpayable debt. Secondly, in a private school in Fairfax, Virginia, I was invited to speak about our campaign to a mixed class of 13/14 year olds: the enthusiasm they showed for the campaign, once explained, was heart-warming. We need to engage the hearts and minds of such age groups.

Coming now to the Caux connection, I highlighted the subject of international debt there at the regular summer International Conferences. I introduced the subject on 1 September 1983 describing deteriorating conditions in Malawi, commending the broad subject for future attention and study. I pointed out that a situation in which a swathe of developing countries, having opted for democracy, was beginning to question whether the open form of government involved, associated with strict adherence to market economies such as the IMF enjoined, was better for them than the closed structures and interventionist policies of the Soviet and Chinese systems; a wholesale switch by such countries already foreshadowed in the changing balance of votes at UN General Assemblies, could have implications as serious as those of uncontrolled nuclear proliferation, then dominating debate in world councils. At subsequent annual conferences from 1984 to 1991, apart from 1990, I continued to press the case for debt remission of developing countries. In 1984 I initiated a paper[3] on the consequences of the debt overhang, proposing the introduction of a two-tier system of interest rates on loans and an international effort similar to the Marshall Plan to relieve the debt burden and open the way to a fresh impetus of development for least developed countries. At App. 3 [4] is the text of a Press Release issued after that event, once again I stressed the danger to world stability of disillusionment among LDCs. In 1985 at a Georgetown University Conference from 15 to 23 June on the theme 'How to Create a Just Society and a World at Peace', I contributed to debates on International Debt (led by Geoffrey Lean, doyen of British environmental journalists), on agricultural problems in Africa and on use of food surpluses.[5]

The 1985 Caux Conference was notable for a number of papers presented on the debt issue, including one by the Japanese economist Nobutai Kiuchi which argued for the acceptance of inequality for heavily indebted countries and a measure of protectionism. My own paper repeated the proposal for two tiers of interest rates, suggested fresh rules for the use of IMF Special Drawing Rights as well as improved compensatory schemes for tropical primary products adversely affected by exceptional climatic conditions, and increased aid; and quoted Barbara Ward's warning 'From the beginning of time people have heard the still small voice of obligation and brotherhood. When they have listened society has worked. When they have refused to listen society has broken up.'

From November 1985 I corresponded with the Director General of the International Labour Organisation (ILO), Francois Blanchard, (and Hans Lundström, Executive Director, IMF) on the debt issue. This led to my being invited to the High Level ILO Conference on Employment and Structural Adjustment in Geneva from 23 to 25 November 1987.

This was an important occasion attended by the principals of a large number of UN agencies and representatives of the Bretton Woods institutions. At this stage under Blanchard's guidance the ILO was taking a leading role in discussion of international financial and economic problems including debt. On that the conference communique recorded 'a major effort of world-wide structural adjustment is needed.' The main conclusions are at App. 4.[6] My own report on the meeting is at App. 5.[7]

At the end of the Conference the next major step was envisaged as an international summit to be called later by President Mitterand in 1990. This, unfortunately, never happened. The French prominence at this time is consistent with their earlier record on debt. It was they who in the 'seventies initiated the Conferences on International Economic Co-operation (CIEC, see Chapter 9) which led to the abortive attempt at Cancun in 1981 to reach a *modus vivendi* between the 'first' and 'third' worlds.

For the 1987 Caux Conference a major but unsuccessful effort was made to bring in leading personalities such as Bob Geldof (who, on receiving the Third World Prize in November 1986 had urged debtor countries to refuse to pay interest and seek a 20 year moratorium on stock repayment), Lord (Harold) Lever, author of a recent book 'Debt and Danger' and Dr Johannes Witeveen, Managing Director of the IMF. The first President of Bangladesh was prevented from attending by unforeseen events. But François Blanchard played an active role, as did Mgr Munnor Garcia, the Apostolic Delegate in Geneva, and Olivier Giscard d'Estaing with whom I shared a platform when the dual topic of Changing Corporate Culture and Addressing Third World Debt was held in uneasy tension.

The Caux Conference from 24 to 26 August 1988 focussed specifically on debt and was accompanied by an earlier expert Seminar. Cardinal Jorge Mejia provided the keynote speech, drawing on the 1986 Pax et Justitia publication 'An Ethical Approach to the International Debt Question'.[8] He was supported by the IMF Rep in Europe, Sr Eduardo Wiesner, a former Finance Minister of Colombia. Among the experts a welcome African presence was Professor Washington Okumu, later to play a crucial role in the final stage before the South African election of 1994 in bringing Nelson Mandela and Chief Mangosuthu Buthelezi [9] together, a major contribution to the near miraculous resolution of the South African political impasse before the eradication of apartheid. His earlier experience at UNIDO and his knowledge of African economies was an invaluable input. My report on the Conference and Seminar is at Appendix 6.[10]   One further event at Caux needs mentioning. This was in August 1996. The conference was notable for the number of distinguished and stirring speakers from Japan who spoke on reconciliation. Among them was Mr Tsutomu Hata who for a few months had been Prime Minister. In personal discussion with me he showed great interest in debt cancellation. He was planning for 2000 a major event at Hiroshima to be focussed on reconciliation. He readily agreed that the theme of debt forgiveness could be a very rational and appropriate adjunct to this, in which Japan might gain much credit from taking a lead.

Perhaps the most critical development to date in this account of the genesis of the Jubilee 2000 campaign occurred at Tirley Garth from 12 to 14 March 1993. Following the Caux Conference in 1991 which centred on the situation of minorities within wider nationalities, the debt theme had been maintained but not much advanced — an element at Caux linked into the Swiss banking system was basically unhappy about its pursuit. A New Zealand colleague there had been developing with me a critical appraisal of Adam Smith's tenet that self-interest is the principal human motive to be taken into account in analysing economic activity. We felt that over the years this had distorted economic theory and, particularly in the then prevailing ascendency in Britain of Thatcherite market economics, led to unfortunate and unacceptable results. The broad range of charitable activities some, like the British blood donor system, wholly altruistic, were left out of account, while the excesses of Thatcherite orthodoxy, like 'there is no such thing as society', were plainly wrong. We decided it would be opportune to organise a seminar on Ethics in Economics. One of my fellow members of the South Atlantic Council (see p. 154) was Martin Dent, a Fellow of Keele University, retired from the Politics Department there. He shared with me an active involvement in Malawi and a background, much earlier, in the Overseas Civil Service as a district officer in Nigeria. I proposed him for invitation to the Seminar; he accepted.

His paper unequivocally advocated a campaign, based on his work with students at Keele, for the cancellation of the unpayable debt of highly impoverished poor countries which would never be able to meet their obligations. Dr Michael Schluter, Director of the Jubilee Centre at Cambridge had offered the idea of using the year 2000 in the name of the campaign to link it with the biblical element of Jubilee. My own paper for the seminar described what was needed to solve the debt problem as a major act of international altruism. The idea of a debt cancellation campaign caught fire at the Seminar with Washington Okumu providing much practical advice on how it should be fashioned to win wider acceptance among academics, governments and the IFIs. At a smaller subsequent meeting we agreed that Richard Pearce would follow up the 'ethics in economics' angle, his special interest, while Martin Dent and I would concentrate on debt cancellation. We also agreed that for the latter we needed the widest possible framework since the required degree of support could not be derived from the rather narrow limits within which our work on debt alleviation had until then been conducted.

When mentioning earlier my official report to the British Government alerting them to the risk of damage to fragile economies implicit in IMF prescriptions for structural adjustment in some developing countries, I promised to enlarge on developments from that. So far as I know the report, part of my Valedictory Despatch as British High Commissioner in Malawi, was circulated in Whitehall, as such papers routinely are, to Departments which might have an interest in the topic and to the Bank of England. I did not expect any response but thought it worth following up at the Foreign and Commonwealth Office. This I did in Spring 1985. Mr (now Sir) Humphrey Maud, then Assistant Under-Secretary of State dealing with economic matters, received me, fortunately a sensitive and sympathetic interlocuteur. He heard me out, I thought with more attention than some might have deemed due to a mere retired Head of Mission, turning up again in King Charles Street like a bad penny. He assured me that HMG was very conscious of the risks of acute hardship I had pointed out in my despatch; they were already adopting policies which mitigated the impact of IMF policies, such as the conversion of many bilateral loans to grants. This process continued progressively leading to a situation in which very few UK bilateral loans except those linked to the operation of the Export Credit Guarantee Department (ECGD) now remain outstanding. Mr Maud assured me that HMG were looking at other ways of easing the debt burden for very poor indebted countries, outlining an approach which eventually led to standard loan conversions for all debtor countries seeking rescheduling at the Paris Club; these were initially known as the Trinidad Terms, having been enunciated at a Commonwealth Finance Ministers Meeting in Trinidad in 1990 and subsequently agreed with some improvements by all creditors as the Naples Terms after the G8 Meeting in Naples in 1994.

Friends at the ODA and in the FCO were able to some extent to keep me abreast of the less sensitive developments, some in the UN Administrative Committee on Co-ordination, but I decided to return to the charge on 31 May, 1995. On this occasion I was received by (Sir) Michael Jay, who is currently British Ambassador in Paris, a nephew of Douglas Jay and cousin-in-law of Baroness Jay. He also was a ready, sympathetic listener; once again I was assured that HMG was finding ways of alleviating the debt burden on poor indebted countries, at Washington, through the British Executive Director at the World Bank, as well as in Europe within the G7.
On an earlier visit to the FCO, on 14 Dec 1989, my interlocuteur was the newly appointed Minister of State, the Hon Francis Maude, a cousin of Humphrey, my first FCO interlocuteur. He, too, assured me of HMG's continuing benign intentions on debt.

Humphrey Maud about this time arrived at the Commonwealth Secretariat as Deputy (Economic) to the Secretary General, Chief Emeka Anyoaku; the latter had been one of three Assistant Directors of the International Relations Division of the Secretariat when I was its Director, 1969-71. Not surprisingly, I began to make some of my calls at Marlborough House, where I received encouragement and advice. At the Whitehall end, however, efforts continued, notably with the proposal by Kenneth Clarke as Chancellor of the Exchequer that a proportion of the IMF gold reserves should be sold to provide resources for IFI debt cancellation. (The price of gold was at that stage very high, but collapsed shortly afterwards. The proposal remains on the table to be considered when market conditions are more favourable to a sale.) In Washington in April 1996 I had a meeting with the British Executive Director of the WB and IMF, Mr Huw Evans, who assured me he and his colleagues were working towards a scheme for IMF debt cancellation. The HIPC Initiative when it emerged was, of course, disappointingly inadequate. Huw Evans' successors proved resolutely uncommunicative. With the advent of a strong Labour Government in May 1997, the prospects for continued favourable attention to the debt issue strengthened still further. As a member of the Labour Party I began correspondence with the new Chancellor, Mr Gordon Brown, as well as with the Secretary of State for International Development, Ms Clare Short; she already knew me, having been my guest in Bombay in 1976. The Mauritius Mandate, launched at the Commonwealth Finance Ministers Meeting in Mauritius in September 1997 went a considerable way to meeting the points I had been putting to Gordon Brown and subsequent policy advances have continued in the same direction.[11]

HMG is, of course, constrained by our position in Europe and as a member of the Group of Eight. Financial prudence requires that HMG should not leap too far ahead of the rest of the Group - which would lead to moral hazard, the problem of the free rider - and are bound by EU agreements about variations in the terms of loans such as those managed by the ECGD. Many of the suggestions by the Jubilee 2000 Coalition, such as a tentative one for unilateral cancellation, cannot be adopted as they stand. But HMG welcomes the pressure Jubilee 2000 is building worldwide, and which has already produced improvements, at the G8 meeting in Birmingham on 16 May 1998 when 70,000 people came out on the streets to demand revision of the World Bank's HIPC Initiative. We can, I believe, operate a tacit agreement under which HMG moves as far forward as the changing political balance in the G8 allows, while we and allied n.g.os. continue to build pressure and ask for more, maintaining as a spur the deadline of year 2000, which even the World Bank now acknowledges.

Notes

1   App. 1, Third World: Debt, Poverty and Starvation; W Peters. 26 Feb 1987.
2   Association of Christian Economists of the United States. *Bulletin No.5*. Fall 1995.
3   App. 2, Hope in a World of Tension, Caux, 1.9.84, Bill Peters.
4   App. 3, Press Release issued at Caux, 1.9.84.
5   I also spoke about 'Second Track Diplomacy' in situations of conflict, of which I had had direct experience as a diplomat, in Cyprus, Tibet and Afghanistan. By an extraordinary series of coincidences friends in Montevideo where I attended a Conference from 1 to 3 March 1985 were able to get for me an immediate visa to visit Argentina although at that time, so soon after the Falklands War, British nationals needed to give three months notice for an Argentine visa. In Buenos Aires I was able to obtain support from a number of leading Argentinian businessmen, including Arnoldo Mussich, a powerful moderating influence, for the work then being started between the All Party Parliamentary Group in London known as the South Atlantic Council and the Argentine organisation Consejo Argentino para Relationes Internacionales (CIAS); this led eventually to the restoration of diplomatic relations between the two countries and to the visit of President Menem to Britain October/November 1998.
6   App. 4, Conclusions of the High Level ILO Meeting on Employment and Structural Adjustment.
7   App. 5, Report by W Peters on the High Level ILO Meeting 23-5 Nov 1987.
8   *'At the Service of the Human Community'*, Vatican City, 27 Dec 1986.
9   Michael Cassidy: *A Witness For Ever*, Hodder & Stoughton, 1995, pp. 146-184.
10 App. 6, International Debt Question, Caux, Switzerland, 25-27 August 1988, Report by W Peters.
11 App. 7, Letter from W Peters to the Economic Secretary to the Treasury, 27 Aug 1997.

15 The Approach to Debt in Other Faiths

Jews and Christians in considering the debt problems of the Third World are very well served by their sacred books. The Torah, the Old Testament and the New Testament have clear texts on the forgiveness of debt, brought to a beautiful summation in the Sermon at Nazareth of Jesus Christ when, at the outset of his Ministry, quoting from the Prophet Isaiah, he declared his mission in the World: to bring good news to the poor, the release of prisoners, to declare the acceptable year of the Lord (Luke, 4, 1-18). Unlike earlier texts, the New Testament makes clear that forgiveness and release are for all mankind, not just fellow Jews. St Paul later asserted (2 Corinthians, 6. 2) 'Now' is the 'acceptable time', and 'this very day' is the 'day of salvation'.

The sacred books of some other faiths are no less clear on the subject of debt. The Holy Q'uran, for example, rejects interest-taking, and advocates 'Sadaka', (compassion, charity). For followers of Confucius a memorable fact is that in his fifties and sixties in the 5th Century BC Kong Fu wandered from state to state looking for a ruler who would give him a post in which he could put into practice his ideas for relieving suffering among the poor. Confucianism emphasises filial piety and respect for ancestral tradition, with a moral order based on observance of the established, patriarchal family and social relationships of authority, obedience and mutual respect in which concern for the less prosperous has a place.

But some other faiths give little guidance. In contrast with the pragmatic approach to ethical conduct of Confucianism, Taoism, the other great Chinese religion, following Lao Tze (6th Century BC) approaches most matters from a mystical base, intuitive and divinatory, characterised by its great handbook, the I Ching. The 'dynamic tension' between the Yin and the Yang, the male and female principles, contributes no less to Confucian thought, but the outcomes are totally different. Again, Shintoism, a version of which, State Shintoism, was until 1912 the dominant religion of Japan, has no philosophy or fixed system of ethics. Its ceremonies appeal to the 'kami', mysterious forces of nature which can be called in aid of human endeavours. State Shintoism upheld the Imperial Family, descended from or, at least, favoured by the Sun goddess. Both Taoism and Shintoism, through their intuitive naturism, share features with the religions of the original peoples of America, Australia and New Zealand, who have a kindred feeling for the poor in highly indebted poor countries based possibly more on common suffering than basic principle.

Buddhism has a very extensive ethical system and a code of conduct based on the Eightfold Way. The third, fourth and fifth elements, right action, right livelihood and right effort have most relevance to debt relief. The scriptures, however, recorded primarily the acts of the Buddha and the Boddisathvas. The reincarnation of the Buddha known as Avaloketisvara is the embodiment of compassion and self abnegation as is the Buddha Sakyamuni with whom the Dalai Lama is identified. Compassionate action however is motivated primarily to the attainment of perfection in life and eventual translation to the state of full purification. Thus in Dharmapada v.131 we read 'He who, in seeking his own happiness, torments with the rod creatures that are desirous of happiness, shall not obtain happiness hereafter.' And again, v.125 of the same 'Whosoever offends an innocent person, pure and guiltless, his evil comes back on that fool himself, like fine dust thrown against the wind.' For 'torments with the rod' in the debt context read 'pursues through the Paris Club'. The Buddha said, for humans there are four forms of happiness.

1. The happiness of enjoying economic security or sufficient wealth, acquired by just and righteous means.
2. The happiness of spending the wealth liberally on himself, his family, his friends and performing meritorious deeds.
3. The happiness of being free from debt.
4. The happiness of living a faultless life, committing no unwholesome actions of thought, word or deed.

The Buddha also said that the first three forms are not worth one sixteenth of the fourth form.

The Jains, whose motto is 'Live and let live', have a code of principles which includes non-violence and reverence for life (ahimsa), limiting possession to personal needs (apanigraha) equality of all souls, friendship to all and malice to none. The central conviction is that 'all life is interdependent for mutual need' (parasparopagraho jivanan). The Jain scriptures summarise ahimsa as follows:

All the Arhats (venerable ones) of the past, present and future discourse, counsel, proclaim, propound and prescribe thus in unison: Do not injure, abuse, oppress, enslave, insult, torment, torture or kill any creature or living being.

The Jains consider that keeping poor countries in debt is a form of violence; therefore they fully support Jubilee 2000. Jains hold that we are trustees of property in excess of our needs, to use it for the welfare of other beings. This is part of aparigraha, non-attachment, not only to worldly possessions but also to sensual pleasures and sorrows. Its opposite, paragraha, is the cause of trouble in the world; it means greed, avarice, egoism, and all forms of grasping after and attachment to power and possessions. It is this, they say, which causes rich countries to keep poor countries in debt.

A Jain leader has suggested that the interest due from a poor country should be frozen for a number of years to be used for developing its infrastructure as it grows and improving its people's education. Also that until the people in a receiving country have agreed loans in referenda the world's banking institutions should not release the loans.

The Zoroastrian faith, very ancient, dating from c1200 BC in Persia, where fire temples were built around 'perpetual flames', springing from surface oil wells, now has a minute and declining population base. They believe in perpetual conflict between good and evil, light and darkness. Ahura Mazda (Ormuzd) and Ahriman. Individually they seek moral and physical purity, regarding life and work as part of worship (yarsna), and await a final universal judgement (Frashokereti). Friends among the small Parsee community in Bombay find nothing in the tenets of their faith which contradicts the aims of Jubilee 2000. Many long established and wealthy charities established by Parsees provide benefits not only to their own community but to others, widely spread.

The Baha'í, another small religious community arisen in the mid-nineteenth century, led by Baha'ullah, seek 'a just and global civilisation in which all peoples and their governments regard the world as one country and mankind its citizens'. They recognise that building such a civilisation will be a long and arduous process, requiring the transformation of the inner and outer lives of each of us and the building of new structures of government at local, national and world levels, to safeguard the unity of humankind and promote justice and equity.

Mindful of this, the Baha'í community is applying its teachings at all levels throughout the world to ensure a spiritually based, sustainably prosperous future for individuals, families, villages, countries and ultimately the whole planet - a major project for a small community. They consider they already offer a model of the genuine engagement of the world's peoples in building their own future. Having observed some of the excellent development projects they promote and finance among small communities in remote valleys of the high Himalayas and the Karakoram Range I am full of admiration for their efforts and sure that their weight is on the side of generous debt cancellation. They wish us well, but feel they cannot make any worthwhile immediate contribution.

Sikhism is the monotheistic religion founded by Guru Nanak early in the sixteenth century in reaction against Hindu tradition and the caste system as well as Muslim dominance in North India where they lived, hence their warrior traditions and the inclusion of the dagger (kirpan) among the five symbols of their faith. Their aim was the removal of inequalities in the society where they found themselves; this continues today in the sharing of food by all equally at the gurdwaras where they gather to worship and where food is always available.

The doctrines of Sikhism are recorded in their holy book, the Granth Sahib, which plays a prominent part in their rituals. Sikhs focus on the household as the basic unit of society. Their devotion to equality predisposes them against financial and economic structures which tend towards inequality at state level and the preservation of a debt system which divides rather than harmonises. Like most Indians, for Sikhs the village moneylender, with his exploitative methods, is a hateful figure; they tend to see similarities between the lending system of the IFIs, particularly the IMF, and those of the money-lender.

The Q'uranic injunctions on 'Sadaka' (compassion, charity), 'zakat' (alms) and against interest-taking have already been mentioned. Among the many names of Allah, pointers to conduct for Muslims, is 'Rahim', the loving, the merciful one. His Godly actions include forgiveness as well as punishment, but forgiveness (Ghafoor) is mentioned much more frequently than punishment. A man's duties are not only towards God, Haqooqulch, but also towards fellow man, Haqooqul Ibad; this is part of the Islamic concept of brotherhood and the unity of the Ummah, the whole Islamic community. The revival of Islam, Muslim thinkers say, comes through the reform of society, combatting corruption and disunity and being led to the spirit of brotherhood, social service and community living by men (and women) who obey God's precepts. This is the main aim, generally not understood, of so-called Muslim Fundamentalists.

Among many texts in the Q'uran which enjoin compassion for the poor and indebted are:

Chapter 2 al Baqarah v.280   'If the debtor is in difficulty, grant him time until it is easy for him to pay. But if ye remit it by way of charity, that is best for you, if ye only knew.' (ie for your salvation).

Chapter 3 Al Imran vv133-4. Be quick in the race for forgiveness from your Lord, and for a Garden whose width is that of the heavens and of the earth, prepared for the righteous.

Those who spend freely whether in prosperity or in adversity: who restrain anger, and pardon all men. For God loves those who do good.

Chapter 90 al Badad vv12-17. These enjoin compassion and kindness to those less fortunate 'even though that path be difficult'.

12. And what will explain to thee the path that is steep?
13. It is freeing the bondman
14. Or the giving of food in a day of privation
15. To the orphan with claims of relationship
16. Or to the indigent down in the dust
17. Then will ye be of those who believe and enjoin patience and enjoin deeds of kindness and compassion.

Chapter 107, al Maun (neighbourly assistance) chastises those who ignore the feeding of the indigent and caring for the orphan, and give of their wealth only to boast of their generosity.

Hinduism, perhaps the religion with the largest number of followers world-wide, is difficult to categorise in terms of a code of personal ethics and social conduct. Over the millennia, it has absorbed elements from many other religions; it is syncretistic, so it apparently offers its followers many gods and many paradigms of conduct. But all gods are aspects of the one God, being, spirit-Brahman - and his three principal aspects summed up as Brahma, the creator, Vishnu, the preserver and Shiva, the destroyer. The doctrine of karma teaches that in the perpetual cycle of life each of us works out his destiny determined by previous lives, leading, all hope, to moksha, ultimate release from the cycle.

Hinduism divides people into castes into which they are born according to their place in the cycle. The four main castes - Priest, Warrior, Trader and Agriculturalist, Servants (sudras) leave aside a vast segment once known as the Untouchables, now described as Dalits (children of God) the Scheduled castes or Harijans to whom are linked the tribal peoples of India, the adivasis, also called tribals. The Upanishads are a very ancient series of ethical treatises which examine, as well as causality in creation, the nature of morality, its relation to eternal life, and place in transmigration, *aliter* or, more briefly, the equation of atman (self) and Brahman (ultimate reality). Mahatma Gandhi, who led the Indian Independence movement in its later stages, once freedom had been assured, turned his great capacity for religious and social creative thought to reform of the caste system, particularly untouchability. He campaigned against all forms of discrimination against untouchables, twice fasting almost unto death. He advocated a return to the simpler way of life of earlier man in Indian history where villages could be virtually self-sustaining through co-operative action and strong communal cohesion. He advocated each household doing its own spinning (to escape the grip of the big textile corporations in Indian industry), the maintenance of village crafts, building co-operatives and preserving traditional forms of agriculture. He regarded non-violent protest and hunger strikes, successful against the Raj, as the main instruments of political change. He strongly opposed the first independent Prime Minister, Pandit Jawarhalal Nehru's, drive to build up heavy industry in India as the most important step for securing her place in the world and in world councils. It is from Ghandhi's social theories that we can trace the impetus among Hindu believers for the campaign for debt cancellation. There can be no doubt that Gandhi would have been wholeheartedly in favour of generous debt cancellation for highly indebted poor countries. Within India the strength of support for the campaign comes mostly from dalits and their supporters and advisers. However such is the pervasiveness of Gandhi's benign influence that even high caste Hindus, senior officials, Government leaders and Indian bureaucrats in IFIs do not oppose debt cancellation though they believe that in certain ways large scale debt cancellation, by reducing the total pool available for sovereign lending, works against India's interests as a middle income moderately indebted state.

Gandhi's influence has spread far across the boundaries of Hinduism in India and to other countries beyond India and Asia. His social theories largely inform those of modern Jainism, Zoroastrianism, Sikhism and to some extent even Islam, at least within India. His ideas on environmental protection are incorporated in Green policies worldwide. His non-violent methods of protest to bring about political and social change have been absorbed by pro-democracy movements everywhere, even in China and Myanmar.

Endnote

Since, for me at least, the starting point, after a long period of thought, preparation and active lobbying in many countries around the world, of the campaign for debt cancellation as opposed to debt relief, was the seminar at Tirley Garth on Ethics in Economics, it may be appropriate to write a little about that topic and its linkage with the rest of the subject of debt. Debt cancellation as it must be presented for the wider economic and financial community is a matter of economics. It is, however, also a philosophical, specifically ethical, and theological issue. What follows attempts briefly to examine some aspects of these dimensions.

The basic question is whether a place needs to be found in economic theory for ethical considerations. Adam Smith's indication in the *Wealth of Nations* that self-interest is the principal human motivation affecting economic decisions, has been broadly accepted as the guideline. It is often forgotten that Adam Smith wrote extensively on ethical as well as economic subjects and mentioned the hand of God from time to time. A modern philosopher and economist, Donald Hay of Jesus College, Oxford asks the pointed question; 'Do Markets need a Moral Framework?'[1] He concludes that markets can dispense with a moral framework only if the conditions are right; these include a continuing market about which sufficient information is widely available to allow suppliers to establish a reputation among consumers. Where conditions are not right it is necessary to rely on either statutory- or self-regulation. But, he points out, regulation can be costly, sometimes ineffective, sometimes inimical to good behaviour. So, 'perhaps a moral code is not such a bad idea after all; at the very least honesty is cheaper.' Another economist, Professor Andrew Henley of the University of Wales takes a modern political assertion as his starting point - Margaret Thatcher's address to the Church of Scotland's General Assembly in Sept 1987. She famously asserted that the creation of wealth is essentially an amoral activity while questions about the distribution of that wealth are matter for private, individual conscience leaving the less well-endowed in society to benefit, sooner or later (often much later) from 'trickle-down'. Hay justly comments that this process in the 'Eighties (and 'Nineties) has not worked in Britain or many other economies. He points to elements such as adverse effects from not investing in human capital, societies' concern for intergenerational financial security for the environment and preserving the values of the extended family in developing societies, which are overlooked by the Thatcher neo-classicism. (See Chapter 7.) His analysis leads him to assert that there are sound economic grounds for positing a continuing need for the jubiliary principle and a bias for the poor in our modern economies.[2]

Professor Ronald Preston, Theologian and Economist at Manchester University, has pointed out to me that the British blood transfusion service (at least until recently) relies on a wide-based altruistic impulse mixed with a very small amount of self-interest (possible future need for blood transfusions). The sizeable results now achieved by charitable appeals on TV and radio, such as Comic Relief which will take up the debt theme in 1999, make it impossible to ignore the charitable impulse in economic matters; indeed by using modern polling techniques the extent of charitable input can easily be quantified for incorporation in economic models. It is a factor which Governments now find it necessary to take into account and to harness for programmes as well as for fiscal policies. In my paper for the Tirley Garth seminar on Ethics in Economics I conceded that, although altruism in international affairs is a difficult concept to support, Ronald Preston[3] was right to urge, in the interest of for example environmental protection, the greenhouse effect and the slowness of nuclear degradation, that governments must look beyond short-term interests on a scale never before entertained; in this line of argument a point comes where it is difficult to demarcate prudence from altruism. My paper went on to argue that the Third World Debt issue called for a massive act of international altruism; I am inclined now to say that it is needed on mainly economic grounds. How can a global economy of which two-fifths is non-functioning produce optimal results? Leaving aside the dubious circumstances in which the debts were incurred and accumulated, what benefit can the creditors obtain from persisting in seeking repayment from debtors who cannot pay? In his paper for the seminar Peter Rundell cogently argued that in neo-classical discourse the terms in which the market is justified prevent challenge to the underlying assumptions; this is not to say however that they cannot be challenged. People, once 'disabused of the fallacy that selfishness is the only efficient way to run an economy' can find 'benefit, both political and social, in looking for and developing those actions and attitudes that enhance unselfishness.'

Regarding the theological base for debt cancellation, Chapter 4 re-examines some aspects of this. The literature on the subject has grown fast in the past few years. I know of no better exposition of the biblical foundation than ' The Great Commission'[4] by Mortimer Arias and Alan Johnson in which they expound and analyse St Luke's exordium of the Sermon at Nazareth in Chapter 4. of his gospel. They conclude plangently 'there is focus in mission; repentance and forgiveness. But this focus is part of the beacon light of the Kingdom of God, modelled on Jesus' holistic ministry and inspired by the vision and challenge of the Jubilee paradigm of healing, restoration and liberation.[5] In this perspective, mission is no less than the holistic proclamation of the Jubilee.'

I will mention two short publications, *'Jubilee and Justice'*[6] by John Atherton, Resident Theologian and Economist, Manchester University, and *'Jesus and the International Financial Institutions'*[7] by Michael Taylor, President, Selly Oak Colleges, Birmingham. The first arose from correspondence I initiated with Atherton on Third World Debt in 1994. The second, delivered as the second David Bosch Lecture, urges that the attitude of the Christian mission to IFIs 'must inevitably be edgy and confrontational as well as consensual'. It ends saying we must seek, not that the debts of the poorest be forgiven, but cancelled. 'We must refuse to be over-impressed by an economic system which is supposed to make us all rich even if some will be richer sooner than others, but which in fact allows the gap between rich and poor to grow wider, and threatens to make all of us poor in the long run as it cracks open our communities and greedily consumes the earth's limited resources.' 'Alternatives to Global Capitalism'[8] by Ulrich Duchrow, using all the biblical texts, propounds the most radical solution; it goes back to Hussite and Hutterite models and involves root and branch reform of societies and economies, with emphasis on the need for coalitions of small organisations such as co-operatives. An African voice, already mentioned is Archbishop Njongonkulu Ndugane's address *'Seizing the new Millennium: Reshaping the World's Economy'*[9] at Southwark Cathedral, 24 April 1997.

Again, Tim Gorringe of St Andrew's University, an Anglican theologian, in

'Capital and the Kingdom'[10] examines all the biblical texts, Old Testament and New, and applies them to the global economic panorama. 'The present system keeps the North awash in capital and maintains the United States' and her dependent elites' dominant position.' To change this system we need not only resistance in the South but 'strong and sustained popular pressure in the northern countries'. He urges that the church should play a leading role in this (as it did at the Lambeth Conference in Canterbury, July-August 1998). His conclusion is stark. 'In the struggle for fulness of life we are called to make a clear option on the side of God and life and against the Baals of profit and power. There are two ways and we must choose.'

Most radical and most fundamental, the voice of Liberation Theology[11], Gustavo Gutiérrez: 'The universality of Christian love is ... incompatible with the exclusion of any person, but it is not incompatible with a preferential option for the poorest and most oppressed.' And again, The existence of poverty ... 'is therefore incompatible with the coming of the Kingdom of God, a Kingdom of love and peace. Poverty is an evil, a scandalous condition, which in our times has taken on enormous proportions. To eliminate it is to bring closer the moment of seeing God face to face, in union with other persons.'

Notes

1   ACE Journal, No.19, 1995, pp. 33-45.
2   ACE Journal, No.11, 1991, pp. 1-21.
3   *Religion and the Ambiguities of Capitalism*, p.124.
4   Abingdon Press, June 1992.
5   Orbis, New York and SPCK, London, 1994.
6   Thinking Mission Series, USPG, London, 1997.
7   Occasional Paper No. 17, Selly Oak College, Birmingham, 1996.
8   International Books with Kairos Europa, the Hague, 1995.
9   Southwark Cathedral Lecture Series, 1997.
10 Orders, New York, & SPCK, London, 1994.
11 Gustavo Gutierrez *'A Theology of Liberation'*, SCM Press, 1973.

16 The International Spread of the Jubilee 2000 Campaign

Chapter 15 dealt with the religious and philosophical approaches to debt cancellation of faiths other than Christian. It is necessary to know these because the campaign needs massive grass roots support from all quarters of the globe to override the entrenched global opposition centred on the bureaucracies of the IFIs and status quo governments. This chapter charts the way in which the campaign has grown worldwide.

The series of conferences in a score or so countries in Africa, Asia, Europe and North and South America, at which I spoke about debt in the 'eighties and early 'nineties had already given the debt issue a considerable international spread. Particularly important among these were the four conferences in North America, primarily the United States, since the weightiest supporter of the status quo was and is the US Government, making it essential to lobby in Washington and assess reactions in centres of power and influence mainly in the capital. Equally it was important to be in contact at the UN Headquarters in New York because of initiatives towards debt reform which already existed there and were to grow through the nineties.

From the Caux connection useful individual links were established in numerous European and African countries, countries of the Middle East and Australia, New Zealand, Canada and the Caribbean. Among these the most important was with Professor Washington Okumu (see p.166), familiar of a large number of leading African personalities; his input was invaluable both in working out the theory of the campaign and in ensuring that the African dimension was brought fully into deliberations.

The Tirley Garth Seminar (p.167) which played such an important role in setting the direction for the Jubilee 2000 campaign in March 1993 had a good international spread. Apart from Washington Okumu the participants included Iqbal Azaria, Pakistan and East Africa, Prof Dt Lorenzo de Angelico, Genoa University, Italy, Jacob Bowman-Larsen, Norway, (who took an active role in bringing the Scandinavian youth movements behind Jubilee 2000) Dr Marc Williams, Sussex University, Canon Bill Whiffen, Secretary, Christian Ethical Investment Group and Richard Pearce, New Zealand. A study by two German economists, Ulrich Duchrow, and Christa Springe, entitled *'Beyond the Death of Socialism: Visions from Germany on Alternatives to Capitalism'* and published in English by the William Temple

Foundation, Manchester, circulated among members of the Seminar.   The book's main purpose was to open up economic discussions after the fall of the Berlin Wall; it argued that the collapse of Communism as concomitant and consequence of the disintegration of the USSR did not mean the total triumph of capitalism if that was taken to mean that neo classical theories bolstering market economics could no longer be challenged.   Duchrow himself presided over a consultation in June 1994 organised by Kairos Europa and drowining its members mainly from leftward-inclined n.g.os. Martin Dent attended this Conference and spoke about Jubilee 2000, but was allowed very little time to do so.   A further international dimension was contributed by Percy Mistry, former senior official at the World Bank, who, as an adviser to the Non Aligned Movement was in touch with representatives of virtually all heavily indebted countries.   He played a leading role in the Movement's Ad Hoc Advisory Group of Experts on Debt, including preparation of their report *'The Continuing Debt Crisis of the Developing Countries'*.

In setting up the Jubilee 2000 charity we drew together a committee drawn entirely from Britain.   But very soon we found it helpful to look beyond the limits of the UK.   Most of the n.g.os. from which our members were drawn had overseas commitments as had the Debt Crisis Network, under Ed Mayo's chairmanship, to which we belonged.

Patrons were sought among MEPs for example, giving us links with the European Union.   Leading members of the Labour, Social Democrat and Conservative Parties agreed to let us use their names and gave useful support, Glenys Kinnock, Lord (David) Steel and Sir Henry Plumb.   John Atherton and Professor Ronald Preston, theologians and economists with a high reputation in Anglican circles throughout the world, also consented to help. The Master of Balliol College, Oxford, Dr Colin Lucas (now the Vice-Chancellor of the University) came on board.   Through my chairmanship of the United Society of the Propagation of the Gospel we got the vigorous involvement of Archbishop Desmond Tutu; at Westminster Abbey on 24 October 1995 preaching at a service to celebrate the success of the South African Elections which allowed that country to resume its membership of the Commonwealth, he inserted a paragraph at our suggestion on 'applying the Jubilee principle by cancelling Third World foreign debt'.   This same USPG connection gave us another valuable link, with Njongonkulu Ndugane', later to succeed Tutu as Archbishop of Cape Town.   He gave a powerful lecture on Debt Cancellation at Southwark Cathedral on 20 April 1997.[1]

From 3 to 12 February 1996 Jubilee 2000 organised a visit to Britain by leading African economists, politicians and Churchmen to express the African point of view on debt to British audiences. Hiltherto they had heard about the debt issue largely from British speakers. It was important for them to hear about it from Africans speaking for themselves. The group included ex-President Kaunda of Zambia, Archbishop Khotso Makhudu, Primate of the Central African Province of the Anglican Church, Professor Onimode Adidedje of Nigeria and Mr Simba Mahoni of Zimbabwe, newspaper proprietor. They visited Edinburgh, Cardiff, Belfast and Dublin and other cities in England, addressing varied but interested audiences. Archbishop Makhudu made a very impressive presentation at St Martin's-in-the-Fields, London on 6 February. Press and other media coverage was light, except for some of the denominational press.

From the point of view of making Jubilee 2000 known to professional economists, social scientists and students of international affairs, the Annual Conference in April 1996 of the International Studies Association at San Diego, California was undoubtedly the most important occasion. Martin Dent and I both attended and delivered papers as did Percy Mistry, Julius Nyngoro, Professor Christopher Barrett of Utah University and Dr Naval Kemal of the World Bank. The session had the title 'Prospects and Problems of African Debt Forgiveness'.

Once the Jubilee 2000 Office was established as the Secretariat of the Coalition, an International Section staffed by Nick Buxton began to pick up contacts already established and expand them. From the Board itself Kofi Klu gave particular attention to Africa and to organisations like the AACPO in the United States and personalities such as the Revd Jesse Jackson. His organisation, the Afrikan Liberation Support Group, has an interesting history. The Pan African Movement was founded in 1957 by Dr Kwame Nkrumah, then Prime Minister of Ghana, ably assisted by James Padmore, based with other activists at the Pan African Institute in Accra, who wrote a book on the subject of Pan-Africanism. After Nkrumah's fall not much more was heard of the movement, although its aims surfaced from time to time in debates at the UN and elsewhere and, of course, at the Organisation of African Unity. The movement's present strength is difficult to estimate; interestingly one of its 'names' is that of Dr Francis Nkrumah, the son of Kwame Nkrumah by his Egyptian wife. A conference drawing representatives from several parts of Africa and involving Archbishop Njongonkulu Ndugane as well as the then Archbishop of Ghana, the Rt Rev Robert Okine, was held in Accra in April 1998. It produced a resolution.[2] Unfortunately official acknowledgment of the Conference by African Governments has not occurred and there was virtually no coverage of it in the

African media.

Much discussion on methods of building up co-ordination among the various national Jubilee 2000 organisations took place between 1995 and 1998 at meetings of the original Jubilee 2000 Committee, the Co-ordination Committee which laid the groundwork for the Jubilee 2000 Coalition and the Board itself. At an early stage it was decided that a formal international Committee would not be appropriate. While day-to-day work went ahead in the International Section, organisation-to-organisation links were forged informally; the presence of many members of other countries' Jubilee 2000s at the 16 May 1998 demonstration in Birmingham enabled positive directions to be outlined, leading to a Conference in Rome from 15 to 17 November 1998. At this representatives of 38 countries with 12 international organisations drafted and agreed two resolutions[3, 4], a timetable and a programme for the remaining time up to Year 2000. It directed special focus on 19 June 1999 when the G8, WB and IMF are to meet at Köln in Germany under the Chairmanship of Dr Gerhard Schröder. Relations and correspondence remain informal; the aim is to sustain a many-fronted volume of pressure on decision takers in the IFIs and G8 governments, to listen to the popular demand for very generous terms for debt cancellation in 2000. At Appendix 11[5] is a list of countries and international organisations which are engaged in the campaign. The petition which is being promoted by Jubilee 2000 currently has over 3 million signatures.[6] The target total is 22 million.

A number of international gatherings have given opportunities for spreading the ideas of Jubilee 2000 and winning support for them. The most prestigious of these was the Commonwealth Heads of Government Meeting (CHOGM) at Edinburgh in October 1997. Jubilee 2000 established a stall in the n.g.o. market near the Conference Centre where several Heads of Government signed the petition. Having myself been Conference Secretary for CHOGM 71 in Singapore, I was given access on a few occasions by the Commonwealth Secretary-General, Chief Emeka Anyaoko. At these I was able to lobby several Presidents, Heads of Government, Finance Ministers and Foreign Ministers on behalf of Jubilee 2000. They included Presidents Mugabe of Zimbabwe, Masire of Botswana and Clerides of Cyprus, Prime Ministers Sheikh Wajid Hazina (Bangladesh), and James Bolger (New Zealand, replaced on return to Wellington), Finance Ministers P Chidambaram (India), Kibria (Bangladesh) and Bangura (Sierra Leone) and Foreign Ministers/Secretary Musyoka (Kenya), Clare (Jamaica) and Robin Cook (UK). The responses to my lobbying were uniformly interested and favourable. I followed them up with correspondence to all my eminent interlocutors. Subsequent activities by Jubilee 2000 organisations in the countries involved, notably Bangladesh, have been assisted by this effort.

At a subsequent, lower key conference in London in February 1998 similar lobbying at high levels in governments was carried out. This was the Conference of Associated States, fragments of the former British Empire still in some form of relationship with the British Government. It was a significant Conference because a change of status for the component countries was announced at it, from Dependent Territories to Associated States, as well as the decision to grant or confirm British citizenship status to all their people. With the agreement of the Minister of State responsible, Baroness Symons of Vernham Dean who invited me to the Reception which concluded the Conference, I was able to lobby, most through their Heads, the delegations of the 11 states. Once again the responses were interested and favourable. I received particularly encouraging follow-up letters from Mrs Pamela Gordon the Premier of Bermuda, and Mr P R Caruana, the Chief Minister of Gibraltar. It was a delight to find that the leader of the delegation from Pitcairn Island was a Mr Fletcher Christian!

The Lambeth Conference of the worldwide Anglican Communion is held once every ten years. The 1998 Conference at Canterbury from 19 July to 8 August paid special attention to the debt issue: virtually every Province of the Communion had given first preference to this issue on a list of topics for discussion offered in the preparation for the Conference. To the Conference over 850 Archbishops and Bishops came from every continent. Within Britain the prominence of debt resulted from action by Jubilee 2000 over several years. In July 1994 I was invited by the then Bishop of Dover, Assistant to the Archbishop of Canterbury, to provide a paper on debt for the House of English bishops then about to meet. The text of this is at App. 12.[7] Thereafter I was approached by two members of the General Synod to help them in drafting a resolution for the November 1996 General Synod. This was duly put forward and carried nem. con. Diocesan Synods debated the same subject during 1997 and 1998, while a number of whole day conferences were organised in dioceses such as Southwell and Lichfield in July 1998. Overseas bishops arriving for the Lambeth Conference were involved in many of these occasions. When the debate on debt began at Lambeth an abundance of well-informed clerics spoke while the specialised group assigned under Archbishop Njungonkulu Ndugane of Cape Town to draft a resolution brought together points of view and experience from all the continents. The first day of debate was graced by the presence of the World Bank President, James Wolfensohn; to allow him to address the Conference he made an heroic effort to escape his web of engagements in Washington flying direct to Canterbury and back. Unfortunately, his speech turned out to be somewhat personalised and dismissive; time did not allow him to exchange views with anyone but his friend, the Archbishop of Canterbury; a number of bishops who wrote to him after the event received no reply.

Following the Lambeth Conference, one notch higher, as it were, on the ecumenical scale, was the World Council of Churches' eighth Assembly at Harare University in Zimbabwe in December 1998. This magnificent occasion drew over 2000 representatives of a wide range of Christian denominations from all the continents. Jubilee could not have been more prominently featured at the opening service on 3 December. The proceedings began with the sound of the trumpet, as is the ancient Hebrew Jubilee celebration (ram's horn), the lessons were from Leviticus and Isaiah/Luke, properly starting the theme of debt with the Sermon at Nazareth. The sermon for the service, in Spanish and English by the eloquent Puerto Rican Priest, Eunice Santana, spoke of the central place of women in Christ's ministry; she offered the miracle of the loaves and fishes as a paradigm for the world financial and economic leaders to follow in dealing with the debt problem. A prayer in Japanese began 'Great God, God of Jubilee'. The Lord's Prayer was begun in Aramaic, Jesus' own language, by a Syrian Orthodox Priest, and spoken by the whole congregation in whatever language was most appropriate for each individual. The effect of this opening ceremony in concentrating Christians' minds on debt could not be other than overwhelming. The whole Council gave a strong, timely impetus to the Jubilee 2000 campaign just before the start of its final year. In a concluding statement it appealed to the leaders of the G8 nations to cancel the debts of the poorest countries and set up a new independent arbitration process. Tough conditions should be imposed on debtor governments but not as prerequisites for cancellation. It recommended a new ethical approach to the system of lending and borrowing, including a tax on financial conversions, and limiting the unregulated flow of capital.

Where, then, does the campaign stand as it enters its final phase? What, realistically, (a favourite word of James Wolfensohn) are its prospects with months, not years to run? Up to 16 May 1998 the prospects, realistically, were perhaps not too favourable. The G8, then meeting in Birmingham, seemed to be heavily balanced towards those, led by Germany and Japan, who saw no reason for speeding up the HIPC Initiative. Britain and Canada were the only proponents of ideas for improvement. The Birmingham event, with 70,000 demonstrating on the streets for improvement, had an effect. The original agenda for the G8 meeting, pre-occupied with events in S E Asia, apparently did not feature Third World Debt. Our demonstration ensured the subject was put on the agenda, was discussed and remained there in 1999. A new category of post-conflict countries designated for special attention in debt management was recognised. Tony Blair, as Chairman of the G8 meeting, came personally to meet leaders of the Jubilee 2000 campaign, to thank them for maintaining their expressions of concern about debt and to assure them that the subject would have his attention and would remain on the G8 agenda.[8] The Bishop of Lichfield, the Rt Rev Keith Sutton, at the end of the Lambeth debate on debt, gave a particularly effective push to the campaign by bidding all 850 of his fellow bishops to return to their dioceses and 'organise Birminghams in all of them'. The weight of grass roots support for generous cancellation around the world will surely be immensely increased.

And there have been significant advances. Since Birmingham a new German Chancellor has emerged from the German elections. Gerhard Schröder made it clear before he was elected that he did not intend to follow the hard line of his predecessor, Helmut Kohl, against those who wished to improve the HIPC Initiative. Now he has been joined in Coalition by the Greens, led by Joshka Fischer, who are favourable towards debt cancellation. Moreover, in the European Union, there are now eleven governments which adopt a programme similar to those of the German SDU and Britain's New Labour. In Japan the hard line of the Liberal Government seems to be modifying under Keizo Obuchi. At the conference in Tokyo from 17 to 19 October 1998, the second Tokyo International Conference on African Development (TICAD II), participants were urged to 'ensure the full financing of the HIPC Initiative, expedite, in a determined manner, the extension of debt relief to more countries .... taking note of the proposal of the UN Secretary-General in his report on Africa to the Security Council'.[9] Japan is the largest contributor to the HIPC Fund and is seeking to encourage others to contribute more to it. By her policy of reducing Bangladesh's debt to her by compensated refinancing, Japan shows that she wishes to find softer methods of dealing with international debt and overcome the very strong bar to write-offs which exists in modern Japanese culture; something more akin to the social concern for the poor which Japanese feudal leaders displayed when times were hard before the Meiji Restoration. The Japanese bishops at the Lambeth Conference proved open to arguments for debt cancellation. They are supplementing an n.g.o. initiative to develop a Japanese Jubilee 2000 which has already produced an impressive handbook for its supporters, while on the political fringe former Prime Minister Tsutomu Hata (see p.166) preserves his enthusiasm for joining debt cancellation to peace campaigning at ceremonies in Hiroshima in 2000.

From the United States, crucially important, amid all the concentration on

188 *The Crisis of Poverty and Debt in the Third World*

working out American policies in face of the recent crises in S E Asia and incipient fresh problems in Latin America, a plea[10] is being made not to forget the 50 odd smaller developing economies which have been suffering from their debt crises for over fifteen years. Even in Camdessus' France, the new Jubilee 2000 organisation appears to be getting off the ground, and there are some favourable indications in Italy. All causes for hope.

Notes

1 He had been a candidate for the Secretary-Generalship of USPG in 1991.
2 App. 8. The Accra Declaration. Accra. 19 April 1998.
3 App. 9. A Jubilee Call for Debt Cancellation and Economic Justice. Rome. 17 Nov 1998.
4 App. 10. Declaration in support of the Southern African Apartheid Debt Campaign. Rome 17 November 1998.
5 App.11. List of Jubilee 2000's supporting countries.
6 By the time of the G8 meeting in Köln on 19 June the total was given as 17 million.
7 App.12. Background Paper on International Debt for the Bishops' Meeting, July 1994.
8 Tony Blair's words are 'I pay tribute to the Jubilee 2000 campaign and its dignified breaking-the-chain demonstration in Birmingham. The most persuasive case for debt relief is that it is only when those countries can escape the burden of debt that they are able to benefit economically'. N.B. 'they' - he could have said 'we all'.
9 Report of the United Nations Secretary General to the Security Council. *'The causes of Conflict and the promotion of Durable Peace and Sustainable Development in Africa'*. UN. 16 April 1998.
10 Cf *'The Poverty Abroad...'* The Washington Post, 28 September 1998.

17 WB Philosophies and Policies: the Unsoundness of the Theoretical Economic Base

In his paper delivered as the Wider Annual Lecture in Helsinki on 7 January 1998, 'More Instruments and Broader Goals: Moving Toward the Post-Washington Consensus', Joseph Stiglitz, Senior Vice-President and Chief Economist at the World Bank, records the circumstances in which in the early 'eighties the Washington Consensus was formed by US economic officials, the International Monetary Fund (IMF) and the World Bank (WB). It was catalysed, he said, by the experience of Latin American countries in the 1980s, when the economies of many of them virtually ceased to function. Budget deficits were in the range of 5-10 per cent while most spending was directed to subsidizing the large and inefficient state sector resulting in productive firms failing. The deficits were financed from abroad in the lending spree of the late seventies until rising US interest rates forced governments to resort to printing money, which of course led to rampant inflation. Quoting Stiglitz, 'The Washington Consensus held that good economic performance required liberalized trade, macro-economic stability and getting prices right. Once the government took care of these issues - ie 'got out of the way' - private markets would produce efficient allocations and growth.'

The great success claimed for the Washington Consensus, notably in the World Bank's somewhat vainglorious study 'The East Asian Miracle' (WB, 1993), was the achievement of the East Asian economies in promoting very rapid development up to 1997. Following the collapse, a reassessment of the Consensus has had to be carried out. It is postulated that the root of the S E Asian problem is over-active state intervention - government directed loans and cozy relationships with the large industrial conglomerates (chaebol). Stiglitz does not agree with this; rather he thinks that it was US, Japanese and European banks which over-lent; the governments 'underestimated the importance of financial regulation and corporate governance' and should have done much more in these areas. He adds that the collapse should not obscure the fact that very real achievements in economic development did occur in the 'Tiger Economies' from 1970 to 1997 in which the governments concerned played a very positive part.

Nevertheless, Stiglitz is forced to admit that the Washington Consensus must now be viewed as highly flawed - 'incomplete and often misguided' are his words. He argues that the focus on inflation resulting from its origin in the Latin American crisis, led to macroeconomic policies which worked against long-term economic growth and detracted attention from weak financial sectors, major sources of macro-instability.   Financial market liberalization might have contributed to macro-instability by weakening the financial sector. 'More broadly the focus on trade liberalization, deregulation and privatization ignored the important ingredients required to make an effective market economy, most notably competition.' Stiglitz also admits that the Washington Consensus failed to give due insight into the importance for economic growth of education and improvement in technology.

Most revealingly, Stiglitz confesses that many economists working within the Washington Consensus took a simplistic view, that by referring to a few economic indicators, viz. inflation, money supply growth, interest rates, budget and trade deficits, they could formulate recommendations for the 'improvement', stabilisation or 'correction' of a country's economy. His most damning admission is that 'economists would fly to a country, look at and attempt to verify the 'relevant' data and make macroeconomic recommendations for policy reform, all in the space of weeks.'   This is precisely the concern which as far back as April 1983 prompted me to warn my Government of the dangers embedded in the methods of IMF teams prescribing for highly indebted poor countries (see p.168) I shall attempt to show that in fact the failure in development and the deterioration in the economies of a large number of poor countries and the appalling collapse in the standard of living of their people apart from favoured elites is largely due to the misdirection of IFI personnel, particularly IMF, arising from the obtuse, doctrinaire leadership they have experienced for the last 15 years.

Credit where credit is due.   Stiglitz admits that a new policy base is needed - he calls it 'a post-Washington Consensus consensus'. One wonders if its architects will be the same as for the original Consensus. He says that whatever it turns out to be it cannot be based in Washington. Sustainable policies cannot be prescribed from afar; they must be freely accepted by - owned by - the developing countries. 'We' (the IFIs) require 'a greater degree of humility' .... 'we do not have all the answers' .... 'Continued research and discussion, not just between the WB and the IMF but throughout the world is essential if we are to better understand how to achieve our (sic) many goals.'

Stiglitz describes some of his pointers for the new consensus.   The

Washington Consensus pursuing market purity urged minimal government intervention: Governments were presumed to be worse than markets; smaller was better. He now admits this is not so. The state's role is significant in appropriate regulation of financial sectors, industrial policy, licence allocation, social protection and welfare. Education and technology transfer are particularly important since the private sector cannot encompass these and never does enough; developed countries, for obvious reasons, are reluctant to transfer technology. The example is cited of Korea where the impetus to rapid development received a major boost from very large-scale government investment in Tertiary Education. Human capital is now one of Stiglitz's watchwords, an element which the Washington Consensus virtually ignored. In all this he is at one with voters across Europe who seeking a balance between market efficiencies and social justice, rejected political parties in their own countries which followed policies analogous to those of the Washington Consensus. Thoughts on what is needed to make governments more effective within their capacities are that:

1. Restraints are crucial for a professional and capable bureaucracy
2. The civil service should be more effective through competitive wages for talented people
3. Government should be closer to the people through established feedback in policy making and service
4. The public sector should embrace market-like mechanisms - performance standards, including standards for environment protection and safety, auctions, selling licences, etc.
5. Policies should be introduced to reduce scope for rent seeking e.g. by curtailing discretionary activities like licensing and trade restrictions; and by auctioning off natural resources or spectrum allocations.

Some of these ideas sound similar to injunctions appearing in Structural Adjustment Programmes but contain positive ideas which, properly introduced, could inform conditionalities for debt cancellation (see Chapter 19).

The President of the World Bank, James D Wolfensohn, has also been doing some reflection. His address to the Board of Governors in Washington on 6 October 1998 shows the direction of his thought. Interestingly, he titles it 'The Other Crisis'. He says, the crises in East Asia and in Russia cannot be overlooked. Nor can floods in Bangladesh and on the Yangtse, and the effects of El Niño. (Even so he can still say 'twelve months ago developing countries as a whole were on a path to strong growth over the next decade.')

They impel him to focus on the need for institutional change and on social issues to bring recovery and sustainable development. Without greater equity and social justice there will be no political stability, without that financial stability is unattainable. A new tune! Likewise, 'when we redress budget imbalances, we must recognise that programmes to keep children in school may be lost' .... as also health care, small and medium enterprises. Would that his predecessors even five years ago could have seen that! Safety nets are, he says, needed (confusingly, on a pillar) and 'we must face full funding for the poorest countries through IDA12 and HIPC ... as a priority in the weeks and months ahead' (before 2000?)

He commends the IMF for the framework in which it reviews the record annually with 'client countries' to evaluate macroeconomic performance. (Evidently he has not absorbed Mr Stiglitz's strictures on the IMF's instant prescribers.) But a second framework is needed, a new development framework. Apart from the essentials of good governance - transparency, voice, the free flow of information, a commitment to fight corruption and a well-trained, properly rewarded civil service - it should specify 'the regulatory and institutional fundamentals essential to a workable market economy'; ..... inclusive policies ('inclusive is becoming one of his favourite words), ... for communications, infrastructure, urban and rural strategies, agricultural services and measures to ensure 'environmental and human sustainability'. Moreover 'countries and governments should be in the driver's seat' - 'people must be consulted and involved'. 'We must never stop reminding ourselves that we cannot and should not impose developments by fiat from above, or from abroad.' (More new tunes) For the next two years he wants to work with two governments in each region, to move from a project by project approach to an approach that 'looks at the totality of effort necessary for county development', in drawing up 'holistic frameworks that sharpen strategies'. Well .....

Perhaps one voice from the IMF is also worth hearing, Jack Boorman's, Director of Policy Development and Review. He used the columns of The Guardian of 9 November 1998 to 'debunk one of the myths' about the HIPC Initiative, of which he is one of the architects. First, he says, it is not true that widespread poverty is due to the debt. He does not specify who says that. Certainly not the proponents of generous debt cancellation. An attempt has been made, however, involving Clare Short, the British Secretary of State for International Development, to create a false antipathy between supporters of poverty eradication and those who want debt cancellation. The two are, of course, perfectly compatible and debt is an important first step towards poverty eradication; one that can, moreover, given the political will which

Jubilee 2000 seeks to encourage, be taken by the Millennium.

Boorman's second myth is that debt is responsible for insufficient social spending. 'In reality debt does not prevent any HIPC from providing basic social services.' He might as well say that the Bangladesh floods didn't prevent any Bengali rice farmers from planting rice. The fact is that SAP campaigns to reduce budgetary deficits forced developing country governments to cut back on education and health allocations, the only ones available to carry the demanded reductions. James Wolfensohn has just been quoted (p.192) as saying that cutting budget deficits can be harmful; in his address he gives an example from Ethiopia of how it can happen. It has been happening in dozens of HIPCs for years and the IMF is just beginning to wake up to it.

The third Boorman myth is that 'wiping the slate clean' would be a panacea. He goes on to say that unconditional cancellation risks debt relief being squandered. Again, who denied that? The proponents of generous debt cancellation have always said that debt cancellation should be on a case by case basis precisely to show that they do not seek unconditional relief. Boorman says critics of the HIPC Initiative might do better to encourage their own governments to transfer resources to the poorer countries. That we certainly do. But is he giving as much thought to working out ways of ensuring that resources available after debt cancellation are used for the restoration of education and health services, as we are? He comes late to the matter.

Boorman goes on to claim successes for the HIPC Initiative. Would he care to say what proportion of Mozambique's debt has been cancelled by the allegedly generous 'settlement' of its case? Or Uganda's? And, turning to the example the IFIs always advance when defending their record, let us take Ghana. That country, the showcase of adjustment, scrupulously implemented a standard package of policies designed to increase industrial production and employment. After the first few years, when increased availability of foreign exchange lifted performance, since 1989 it has stagnated. By 1993 industrial production had fallen to 8% of GDP from 10% in 1987 and employment in industry over the same period had fallen by two thirds to 27,000. Parallel with this the output of graduates from the University of Science and Technology in Kumasi, the only college in Ghana granting engineering degrees, rose from 125 in 1984 to only 193 in 1991. In a different range, look at Chile, claimed at one stage as a bright star of neo classical-directed economic success by the IFIs. It was not the Friedman-inspired market directed policies of the Pinochet régime which caused Chile's modest revival. In 1982/3 GDP declined by 19%. The State Banks were sold off at a 40%

discount. Two speculative conglomerate empires bought up manufacturers and then defaulted. It was by bringing in policies Allende had proposed - minimum wage, job creation, restrictions on inflow of foreign capital - harking back to Keynes - that Chile began to climb back to modest competence.[1]

The IFIs have, of course, a great deal to defend. Their decisions crucially affect the economic fate of countries around the globe. Taking the whole sweep of action since the Bretton Woods agreements they have a record of achievement to be proud of. Reconstruction in Europe and Asia, the consolidation of the development process in the developing world which they took over from the former imperial powers; effective first aid remedies for numerous countries facing balance of trade or budgetary problems all stand very much to their credit. To quote James Wolfensohn again, 'Our international economic institutions have served us well .... The Fund's mandate covers surveillance, exchange rate matters, balance of payments, growth-oriented stabilisation policies and their related instruments. The Bank has a mandate for the composition and appropriateness of development programmes and priorities, including structural and sectoral policies - and, therefore, by building a good basis for development, a responsibility for crisis prevention.' On the whole, crises have been few and most contained without too much permanent damage. But the recent crises in South East Asia, and now in Russia, the successive crises after settlement of the Latin American crisis, in Mexico and Brazil have all left palpable damage. To take one example only, the takeover of segments of Korean industry by US, Japanese and European capital has created deep resentments and criticism of the system that produces such a result. Regarding Third World Debt, the crisis has continued for over 15 years, many countries are now more deeply in debt than they were at the beginning of the crisis and the number of people moving into extreme poverty increases daily. The HIPC Initiative, despite what its proponents and defenders say, is inadequate for its purpose, a fact once more recognised by the IFIs in their decision to revise the scheme yet again. It remains to be seen how that will be done and what meaning can be placed on James Wolfensohn's assurance that 'full funding for the poorest countries through IDA 12 and HIPC is a priority in the weeks and months ahead'.

One of the points which troubles the organisers of the Jubilee 2000 campaign is that the IFIs have never acknowledged that the debt problem is also a justice problem. As Professor Tony Thirlwall maintains 'since three parties benefited from the debt creation process, the same three parties should share the burden of relief - the debtors, the banks and the whole world community which received an external benefit when the debt was created by the on-lending process in the 1970s preventing output contraction in countries with balance of payments deficits. It is simply not fair that debtor countries should bear the whole of the adjustment burden'. Thirlwall also makes pointed use of Keynes analysis of the transfer problems - of which the debt problem is an example - that arose over the reparations payments imposed on Germany by the Treaty of Versailles in 1919. Keynes mocked the folly and futility of the whole exercise on the grounds that it would be likely to be self defeating, as it turned out to be. The attempt to continue extracting large transfers from Latin America in the 'eighties and from Africa for the next 15 years is similarly leading nowhere. Writing in 1989 Thirlwall said that IFIs were in a state of virtual paralysis while the economies of Latin America and Africa slide further into chaos, and the poor in these continents became progressively poorer.' Latin America's problem and those of a few countries elsewhere like Nigeria was addressed by the US Government through the Brady and Baker plans. Those of Africa as a whole remain to be comprehensively settled.

Not only does the justice issue remain unaddressed but also, along the way, the IFIs, in attempting to manage the debt have compounded it by a series of fundamental errors. These range from simple errors of judgement or economic interpretation such as the exploded view that subsidies in agriculture and lower tariffs necessarily have a negative effect on economic growth to colossal errors of judgement in development such as the Narmada dam project in India, to take a single example of its type; multiple lesser errors involve projects resulting in costly feasibility studies but no further action, projects which were completed but failed to produce the expected benefits, projects which have been frustrated by cumbersome procurement and control methods. Much more serious is the egregious policy they adopted, following their neo-classical, market theories, of encouraging at the same time a large number of primary producing countries to increase their export output in a small number of products, primarily agricultural. Inevitably this led to gluts, to price collapse and in fact to the fundamental swing in the terms of trade of primary producers which began 15 years ago and has continued ever since. In Africa they declined by 6.2% 1980-85, 2.5% 1986-90 and 3.2% 1990-95.[2] The ratio by value of exports to GDP was 31% in 1980, 28% in 1995. Another serious failure has been the inability of the IFIs to adjust for what has become known as their institutional optimism. Because of the absence of knowledge of local conditions, political systems and cultures of the people in the countries for which they prescribe and their mistaken confidence in the economic runes by which they are guided through the statutes of their institutions, they have chronically over-estimated the ability of debtor countries first to repay their loans and secondly to meet interest charges whether on first receipt or through rescheduling. To give a single example, IMF teams rarely understand the informal sectors in the countries they study, nor their use at times of hardship to supplement any regular incomes; thus they are too easily reassured on the basis of past experience when they call for price controls, wage restraint, pruning of subsidies and public service about survival capacity after the reduction but also too careless of the nearness of disaster for families which may tip over into indigence. In 1988 the WB predicted that by 1995 sub-Saharan Africa would owe only $29 billion. In fact the total owed by that year had multiplied seven-fold.

This examination of the Washington Consensus together with proposals from the Bank for its radical overhaul and the criticism of the IFIs by campaigners for generous debt cancellation would be incomplete without attention to alternative economic theories. The principle instrument of the IFIs is the adjustment programmes they have imposed for the past 15 years in search of stabilization. These are based on neo-classical, market driven development economics. The result has been disastrous. Africa's economic malaise is deep. Is it possible to conceptualize the process of development on a different theoretical economic base? There may be several. Jeffrey Sachs of Harvard outlined his ideas in the Economist.[3] A fuller exposition came from Howard Stein, Fellow of Roosevelt University, Chicago whose paper, delivered in Cambridge on 26 October 1998, entitled 'Rethinking Stabilization in Structural Adjustment in Africa: Towards a Critique of the Classical Development Economics' caused quite a stir. His starting point is that neo-classical development economics have little understanding of how to develop Africa's economies or how better to integrate them into the global economy. This warms my heart since it is precisely the point at which my own critique of the IFIs began in April 1983 (see p.168).

Stein quotes a 1996 article by Robert Wade which traces how the WB became increasingly dominated by neo-classical economists with degrees from North American and British Universities where the neo-classical approach dominates the curriculum. By 1991, Wade says, 80% of all bank economists were trained in such institutions. Through the retirement and removal of engineers, agronomists, health and other specialists the neo-classical economists 'took control of the Bank from top to bottom' leading to 'a meta-policy whereby agency problems at the lower level are reduced to a concatenating set of beliefs and constructs.' From internal evidence it is possible to see how a similar process worked out in the IMF. Agnès Carlet

Fermée was a trainee for the IMF economist cadre in the IMF in the mid-nineties. During her traineeship she became disgusted by the arrogance and disregard for external criticism displayed by her tutors, particularly the Director-General of the IMF, Michel Camdessus, who regularly dismissed quoted remarks by authorities who did not view the IMF as he did, as the result of failure to understand and study the Fund; Camdessus presented his organisation as humane and based on the highest moral principles. Agnès Carlet-Fermée records in her doctoral thesis that he would send out the trainees with strong words. An example from February 1994:'Our responsibility is enormous; we must make the world a better place. Ask yourselves the big question, and take it as a fact that our organisation is incredibly flexible, able to adapt itself to new challenges because of the wisdom of its founding articles. Always have with you the Charter of the Fund and refer to it often. As they are described there, the six raisons d'être of the Fund are for me revelations of God. Pascal said, 'Joy, joy, weep for joy ...' You are the high priests of capitalism. You must persuade all countries that, if they do what we tell them to do, all will be well ..... Our mission is to secure growth without inflation and so bring an end to poverty at the same time as we protect the environment. - This organisation exists to restore confidence for its members and the rest of the world, to make them understand that when the Fund says that a country is acting as it should they can trust our judgement; your work will be to help countries make the great leap towards good action - The world wants us to satisfy ourselves that each separate country does what is best for itself and best for global development.' Thus spake the Enarque. Thank heavens for James Stiglitz who says (p.190 above) 'We require a greater degree of humility, ... we do not have all the answers' and even James Wolfensohn who says (p.192 above) 'We must never stop reminding ourselves that we cannot and should not impose development by fiat from above.'

So what does Stein criticise in the neo-classical theories and what does he offer in their place? A few basic points on outcomes:

a) In the years since adjustment policies began flows of direct foreign investment to Africa have fallen; according to UNCTAD from 11% in 1986-90 to 5% 1991/6 and a mere 3.8% in 1996. In 1991-5 the total for Africa was 2% of the global flow;

b) Although stock exchanges in Africa have increased from 7 in 1990 to 21 in 1998, presumably gaining access to portfolio capital, few had more than 50 companies listed, Nigeria with 200 being the largest outside South Africa; but Nigeria's total capitalization was only 1% of GDP compared with 90% in Malaysia. 94% of foreign portfolio equity capital in sub-Saharan Africa went to South Africa;

c)   Africa's share of global trade has fallen from 3% in the 1950s to around 1% in 1995 while its contribution to global manufacturing in 1995 was 0.3%. Exports relative to GDP declined from 31% in 1980 to 28% in 1995 while the percentage of primary products including fuels, minerals and metals remained static at 92% from 1970 to 1991.[4] (cf East Asia and Pacific where primary products declined from 63% to 23% in the same period.);

d)   Terms of Trade, as already indicated declined by -6.2% 1980-85, -2.5% 1986-90, and -3.2% 1990-95. Stein comments 'the very act of flooding the world with resources in response to IMF pressures (SAP-enjoined export crop increases) has a fallacy of composition effect of exacerbating the export position of resource producing countries, where low demand elasticities also play a part. He also points out that synthetic substitutes resulting from advances in biotechnology and material sciences augur badly for any recovery in the African terms of trade relating to the primary product component of exports;

e)   Manufacturing production for export increased by only 0.9% between 1980 and 1993 compared to the pre-adjustment decade of the '70s when it increased by 4.3%. In the '90s African industry in SSA grew by only 0.2% (cf 15% in East Asia and the Pacific). In 1960 the percentage of the labour force in industry was 7%: this had increased to only 9% by 1994[5];

f)   After independence in African countries' primary enrolment for girls rose from 30% in 1965 to 69% in 1980 and for boys from 52% to 91%. Under the malign influences of the recent 15 years including SAPs these figures had fallen by 1993 to 65% for girls and 78% for boys. The largest number of ESAF (IMF soft loans - see g) below) loans during the last 15 years have been for agriculture;

g)   It was not until 1986 that the IMF introduced the structural adjustment facility which displaced standby loans for stabilisation, short term and at market rates; this eased terms to 0.5%, a 5 year grace fixed with principle repaid over 5.5 to 10 years. IMF agreements based on Policy Framework Papers (PFP) have become prerequisites for IMF and WB teams but also for rescheduling at the Paris and London Clubs. (I would add that a number of observers question the legality of loans in these terms linked to SAPs since the WB may only lend for economically and financially viable projects.)

Stein examines the question why structural adjustment policies have not led to their intended consequences. This follows an examination of the literature relating to adjustment from which he concludes that adjustment has not improved conditions in poor countries, with considerable evidence that it has exacerbated the underlying structural weakness of Africa's economies. 'Perhaps the most significant legacy of adjustment in the huge, mostly multilateral and bilateral debt accrued since 1980.' His overall judgement is that the policies have failed because the initial theories are wrong. 'Neo-classical economic theory is badly flawed as a guide to understanding how to build economies capable of structural transformation and sustainable development.' The weakness is conceptual not implementational.

Because neo-classical economic thinking trains its practitioners to determine their actions and policy by using a set of rational rules deduced from its basic market principles they respond to a set of market signals, normally reflecting scarcity and choice. Decisions on what and how to produce are then determined by the endowment of societal resources. If there is an economic crisis it must be due to distortions of market signals. Consumers are presumed to respond efficiently to market signals. But the public sector's approach is deemed to be markedly different, either because the state is predatory or because state agents select politically rational policies which are economically irrational. The public sector must therefore be the source of barriers to efficient operation of markets. The solution to economic malaise must be to reduce state intervention in markets.

Stein produces six main reasons why these concepts and the deductions from them in economic policy making and management create rather than solve problems.

The model by its nature leaves out elements necessary to understand the crisis in Africa. The most important of these is structure itself - a framework which contains choices and often determines them. The model allows an insufficient number of variables to explain the economic crisis in Africa. The missing factors include *first* the structure of aid which is determined by many external as well as domestic factors. Poor balance of payment will not be reversed if the structure of aid, involving the WB and IMF, does not change. *Second*, the structure of multinational capital development; private sector capital is important for economic success and the reform which may be needed to achieve it, but IMF/WB prescriptions frequently rule out the means for attracting foreign capital. *Third*, declining terms of trade obviously affect balance of payments, and global trading conditions plus advances in technology operate to reduce demand for African resources. *Fourth*, the fallacy of composition - over production of traditional items allied with items allied with inelasticity of demand drives down prices and lowers total revenues however much is produced. *Fifth*, the structure of world finance has ensured over the last fifteen years a net outflow of capital to the IMF from Sub-SaharanAfrica. The IMF's central role is unfortunate since primarily it offers short-term finance while Africa needs 'instruments with a long term developmental orientation'. Moreover Africa has long passed the level where debt ratios can be sustained. Nor can the debt be sold at a discount on world markets 'since its later expansion is multilateral'; the WB debt forgiveness programme, the only way out of this impasse, is inadequate in volume, and too slow in action. *Sixth*, Bank and IMF policies are predicated on the existence of an entrepreneurial class which will respond with investment and production. The IFIs expressed hopes based on widespread informal activities in African economies are completely wide of the mark. The groups involved in informal activities are so involved to enable families to survive, mostly undertaken by women to shore up the husband's declining purchasing power or by children withdrawn from school thus reducing the competitive labour force.

There is much more in Stein's analysis. Trenchant examination of inconsistencies in the neo-classical model used by the WB/IMF leads to some notable aperçus such as 'The IMF (says) countries must not live beyond their means. Unfortunately the very act of forcing countries to fall within the domain of their means leads to a reduction in the size of that domain'. (cf. the consequence of recent IMF loans to crisis-ridden Asian countries); or 'Liberalization with its efforts to create a financial system based on the image of pure competition has engendered enormous financial problems. Moreover factors beyond the issue of market imperfections are *sui generis* to developing countries. These include the questions of politics, institutions and macrostability;' or ' ... in the fragile economies of Africa and elsewhere, which are subject to the vicissitudes of international commodity prices, rapid shifts in financial flows and frequent transformations of political regimes, periods of macro instability are likely to be common. There are serious questions concerning the merit of completely liberalized financial systems. .... An unfettered private sector banking model will not generally lead to activities that generate growth and development'.

We must be grateful that the leadership of the World Bank, learning from mistakes, is looking for ways to avoid them in future. Welcome are the emphases on human capital, on involving receiving governments and people in decision making about their economic destiny and on recognising the role of the state in regulation of financial sectors, industrial policy, social protection and welfare. But Stein's criticisms to my mind make it abundantly clear that re-examination and reform in the IFIs has to go very much further than Stiglitz and Wolfensohn foreshadow. Whole areas of their basic approach need to be rewritten and subjects they have totally neglected in Africa such as planning for industrial growth must be opened up. The question arises whether the structures of the IFIs are adequate, whether their ability to supervise themselves can be relied upon, whether they are capable of the transparency they enjoin on others. This matter will be taken up in Chapter 20. Meanwhile an examination follows of other areas of activity and management in which the IFIs are open to fundamental criticism.

Notes

1   Gregory Palast: *'Miracle cure, but the medicine was bright red.'* *Guardian*, ? Nov 1998.
2   African Development Bank. African Development Report 1997 (Oxford: OUP).
3   *Economist* (London) 12 Sept 1998.
4   World Bank statistics 1993.
5   UNDP, Human Development Report, 1997 (Oxford: OUP).

18 Other Areas of Activity and Management Where the IFIs Fall Short

In the preceding chapter the doctoral thesis of a former IMF trainee is quoted as an example of how one individual reacted to the approach to her work and the method enjoined in her training course. While pursuing the campaign for debt cancellation I have come across many other disaffected former trainees and senior staff of the IFIs who got out because they disagreed fundamentally with the way the WB and IMF were carrying out their tasks. Notable among these is Percy Mistry, who was Chef de Cabinet in the Office of the WB Senior Vice-President for Finance when the Third World Debt Problem first broke in 1982; he left the Bank in 1987 but continues to work in the same field of development; he has written extensively on the subject;[1] he is one of the ad hoc Advisory Group of Experts on Debt advising the Non-Aligned Movement. Chapter 17 draws on the views of such informants.

Another category of informant comprises technical experts who have been and in some cases still are employed by the WB or IMF in project management. They voice grave concern about the waste and misuse of project loans which they have experienced; some they attribute to the size of WB and IMF operations and to the standards they set for themselves in a search for 'objectivity', 'transparency' and 'impartiality'; some they attribute to naïveté in dealing with contractors around the world, plus a failure to realise that in many cases complexity of administration, perhaps for worthy fail-safe and supra-national motives, lay the way open for corruption as well as for the failure to recognise strengths and values in local systems. This last point leads back to what is said in Chapter 17 by WB leaders about it being impossible to prescribe sustainable policies from afar: 'they must be freely accepted and owned by the developing countries' (Stiglitz p.190). For obvious reasons some informants quoted in this chapter cannot be named. One of them presses for independent auditing of development projects by an international body. He asserts that, if undertaken, this will reveal 'that the appalling interest burden (of debt) is being paid largely on wasted projects. Many have been poor in design, almost all have cost far too much and large numbers will not have lasted more than five years after the withdrawal (cessation?) of Aid funds. The only real beneficiaries have been the donor countries .... You could justifiably argue for wholesale repayment of the project cost, as well as interest'. This informant considers the audit should examine projects in the pre-contract stage, during actual execution and, for performance, after completion before aid money ceases. The audit should be independent and should be published. Further he argues that bidders for development projects should be evaluated and their performance recorded against future occasions when they may bid again for contracts, something which, surprisingly, does not happen now. The IFI failure to do this, said to be in the interests of objectivity is, he believes, misguided, leading to loss and unrequited corruption. The same should be done for the same reasons for contractors' personnel. Again the reason for not doing so is given as objectivity, but the penalties for not doing so can be great. He cites the case of a project in Kazakhstan to set up a Rehabilitation Bank. The contract had been given to one of the world's six leading accountancy firms. He had doubts about the cv of the person nominated by the firm as its leading banking expert for the project; the informant's enquiries to the previous employer fully confirmed his doubts; the man had described himself as Chief Executive and Executive Vice President of a respected national bank; on enquiry he was informed, contrary to normal phraseology, that the man had worked for the bank only 'in a humble capacity'. When my informant reported the matter to a visiting senior WB official he was told to say nothing further as it would reflect on the successful bidder and prevent them from bidding again for three years which 'could not be considered'. Instead he was to place the man on three months' probation; in fact the man was sacked after five weeks while most of the rest of the team were sent home within six months. My informant's comment, justified in my opinion, is that the leading accountancy firm would never have attempted such action in a less remote location and, in fact, behaved corruptly, and that it was totally wrong for the WB to suppress his initial report.

Another case,[2] cited in similar circumstances is no less worrying; it shows how IFI routine adherence to transparency and objectivity can lead to the virtual nullification of an excellent project with great potential for improving the lives of humble folks, in this case fishermen and rice cultivators. The near failure of this project, known as the Third Fisheries Project in Bangladesh, is so well described that I quote it in full at Appendix 3.[3]

The most worrying aspects are that the cumbersome methods used in a simple environment, for making the contracts to supply fingerlings, on which the project depended, insisting on full 40-page contract documents in

English, which had to be purchased, inevitably took the ability to tender away from the people intended to do so and placed it in the laps of middlemen (in Bengali 'mastans' = 'musclemen'), who pushed up the price from an expected 65 takas per kilo to 120 takas. Still worse perhaps, when the consultants employed for the project, a British university, decided to issue some contracts to actual small scale breeders, whose prices were lower and quality higher, they were strongly criticised and told to revert to prescribed methods.

This informant, troubled by corruption arising from WB and IMF elaborate contracting procedures, also insists that the WB and IMF should persuade all countries which provide aid to pass a Foreign Corrupt Practice act like that already existing in the US (and apparently under threat). Interestingly something similar appears in the Resolution on Debt passed by the Lambeth Conference at Canterbury of the 850 bishops and archbishops of the world-side Anglican Communion on 6 August 1998, but they urge the legislation be passed by loan-receiving countries, relating to their own political officers and bureaucrats.

A different informant describes an airport project in Cameroon in which the major beneficiaries of the scheme were suppliers of equipment in the donor countries and the major losers former workers at the airport whose jobs disappeared when unnecessary high-tech equipment, e.g. for loading baggage, was introduced. The same expert shows how an agricultural project in Madagascar resulted in 80% of the project's value going on building and equipment, mainly off-shore costs, and the IFI personnel, with only 20% getting through to the farmers.

The method of advertising WB and IMF projects to bidding firms is publication in 'Development Business'; this is a UN official journal, which is expensive and not widely disseminated except to habitués of WB/IMF offices and sub-offices and professional consultants; the method excludes many potential bidders on grounds of cost - the next step after seeing the advertisement is to buy the bidding documents which are expensive - and inconvenience. Admittedly the existing procedure may deter frivolous bidders but limiting the field through cumbersomeness and remoteness also has disadvantages. Issuing the documents free might be cheaper in the long run. It has been estimated that the cost of a loan could be doubled because what some consider to be inevitable and extremely costly commercial methods are imposed on aid contracts. Further because estimates of a consultant's work are excluded to eliminate 'subjectivity' and satisfy criteria for transparency the cost of considering good and bad consultants on an equal footing must also be added to the cost of contracts.

Lastly in the field of procurement, a vast area of activity dependent on WB and IMF projects, a method has grown up, now virtually hallowed like the methods for bidding contracts, and even copied by other major organisations outside the WB/IMF nexus; this, if viewed by an independent body, might well be found to be over-elaborate and very expensive. When debt repayments by poor countries arising from loan funds are in question there is surely no justification for allowing costs to be increased by procedures which may owe more to comfortable acceptance because of familiarity and the protection they provide for those who operate them when an independent reassessment might lead to very substantial savings. If a professional adviser who has been deeply immersed in procurement for WB and IMF projects can write that sometimes it seems that 'an open paper trail in all that matters to the Bank's Task Manager' but that such a trail 'can conceal corruption, suppress awkward evidence and even protect the guilty', is it not time for those who ultimately pay for the WB and IMF to begin to ask hard questions and demand greater accountability?

Two examples of justified criticism of WB/IMF results may be worth mentioning separately because they arise, not from the methods enjoined on field staff, over the course of experiential development of the system for devising projects and handling the contracts, procurement, etc these entail, but from the basic economic theories on which the work of the organisations is based, as examined in Chapter 17. They are single examples only but could be multiplied. One concerns an agricultural scheme in which increased production was achieved by allying a newly developed type of seed with a fertiliser which had been designed to give it maximum productive growth. For a number of years the scheme brought excellent results. But a reappraisal by economic staff revealed that supply of the fertiliser was being subsidised and this, of course, ran counter to neo-classical doctrine. The subsidies were accordingly requested to be countermanded, the farmers could no longer afford the fertiliser and the scheme collapsed. The farmers were heavy losers because they no longer had the skills and markets on which their earlier type of production depended and there was no substitute crop to which they could turn.

The second concerns the absence in WB/IMF circles of knowledge of traditional methods which have sustained African populations in times of hardship for centuries past. For details of this I am indebted to Mr James Gibb who drew my attention to a paper by Michael Barratt Brown 'An African Road for Development: Are we all Romantics?'[4]   In this Barrett Brown draws on the UN Economic Commission for Africa's Khartoum Declaration of 1988 which emerged from a meeting called by the

Commission of more than 200 leading African scholars to present papers and debate the declaration. That declaration, 'The Human Dimension of Africa's Economic Recovery and Development', had resulted from the 'Beyond Hunger Project' of the famous Nigerian author, Chinua Achebe, leading a small group of African intellectuals at a workshop at Kericho in Kenya in 1987. They compared with the conventional (economic) wisdom of 'the North', their own conception, dialectic not unitary, their methodology inductive and not deductive, their vision, people-intensive not capital-intensive', summed up in the term 'co-operative capitalism'. The Khartoum Declaration highlighted how large cutbacks and constraints of government on urban production had stimulated communities to devise their own solutions to the problem of meeting basic human needs; examples of this could be found in almost every village. After Khartoum a document, 'The African Alternative', was published in 1989; it recommended, inter alia, 'the development of the informal sector which has a high potential for employment creation in African countries and is a rich and fertile ground for the development of indigenous entrepreneurship.' At this stage neo-classical market economics was in the ascendant, as virtually the sole theory guiding WB and IMF leaders and personnel. 'The African Alternative' accordingly found little favour. Chapter 17 makes clear why. Little work was done therefore on possible alternative paths for Africa by IFI staff, although some attention was given to the informal sector as a supplement for employment in sectors which IFI policies were driving to the wall. It is encouraging, however, that both Wolfensohn and Stiglitz have recently (see p.190), called for a re-examination of possible local initiatives and methods in HIPCs and admitted that in the current economic phase policies can no longer all be devised in and applied from Washington. Moreover, Wolfensohn has clearly affirmed that micro-credit is an area which appears to have good possibilities, wrongly neglected hitherto by IFI policies (although a number of micro-credit projects have recently been supported in Eastern Europe). Michael Barratt Brown's article recognises the significance of 'the participative tendencies of African culture' linked with the extended family system spread across much of Africa, and the traditional sanctions there on leadership. He sees the strengths of 'long-standing indigenous African co-operative practice in social and economic organisation' and the failures of industrialists who thought they 'could transfer modern European technology to Africa without adaptation in consultation with local people' (like IMF structural adjustment teams with their theory-driven solutions). 'Human-centred development' had more roots in Africa than 'the orthodox development paradigm' anchored to things, not people and driven by exports as source of foreign exchange.

Moreover Africans, like indigenous people in other continents, were more concerned with ecological factors and so better adapted to changing current circumstances. Importantly African women played a major role, both traditionally and in the circumstances brought about by SAPs, in sustaining African economies.

There is a rich source of examples of development which succeeded through synergy of knowledge of traditional African methods and the technology and concepts derived from more advanced economic systems. It is to be found in the post WWII pre-Independence experience of emerging African countries, still governed from metropolitan capitals and managed by cadres of officials, trained to analyze, to speak the languages of the societies in which they worked and to understand their cultures, as well as to apply the experience, techniques and concepts of their own cultures. The colonial services of Britain and France, and, to a lesser extent, of Holland and Portugal are frequently characterized as agents of exploitation, concerned primarily to win advantage for their metropolitan governments, only incidentally to foster economically viable autonomy, then independence in the countries where they worked. Certainly there are examples of continuing widespread exploitation and of heavy-handedness in managing the difficult political transition from dependence to independence. There are also examples of large-scale economic disasters in development such as the Tanganyika Groundnuts Scheme, once billed as a shining example of British innovation in tropical, large-scale agricultural production. But the whole episode of the advance to independence first in South Asia, then South East Asia, later in Africa, the Caribbean, parts of Latin America, and finally the Pacific, is a remarkable one, for which its principal architects and managers have still not been given full credit. The movement initially was reluctant, impelled by economic realities resulting from the devastation and cost of WWII, as well as by US determination to bring an end in particular to the British Empire, so clearly delineated in the massive 'Transfer of Power', edited by Nicholas Mansergh, which chronicles in detail the steps to India's Independence in 1947. It was also enormously helped by the establishment of the International Bank for Reconstruction and Development and through the Marshall Plan for which the Bank was the principal agent. But as the lessons of India sank in and the metropolitan powers understood the strength of the winds of change in Africa, the removal of colonial controls was increasingly administered by enlightened and frequently liberal services which saw their major objective as that of ensuring that, when independence came, even on the speedier track events required, the countries where they worked would have the structures, resources, services and personnel which would give them a reasonable chance of surviving economically as well as politically in the environment that then existed. This was the time also when remarkable indigenous talent was found, fostered and given authority; the indigenisation of many colonial services was carried out in a surprisingly short space of time, producing, to quote from only one small country, Ghana, which was, however, the first in Africa to gain independence, such world figures as Robert Gardiner, Yaw Adu, Kenneth Dadzie and Kofi Annan.

Three development projects in my personal experience may serve as illustrations. The first is the Kusasi Agricultural Development Co-operative set up in the Bawku District in the extreme North East of the Northern Territories of the Gold Coast in 1951 by one of the unsung geniuses of the British Overseas Civil Service, J H F Macgiffin. The co-operative, within the space of five years, brought the agriculturalists of the Kusasi tribe from stone-age, hoe-cultivation of groundnuts to a form of simple mixed farming which was modern in its techniques and organisation. With a very small input of government funds, most of which were later repaid, it used the fluctuation in the price of groundnuts between harvest and the onset of the growing season to accumulate capital for the farmers; they joined the co-operative in large numbers — voluntarily — when the value of the scheme became apparent. They were paid the market price of their crop at harvest and the initial capital was used to build groundnut stores. The crop was held until the market price peaked and then was sold. The credit balances were banked by the co-operative in separate accounts for each farmer. These were used over the next few years to enable the farmers first to buy bullocks and ploughs, then other equipment and supplies such as fertiliser. Eventually small bullock carts and other larger items were brought in. Selected farmers were helped to begin mixed cultivation, and the system spread, once again, as success was confirmed. In the last stages land planning was introduced into the scheme with small, clay-cored dams being built in suitable locations across the Kusasi area. The effect on the standard of living of the communities concerned was very considerable. This project, of which I became chairman for a couple of years, 1954-5, worked along the existing divisions of the tribe, using its chiefly hierarchy into which was melded the democracy inherent in a co-operative society; such an arrangement could be described as a development of the communal collaboration based on extended families which are traditional in the area. The veterinary, agricultural and land planning skills brought in by expatriate staff were supplemented from the beginning by training young Kusasi men (primarily) and were absorbed without upheaval over half a decade by the farmers themselves. The scheme, I think speaks for itself. It would not have been countenanced by latter-day neo classical economists from the IFIs.

The second example was in Bangladesh at Comilla, beginning in the late 'fifties under another, largely unknown, genius, Akhtar Hamid Khan. He was a member of the ICS at the time of Indian Independence, a Muslim and a Gandhian, with a bias towards advancing rural communities by incorporating modern techniques into the traditional culture. Eighty square miles around Comilla were designated as a special agricultural development area and put in Hamid Khan's charge, with a remit to improve the basic, peasant rice cultivation there by any means available; he had a free hand to bring in specialists from abroad such as rice cultivators from Japan and fish farmers from South East Asia. Here also, the principal instrument was the co-operative both as a channel for capital formation and for education in agricultural techniques. Hamid Khan, with charisma, was able even to get the Mullahs on his side over birth control by quoting suras of the Q'uran which advocated "asl" (withdrawal) as a method of contraception. He empowered women to make contributions in the economy of their villages, fostered local crafts on the Gandhian paradigm and transformed not only the basic rice culture but the whole agricultural effort by winning acceptance for new forms such as fish farming. It was from the work of Hamid Khan in the Comilla area that the Grameen Movement, so ably developed and directed by Professor Muhammad Yunus, eventually took off; and the proliferation of n.g.os. which is now helping to transform Bangladesh from a basket case to a viable national economy had its earliest impulse in Comilla. The lessons for IFI staff interested in incorporating local experience into development work should be obvious.

The third example I will merely mention; but as it is industrial in character at least a brief note may be appropriate. The milk supply of the megapolis of Bombay depends on a remarkable scheme in Gujarat, to the North, devised by V V Kurien, an agronomist and industrial economist who largely transformed the rural scene in Gujarat. He was able to co-ordinate a system of collecting milk supplies over a wide area from villages to intermediate collection points to rail heads and finally into the dispersal points in the city. The collection system was skilfully allied to a veterinary service for cattle and other livestock, and, by extension, to other requirements for farmers and their families. But there were also industrial applications extending even to a chocolate factory producing the first commercial chocolate for the Indian market entirely from local products; this in part was made possible by the development of laboratories for research in local materials. The whole project was sustained and marketed using modern advertising techniques. Its success was such that the then Indian Prime Minister, Lal Bahadur Shastri, asked Dr

Kurien to replicate his system for other states of the Indian Union in a scheme known as 'Operation Flood'. Again, surely, there are valid lessons for IFI staff on how traditional forms and structures can be effectively moulded into development such as they seek to foster.

In this and the preceding chapter it may appear that I have been subjecting the WB and IMF to a critique that centres solely on their faults and shortcomings, unavoidable given the starting point and the nature of the critique. This is the place, therefore, to recognise the strengths of the Bretton Woods institutions and their staffs. Since 1947 they have made enormous advances, mainly from post-colonial development and welfare parameters to a global system of development; they have helped countries through innumerable financial crises; because of their reputation and status, they have been able to provide finance on a massive scale, at remarkably low rates of interest, where it has most been needed. It would be surprising if some faults of over-elaboration and bureaucratisation had not emerged in the course of this saga, involving staff in the tens of thousands working in virtually all the world's countries. A multinational cadre, on the whole highly dedicated, has worked not only in the Washington and regional headquarters, but also on project sites often in remote and difficult areas throughout the world. Several of them have protested that the thrust of the Jubilee 2000 campaign appears to be inadvertently directed against them and their colleagues. This is not the intention, as I have been at pains to point out. Perhaps it would be appropriate to quote here from a letter to one of them from which, I gather from his reply, he found some comfort and a clearer understanding of what we are about.

'It is true, as you say, through World Bank efforts much has been achieved. This is charted in UNDP's Human Development Report 1997. But whereas one finds in looking at the global trends that their direction is broadly upwards, if one examines in detail many of the social indicator tables eg infant mortality, life expectancy, literacy, various health aspects, it turns out that for the countries in the lowest segment (h.i.p.cs.) the direction is down, not up, and has been so since the mid-eighties. I am particularly conscious of this because I was serving in h.i.pcs. from 1974 to 1983 - India, Uruguay (a base for observing countries like Bolivia and Paraguay) and Malawi, where not only was I High Commissioner but also had under my wing the Southern African Development Division covering from Dar-es-Salaam to the Cape. I witnessed personally the start of the downturn as debt servicing began to bite, terms of trade swung against primary producers and capital flows diminished. My valedictory despatch in 1983 for the Secretary of State drew attention to the adverse effects already resulting from WB and IMF prescriptions for recipients of their loans because of insensitivity among visiting teams to the political and economic parameters which affect the welfare of their populations, especially the poorest segments, not always at the forefront of the minds of the elite senior officials with whom they negotiate. This was where doubts about structural adjustment programmes began to arise. From the lobbying in Whitehall which I undertook after my retirement came the germ of the mitigation soon known as the Trinidad Terms, which later became the Naples Terms. I readily acknowledge that much good work goes into project preparation, but how many feasibility studies result in actual development work? I can recall many which merely mouldered on office shelves.

The Treasury and the DFID both acknowledge that they are greatly indebted to Jubilee 2000 for the work we have done on debt remission, some of its theory from my own pen, and there have been personal communications to Gordon Brown, Helen Liddell and Claire Short. You will find in the 'Mauritius Mandate' much of my thinking. Equally, in producing the HIPC Initiative, the WB/IMF admitted that they were finally conceding to the sustained pressure of n.g.os., having previously maintained for years that remission of multilateral debt was impossible. I am glad you cite these advances as important progress but please don't think they were made merely out of the goodness of heart of their proponents. As far as concerns the paragraph immediately preceding your social indicators paragraph, as you know the WB was set up in 1944; its achievements over 50 years are perhaps not proportionate to the time and money expended and in many cases - cf e.g. the Narmada Dam saga - wasted. I have no doubt that you are right to praise professional advisers who have produced great results; our attitude to the IFIs is based more on their central management and philosophy, particularly those of the IMF. I attach a commentary on M Camdessus for your interest. Similarly, in drawing the parallel between the slave abolitionists in the Nineteenth Century and the J2000 campaigners, we are primarily intent on making people aware that there is a world situation now over debt comparable to the continuation of slavery last century, and requiring a similar effort to correct; like the abolitionists who carried their campaign to success by going to the churches, then much more inclusive than they are now, we are going to the churches and n.g.os. for the support we need for success. It is not intended to use the parallel as a criticism of individuals or institutions, although, of course, if the cap fits ....

Finally may I offer you a few pertinent observations by a well known German academic and international lawyer, Kunibert Raffer. a) On debt reduction as practised hitherto, 'Unhampered creditor power has produced too small reductions prolonging rather than solving the problem, as the Paris Club and the H.I.P.C. Initiative prove. ... a neutral and fair body is mandatory to guarantee a minimum of fairness, debtor protection and economic efficiency'. b) On moral hazard resulting from debt reduction 'The real moral hazard is on the creditor side, who are allowed to put their own interests above fairness, economic sense and humanitarian concern.'

c) On insolvency 'In all cases of insolvency - be it private or public - the reduction of creditors' claims is one essential means of reaching a feasible composition plan. Present (- ie the programme for Third World Debt reduction -) debt management on the other hand has precisely an exclusive fiscal perspective without exemption to protect debtors (with) its barbaric effects on the population and the future of debtor countries.' Two further observations on my own account. d) IFIs, in calculating debtor countries' ability to repay, for several years egregiously overstated prospective income from exports. There has been no counter-adjustment since, under n.g.o. pressure, they agreed to revise current calculations. d) The IFIs claim that they bear no responsibility for the catastrophic deterioration in the terms of trade of most primary producers. For an impartial economist it must be apparent that if 50 producing countries are urged over the same years to increase their exports of dollar-earning products, although no specific indication of which products to increase may have been given, there were bound to be gluts leading inevitably to severe income-reduction. Do the IFIs bear no responsibility for this? Are their contrary claims not highly suspect? Should they not be brought to account?

In short, it's not the hard working consultants on the ground and the kind of high street bankers whom you have met, who are the target of Jubilee 2000; it is the IFIs and all who support their practices in the larger framework of their relations with poor countries.

Notes

1 e.g. Percy Mistry: *African Debt Revisited* (1991, the Hague) and *Multilateral Debt: an Emerging Crisis* (1994, the Hague).
2 *Public Procurement: Global Revolution* ed. Sue Arrowsmith and Arwel Davies. Klunder Law International, Oct 1998, The Hague. Chapter by T. Tucker '*A critical analysis of Procurement Procedures at the World Bank*'.
3 Appendix 13. The Third Fisheries Project in Bangladesh. Private communication.
4 Leeds African Bulletin No.62, 1997, pp.13-39.

19 Conditions for Remission: Is a Grand Concordat Possible?

Chapter 7 considers in general terms the conditions which generous debt cancellation on the Jubilee 2000 model would encourage, for application in the context and at the time of the cancellation. This chapter attempts to sketch a broader reform which might result from discussions at high level between the leaders of debtor and creditor countries once generous cancellation has been agreed.

An unsuccessful attempt to reach a broad economic agreement between developed and developing countries had been made before the debt crisis started. This stemmed from a recommendation in the Brandt Commission Report for a summit meeting of 'First' and 'Third' World countries to achieve a consensus on future global economic co-operation. Following meetings of the French inspired Conference on International Economic Co-operation (CIEC) a summit took place. It was held as the Conference on International Co-operation and Development at Cancun in Mexico 22-3 October 1981. Among the industrialised countries were the USA, UK, Germany and Canada; among the developing countries, India, Zimbabwe, Nigeria and Malaysia. The USSR stood aside, calling the Conference a 'dialogue of the deaf' unless the capitalist powers were prepared to commit to radical change. Monetary and financial issues formed one of four sections on the agenda. At the opening of the Conference, President Reagan who had diverged from his two predecessors in countenancing the summit, called his audience's attention to the 'responsibilities (they must) face, if the world is to be an acceptable place for six billion inhabitants in year 2000'. However, progress was prevented over the international structures to deal with economic and financial matters. The developing countries considered that all UN agencies, including the Bretton Woods Institutions, should come under the final direction of the UN while the industrialized agreed with Reagan's ukhase 'Decisions reached by these agencies (the WB and IMF) within respective areas of competence are final'. An UN Resolution supported by almost all developing countries in December 1981 for continuing North-South negotiations on restructuring the international economy was never put to the vote. The Brandt Commission reactivated itself in Kuwait on 9 June 1982 but failed to break the deadlock. A meeting called by Indira Gandhi of African, Asia and Latin American countries in New Delhi, 22-4 February

215

1982, got no further than appealing for 'collective self-reliance' among participants. So the matter rests.

Would a similar effort made in the context of the Millennium have a better prospect of succeeding if our campaign to improve the terms of debt cancellation very substantially achieved its objective? The debtor countries, could they truly believe that their people were being given a fresh start, debt free, at the onset of the Millennium, might well be in a frame of mind to establish for themselves norms of behaviour in the political and economic fields which could help to rule out or considerably diminish the failures of confidence and conscience which contributed in part to the debt crisis. As Martin Dent records, already in many parts of Africa voices are heard saying that leaders in future should be accountable at the outset for economic burdens they bring to their people, such as the debt overhang: and that in future a system must be constructed which would make it much more difficult for corrupt leaders and bureaucrats to enrich themselves at the expense of the people they are supposed to serve. On the creditor side hard questions also are being asked: how much of the suffering from the debt burden is due to carelessness on the part of the creditors in distributing the surpluses which were the prime cause of the crisis? Were adequate calculations made beforehand about the revenue-earning capacities of projects which might have averted the build up of interest arrears? Why were the neo-classical principles on which the Washington Consensus was based applied with thoughtless 'rigour' without concern for the local context in which adjustment was enforced? Other issues are now on the agenda: we have seen the beginnings of an attempt to register the details of international arms sales, which, perhaps, foreshadows a greater readiness than has hitherto existed to provide a moral check on the indiscriminate sale of arms to Third World countries by the major arms producers. An international court has begun to operate from Rome: can the scope of the international laws it administers be extended to take in kleptocracy, to provide a means of redress for peoples who have been beggared by unscrupulous, plundering leaders intent primarily on their own and their families' enrichment? The widespread debate surrounding ex-President Pinochet of Chile during the extended hearing in London of the Spanish case for his extradition from Britain to face charges of torture and human rights violation have manifested a strong build up of feeling in favour of legal mechanisms to bring even Heads of State to book for atrocities for which they can be held responsible. Many believe that economic as well as human rights violations and political atrocities should come within this ambit.

Progress has already been made in the 'south' towards preparing guidelines to improve co-operation and collaboration among Third World countries. Julius Nyerere's South Commission has now been working for over ten years, exploring methods by which poor countries can help each other through technical advice, joint projects, shared services and training facilities, commercial collaboration and action in international fora. The non-Aligned Movement similarly has accumulated a body of analysis leading to recommendations on how to tackle problems like debt, both domestically and at regional and international levels. They have created a framework for a comprehensive approach to debt reform and begun to lay out a programme for change in institutional arrangements for debt reorganisation; speaking of the existing system they assert 'the entire process is inherently unjust: most of the meetings are prepared, staged and managed exclusively by the creditors.' For the avoidance of widespread debt crises in the future the Movement, inter alia, recognises that 'improvements in internal management .... are necessary, both in handling projects and operating government enterprises, and in macro policies as they affect major markets, foreign trade and capital flows. These improvements, to be effective, must be domestically generated and formulated and seen to be such: the borrowing countries must 'own' the programmes they are expected to implement. The ... 'explosion of conditionality' is not conducive to effective co-operation between capital exporting countries and agencies and capital importing countries .... A reform of conditionality doctrine, practices and modalities is needed. The right of creditors to be concerned with developments and policies of their debtors cannot be denied; nor can the need for adequate policies in debtor countries' own interest. On the other hand, the responsibility for those policies and their results belong to the government of the country, not to outside powers. Serious work is urgently needed to find the line of compromise between these different considerations and interests.'[1] It is encouraging to note that one of the recommendations of the Movement's Ad Hoc Group of Experts on Debt about intra-South debtor-creditor relations is already being applied. The South African Government has forgiven the debts owed to its own apartheid-based predecessor by Namibia on the grounds that they were incurred in the pursuit of policies now totally rejected by the present South African Government, to be classified as 'odious' and therefore not to be pursued.

As an example of how a debtor country can forestall criticism by volunteering a bold policy of transparency, President Museveni of Uganda has given access to his Finance Ministry and Central Bank to WB and IMF officials. So far as he is concerned they can observe and discuss operations as they occur, monitoring and auditing on a continuous basis. Transparency has been much touted as a condition to be applied in negotiations for debt relief.

'Transparency International' makes this its main target. The Berlin-based organisation has recently appeared to alter its approach. Initially it urged that tackling corruption was the ineluctable first step towards relief and argued as if corruption (and economic maladministration) were defining characteristics of debtor governments. More recently they have begun to admit that corruption occurs in developed countries as well as poor ones. Perhaps they were helped by the so-called 'Nazi Gold' case through which it become apparent that, among others, Swiss banks and the Swiss government, held up as paragons of financial rectitude, had for over fifty years been sitting on and profiting from looted wealth obtained in the most despicable circumstances imaginable. The old saw about people in glass houses applies in the financial and economics fields as much as elsewhere! The vast total of the EU's untraceable missing funds from the CAP and elsewhere is another useful reminder of corruption and malversion in developed countries. There is no question but that corruption must be dealt with and rooted out to the maximum possible degree. But surely it is not desirable to tackle corruption by imposing even greater deprivation on people in indebted countries who have already suffered grievously from the defalcations of their leaders (and, perhaps it should be added, by the weakly managed, theoretically questionable prescriptions of the IFIs).

The elements of a possible, wide-ranging agreement between leaders of the Third World and the First are beginning to define themselves. It must not be imposed by either side. It must be balanced in its benefits and trade-offs. The commitments it records must be self-policed. Some form of impartial arbitration or even regular audit may be necessary. Anti-corruption domestic legislation in all participant countries could be called for. Similarly participant countries would need to spell out the democratic modes for making more transparent the providing and receiving of loans. A few basic rules might be agreed and promulgated. For example, most large project loans should include in their planning and execution provision for a revenue earning component which would ensure the servicing of the loan would be at least partly covered by project income. When funds are released in a debtor country either by cancellation, rescheduling or discharge, at least 20% of them should be ring-fenced for health services and 20% for education. Before loans are agreed a careful assessment should be made of the debtor country's ability to repay over the long term, using best available forecasting techniques. Such measures could be beneficial for all the parties concerned, and have already proved acceptable in part to one highly indebted poor country as the example set by President Museveni in Uganda has shown. They would give a ready riposte to those in the developed world who oppose generous debt cancellation, answering the objections they so readily raise, that cancelling debt is 'pouring money down an open drain', that it will only benefit the kleptocrats and economic malefactors, that it will merely lead to the recreation of another debt crisis in another decade or two, that its benefits will never reach those who truly need them at the lowest poverty level in poor countries.

The '*grundlelgung*', as Kant would have called it, the groundwork for the foundations of a grand concordat such as I describe has already been done. A number of visionary politicians, not least Nelson Mandela, has already been talking along these lines. Julius Nyerere speaks of a new, responsible spirit being abroad in Africa. Active mediators like Professor Washington Okumu have brought up the subject of economic reform in the context of debt cancellation with Heads of State and Government with whom they engage. Topics like expanded debt-for-development schemes are being extensively discussed. The World Bank President himself has praised those who through microcredit enable women to find their dignity and 'empower people to take charge of their destinies'. Businessmen in developed countries, well aware of the effect of the adverse swing in the terms of trade on primary producers, are looking for ways of directing private foreign investment flows towards local businesses and agencies, to move a larger proportion of development out of the state sector. In 1996 the African Trade & Investment Caucus in the House of Representatives in Washington was pioneering this line, but appears to have been absorbed elsewhere. There is a clear need for renewed efforts to widen the economic base in most developing countries by starting new enterprises, whether for more import substitution or for export. To achieve permanent improvements in this way a degree of protection for nascent industries would have to be allowed, breaching market principles but only for a limited time and in places of special hardship. Some consideration might be given to temporary privileges including tax concessions in the receiving country or the home base for multinational corporations and other organisations, some perhaps charitably oriented, in return for technology transfer, training and any required expertise.

The UN Secretary-General, Dr Kofi Annan, has proposed that an UN programme should be worked out to mark the Millennium; he has invited suggestions for themes; that of Jubilee 2000 has already been put forward. He has also called for a Millennium Assembly (of the UNGA) and a Millennium Forum, in which civil society would have space to debate some of the ideas in the UN Millennium programme. The summit of the Millennium Assembly would be an obvious location for leaders of all UN member states to forge a grand concordat; some details and non-official proposals could be worked out in the Millennium Forum. Time is short, but the ideas are already fermenting. May they 'lead on to fortune'.

Note

1   Report of the Non-Aligned Movement Ad Hoc Advisory Group of Experts on Debt, 1994.

20 Reform of UN, Including Bretton Woods, Structures

'Fifty years is enough' is a slogan of recent years which has challenged the Bretton Woods structure. After all, when the post-War regime of fixed parities ended in 1971 one of the prime functions of the IMF ceased with it. As Milton Friedman said in Hong Kong in September 1998 'The IMF has long outlived its purpose. It should have been absorbed in 1971 and if not then now .... the IMF now does more harm than good,' [1] It was not until November 1985 that the G5 (as it then was) undertook the task of some exchange rate co-ordination, and that in a very loose manner; extensions of this type of oversight have been spectacularly incapable of providing any type of fail-safe procedure. The crises in S E Asia have stirred up strong criticism of the Fund, with accusations that in the early stage their action in causing restrictions to be imposed on bank credit exacerbated the problem. Adherence to strict market principles leading to the acquisition of large segments of hitherto flourishing industries by foreign capital has prompted bitter reactions. In relation to the Third World Debt Crisis Chapters 17 and 18 attempt to show that the ministrations of the IFIs in many ways made it worse in part because their predominantly neo-classical theoretical base from which policies were developed by rote was unsuitable, applied insensitively, for the economies they presumed to guide and in part because many of their methods were unsuitable for some types of economy or culture or have become over-bureaucratised.

In support of the HIPC Initiative in October 1996 James Wolfensohn launched a publicity campaign. He, Michel Camdessus and other leaders of the Bank and Fund began a series of meetings and conferences with prominent people around the world, including religious leaders, to explain IFI policies and initiate dialogues about the world economy and matters such as environmental protection. This was accompanied by a campaign in the media and the establishment of an organisation for consultation with civil society, Structural Adjustment Participatory Review Initiative (SAPRI). As we have recorded in Chapter 17, the Bank at least has also begun some reappraisal of fundamentals. This is a praiseworthy and justifiable effort. If its purpose, as it developed, has also been to head off external demands for reform of the Bretton Woods Institutions, this appears to be failing. The opening up to civil society through SAPRI is unconvincing: apart from anything else the IFIs are very selective in the organisations and other interlocuteurs with whom they are prepared to engage. Dialogue at higher levels has not been trouble free. For example James Wolfensohn's episode at the Lambeth Conference in Canterbury on 24 July was counter-productive because he over-reacted and in a personal way to mild criticism and allowed no opportunity to the 850 bishops assembled from all the continents to comment on or question his address.

With an intimate practical knowledge of the financial markets George Soros proposes an open society coalition - he is a keen supporter of Karl Popper's theories - focussed on 'freedom of information and association, due process and transparency in state procurements'; it should be based on a 'worldwide alliance of democratic countries but open to candidate members reaching their standards of commitment to the open society.

Meanwhile political leaders like Tony Blair and Michel Jospin have begun to call for reform of the IFIs. The initiative was launched by the British Prime Minister in Washington on the day when the Monica Lewinsky tapes were launched on the American (and world) public. Oscar Lafontaine suggested making the Interim Committee of the IMF into a Council of Finance Ministers, presumably with greater powers of control. The Lambeth Conference's resolution on international debt advocates establishing a Mediation Council which would arbitrate over debt issues both in the initial stages and if need arose later to consider rescheduling and cancellation. On 1 December 1998 at the World Bank office in London, when launching the latest WB Annual Report (which predicts the lowest growth rates for developing countries since the Eighties debt crisis), Mahsood Ahmed, Director, International Economic Dept of the WB, admitted during questions that the IFIs needed reform, for which they were planning.

Aside from the theoretical and methodological weaknesses of the IFIs themselves, the dissatisfaction which produced the 'Fifty years is enough' campaign arose also from a number of factors within the institutional framework where the IFI's operate. It is fairly obvious that when the Bretton Woods institutions were set up, although they were part of a wider UN complex, they were in many ways autonomous and self-regulating. Whereas most UN agencies respond to committees of the UNGA, and ultimately, if necessary, to the Security Council, there is no such over-riding mechanism for the WB and IMF. Their own governing body fulfils that function if needed, but has not been prominent in the role. In consequence subordinate elements such as the London and Paris Clubs have needed to operate to the satisfaction of their parent body only, without regard to voices from outside which criticise or question them. When Martin Dent and I visited the then Secretary General of the Paris Club, Jerome Haas, and his Inspecteur de Finances friend, Daniel Dommel, at the French Finance Ministry on 11 April 1995 to talk over debt cancellation we found him charming and hospitable but quite clearly running on rails laid down by his own organisations in Paris and Washington. Yet the volume of criticism of the slow pace of the Paris Club was already large; the inequality of its proceedings was patent with a small delegation of officials or ministers from a debtor country having to face a large battery of weighty experts from creditor countries and the IFIs. On the other hand, no less patent was the absence of monitoring the pursuit of the interests of the creditor countries. When matters such as extending further loans to rulers like Mobutu arose, the overriding political interests of the principal parties appear to have prevailed regardless of the high risk of sequestration of these disbursements like their predecessors, with no benefit to but rather an enlargement of their burden of the unconsulted poor of Zaire. When problems arose over countries reneging on debt or failing to maintain rescheduling targets, the IFIs were effectively judge, jury and executor in their own cases. This, apart from its obvious unfairness, made for anomalies; for example, when a debtor country, to assist compliance, was obliged - (some suggest, with doubtful legality on the part of the IMF) - to accept a structural adjustment programme in return for further loans, but thereafter still failed to meet its obligation, it was still pressurised into continuing the programme. Despite the obvious need for workable legal sanctions on kleptocrats the IFIs have produced no answer to popular demands for restitution when the kleptocrats die or are superceded, regardless - or perhaps because - of their own complicity; the fact that Imelda Marcos has successfully appealed against her part in her family's defalcations, or that the Presidents Chun Do-Whun and Rioh Tae-Woo of Korea, having been condemned respectively to death and life imprisonment for similar offences, were pardoned in an act of clemency: (the legal prestigitations of the Duvalier family are too complex to summarise succinctly) have not appeared to spur the IFIs to back the new Court of International Justice in Rome as a place for judgement for state economic offences as well as those involving torture and breach of human rights. This would nevertheless seem appropriate and would complement results from the calls for domestic legislation in debtor and creditor countries to create offences with which to charge civil or political officials who misappropriate public funds.

A plan[2] has been put forward by Christian Aid for the creation of a second

Security Council which would be a counterpart in social and economic affairs for the existing Security Council in its role in political matters. Article 63 of the UN Charter provides for the Economic and Social Council to enter into agreements with any of specialised agencies which include IMF and the WB, but ECOSOC's powers are only consultative and advisory. Failure to give it any power was a grave omission by the drafters of the Charter. The Administrative Committee on Co-ordination (ACC), later set up to attempt to rectify the omission, has brought little amelioration. The Executive Heads of the Specialised Agencies including the WB and IMF who form it under the Secretary General's chairmanship all have their own agendas and territories to defend. Something else, like the Christian Aid suggestion, is needed. A body, such as they suggest, would in effect supervise and control the WB and IMF. It could set up a fresh organisation as arbitrator and conciliator, to act when disputes arise in future over economic and social matters such as debt adjudication. By its constitution such an organisation could be carefully composed to give equal representation to debtors and creditors and their advocates and to ensure that democratic transparency prevailed, thus eliminating the charge that the WB and IMF are both judge and jury. When an international law to deal with state insolvency is instituted, (see Martin Dent's comments on Kunibert Raffer's proposals, p.132), the new organisation could administer that. None of this, it should be clear, is preliminary to debt cancellation. Up to December 2000 the primary target must remain, the most generous possible cancellation of debt. But as study of the debt issue has revealed weaknesses in the existing system of debt management leading to calls for reform it is worth noting the areas where changes are needed as well as ideas for their accomplishment.

A process has already been outlined within the broad UN framework, within which these ideas may be developed and given concrete form. The Secretary General has called for ideas appropriate for the celebration by UN of the Millennium. These are being put forward by UN Associations in different countries, and processed. Through the British UNA, Jubilee 2000 has proposed, as suitable for the Millennium programme, the theme of generous debt cancellation. This idea appealed to Nitin Desai, the Secretary General's Deputy (the Sec Gen had been summoned urgently to Nigeria after General Abacha's death) when I offered it at a meeting in New York on 24 June 1998. Complementary to this a number of governments are considering a proposal for a UN Resolution to proclaim a time in 2000 - a month, a week, a day - when people may be reminded of the pressing urgency of reducing the debt burden in HIPCs. The Resolution would be along the lines of others commemorating special events or drawing attention to special human problems.

More substantially from the point of view of UN structures, the Secretary General in his Note of 31 March 1998 proposed that the fifty-fifth session of the General Assembly should be designated a Millennium Assembly. He goes on to suggest that there should be a high-level segment for this Assembly - a Millennium Summit - devoted to in-depth consideration of the theme 'The United Nations in the Twenty-First Century'. It would 'facilitate the participation of Heads of State and Government while maximising continuity in the Assembly's normal procedure and work'. This surely would be the occasion for drawing to conclusion a reappraisal of the structures within which the WB and IMF operate, and setting a better course for them within the wider UN framework for the next 50 years. We saw in Chapter 19 how at the Cancun Conference in 1981 President Reagan's ukhase about decisions of the WB and IMF being 'final in the area of competence' stymied the effort to find a *modus vivendi* between the rich and the poor. He also said responsibilities had to be faced if the world was to be an acceptable place for 6 billion inhabitants in year 2000. Can that ukhase continue unchanged? Are there no limits to the determining power of the hegemon? A leader in the Washington Post of 28 September 1998 suggests that a more generous, less rigid spirit is abroad in America. Discussing US action in the crises of S E Asia, Russia and Brazil it asserts the priority of getting that right but recalls the commitments to HIPC debt cancellation of the IFIs and President Clinton; by country 'the amounts each needs are miniscule' but to overlook them 'would consign millions of people to unnecessary hardship'; (more accurately, starvation or even death). Donald Soper's 'all this talk of enlightened self-interest is merely a way of justifying greed' could just be relevant.

Linked to the proposal for a Millennium Summit and Assembly the Secretary General will, by midsummer 2000, submit to Member States the promised report, 'The United Nations in the Twenty First Century'. It will answer the question 'how should the United Nations relate to and interact with the increasingly densely populated universe of international institutions, an increasingly active global civil society: ever more integrated global markets and systems of production?' He wonders whether the unity of purpose and coherence of action necessitated by the new challenges facing the United Nations can be monitored within existing arrangements by the UN Administrative Committee on Co-ordination (see above) and refers to the consultations on the reforms already being undertaken by individual agencies in their respective roles within the total system. He envisages the likelihood that when the Millennium Assembly considers the report of this Committee on Co-ordination it will wish to consider establishing a Special Commission to examine the UN constitutional framework such as he outlined in his reform report.[3] Once again the ideas for structural change surrounding the WB and IMF discussed earlier in this chapter could find a place on the agenda. As I wrote to Kofi Annan in a letter of 13 Oct 1998 ' ... we (Jubilee 2000) greatly welcome your imaginative suggestions for linking a Special Commission .... to the proposal for the Millennium Assembly. Our study of the reasons for the debt overhang has made it clear ... that a great need exists for new structures to deal with both loan making and debt settlement; also for arrangements in international law to handle insolvency at state level ....'

Thirdly the Secretary-General proposes that non-governmental organisations and other civil society agencies should organise a Millennium Forum to be linked to the Millennium Assembly and perhaps immediately precede it. He wishes liaison mechanisms to be established. This will, he is certainly right to claim, ensure that the United Nations continues to play a vital role in the century ahead, 'benefiting from the imagination and engaging the support of the world's people'. The scope this gives for Jubilee 2000 as the Millennium ends is most welcome.

To end I quote from a recent interview[4] given by ex-President Julius Nyerere to the US journalist Ikaweba Bunting for 'New Internationalist'.

Bunting: Why did your attempt to find a new way founder on the rocks?
Nyerere: I was in Washington last year. At the World Bank the first question they asked me was 'how did you fail?' I responded that we took over a country with 85 per cent of its adult population illiterate. The British ruled us for 43 years. When they left, there were 2 trained engineers and 12 doctors. This is the country we inherited.
When I stepped down there was 91-per-cent literacy and nearly every child was in school. We trained thousands of engineers and doctors and teachers.
In 1988 Tanzania's per-capita income was $280. Now, in 1998, it is $140. So I asked the World Bank people what went wrong. Because for the last ten years Tanzania has been signing on the dotted line and doing everything the IMF and the World Bank wanted. Enrolment in school has plummeted to 63 per cent and conditions in health and other social services have deteriorated. I asked them again 'what went wrong?' These people just sat there looking at me. Then they asked what could they do? I told them, 'Have some humility.'

Notes

1   *Times*, ? Sept 1998.
2   Christian Aid, Viewpoint Series 10. Jan 1996. *Global Challenges: The Case for an UN Economic and Social Security Council* by Frances Stewart and Sam Daws.
3   UN document A/51/950 para.89.
4   New Internationalist, No. 309, January/February 1999. London pp.12-15. *'The Heart of Africa'*.

List of Appendices

Appendix 1

Third World: Debt, Poverty and Starvation

Three cameos. First Bob Geldof on stage in London at the Queen Elizabeth II Conference Centre, close by Westminster Abbey and the 'Mother of Parliament'. He has just received the 1986 Third World Prize in recognition of his efforts for the Sahel and is making his speech, product of midnight oil and much effort. He wears 'the first suit I have ever bought' for the occasion. (It would have served Cyril Smith, the Liberal MP!) Referring to Third World Debt in Africa he says 'I would go further (than Julius Nyerere in 1985) and say that they, i.e., Third World debtor countries, should refuse to pay it. There should be an immediate refusal to make any interest repayments and there should be a moratorium on the capital, at least for twenty years'.

Second, Cyril Townsend, Conservative MP, a liberal thinker, Chairman of the South Atlantic Council where I support him in efforts to keep open the lines of communication to Argentina. He says, obviously deeply worried, 'Bob was a bit off course over debt, wasn't he? Surely if everybody refuses to pay interest and withhold capital payments the world economic system will collapse.' I say, 'Yes, indeed, but there is another way, difficult to chart but possible with goodwill all round.' We talk.

Third cameo; Bernard Russell, formerly senior economist at the World Bank now one of their trusted consultants. (He wrestles with Turkey among other client countries). He was the Brackenbury Scholar at Balliol in the year I got my Domus Exhibition there. We are old friends. He says, 'What I find dangerous and disturbing is people who don't know thoroughly the fundamentals of international banking and finance but who produce bland solutions to the problems of the poorest countries and press them on a listening world with high flown moral arguments in support. Our effort is to keep the world economy on its precarious balance. They blindly urge courses such as debt forgiveness which would endanger that balance - quite possibly bring economic disaster.'

Francis Blanchard, Director General of ILO will take part in a dialogue on World Debt at Caux around 27/28 August 1987. Dr. Johannes Witteveen, former Secretary General of the International Monetary Fund says he would participate only if 'the monetary and economic realities are also dealt with.' Others have been invited to join. They include Harold Lever (Lord Lever) former Financial Secretary in the British Government, and (Sir) Bob Geldof. Groups visiting Latin America in the Spring will try to involve some senior financiers/economists from that area. The first President of Bangladesh, Mr. Abu Syed Choudhury, has agreed to talk about his country.

What basis is there for a realistic dialogue? We have deeply pondered Barbara Ward's words. 'From the beginning of time, she says, people have heard the still small voice of obligation and brotherhood. When they have listened, society has worked. When they have refused to listen, society has broken up.' Geoffrey Lean ends his book 'Rich World, Poor World' with that quotation. But the words don't get through to decision-takers in the world of international finance. Individuals like Tom Clausen, former President of the World Bank, and his forerunner, Robert Macnamara, encourage others to press their case on such grounds.

Harold Lever answering questions I put to him on corruption and the flight of capital which have halted earlier aid efforts writes to me 'We must not allow corruption or export of capital to divert us from our central understanding of this matter. Past experience shows that the transfer of resources did foster economic growth to great advantage to all our purposes. Equally, the negative transfer of resources has produced injury for both sides. We must therefore correct the present anomaly by providing institutional surveillance on the terms of lending to keep misdirection of resources as low as possible'.

Do we think the transfer of resources to the Least Developed Countries (LDCs) desirable? Surely the answer has to be 'yes'. How could it be otherwise when we note the recurrent spectre of famine in Africa, the fourfold swing in the terms of trade against primary producers who form the majority of the LDCs, the clear political danger that Third World leaders who have presided over the disasters which the economic systems of both East and West have wrought on their people -that these leaders will turn away from both the capitalist and the communist blocs and find a third alignment perhaps with the emerging East Pacific force which Lee Kwan Yew foresees as the major new element by the year 2000. If we agree that the transfer is necessary and would be beneficent, for example in terms of increased employment in the industrialised countries, can we not design a programme which would open the door of hope for the Third World? Quoting Harold Lever again, he said that in 1945/46 when the Marshall Plan was being forged for European reconstruction, many financial pundits declared that along that path lay disaster. Yet even while agreement on the Marshall Plan was still being thrashed out conditions began to improve in Europe and the economic miracle of the 'fifties and 'sixties took shape. We need now, urgently, a Marshall Plan for the Third World and should spare no effort to work one out.

Many elements of such a plan are already clear. But what about the hurdle of 'the monetary and economic realities' of which Dr Witteveen speaks? Two events this weekend (21-22 February 1987) help to concentrate the mind. Brazil declared it would not continue to service its colossal debt. The leaders of the Group of Seven, US, Japan, West Germany, France and Britain with support from Canada (but not yet Italy) have agreed to stabilise their currencies at about the present level; while Japan and West Germany will seek to expand their growth rates, America will aim to reduce its deficit from 3.97% of GNP to 2.3% in 1988. Clearly a plan for world poverty needs the beneficent cycle which the Group of Seven is trying to start but not the malignant cycle which would result from Brazil's and other major debtors' reneging (as Zambia has already done with dire consequences for herself). Financial trust and good order should be maintained. Market forces must be allowed to operate. But this does not mean that, where necessary, exceptions can not be made or new solutions devised.

In August 1986 at Caux, Masaki Nakajima, Founder and Senior Adviser of the Mitsubishi Research Institute, spoke about his concept of a Global Infrastructure Fund. This concept, developed over eight years, is for a programme funded by a specific levy in the main industrialised countries to be used for major development projects in the Third World.

Examples are the Kra Isthmus Canal (across the narrow part of Malaysia and very important for Japan), massive solar heat collectors for energy in the tropics, a new super highway along the old 'Silk Road' across Asia. These and many more would have the advantage of bringing the more developed and the less developed world into collaborative contact, creating work in both and improving the economic climate in their localities. Such a scheme would avoid some of the danger of massive cash or material (e.g. grain) handouts to Third World countries often paid as conscience money by the rich. Handouts like this are now recognised to be mainly harmful and are, in fact, subsidies for the giving countries' own industry since they maintain the recipient countries in a state of dependence, without developing agriculture or industry and thus being able to compete with richer countries. What is needed is not conscience money but a structured programme to which the richer countries would contribute and on which the poorer countries could draw as a matter of right, for mutual benefit. Cf. Mao's dictum 'Give a man a fish and you feed him for a day; teach him how to fish and you set him up for life'. (Senator Bradley has pointed out that in 1986 loss of Latin American importing capacity cost 800,000 jobs in the USA).

But the Global Infrastructure Fund is only one element in a series of structural changes which could be considered for the international financial system, recognising the real interdependence which exists among countries of all economic levels and forces within countries in the economic, financial, social and political fields. (During 1986 the ILO was attempting to provide a forum where key actors in decision-making processes at national and international levels were encouraged to examine the issues here discussed as a means of fostering the debates and reflections necessary for advancement towards a more just and prosperous world). Other structural changes are:

At the macro-economic level

(i)   (By the World Bank, IMF, the Regional Development Banks and private banks) a two or three-tier system of interest rates allowing new loans for the poorest countries to be made on less crippling terms (some banks have already done it);

(ii)   (By GATT) a recognition during the Uruguay (Punta del Este) Round that for the poorest countries there should be some 'acceptance of inequality' allowing them a limited 'freedom to engage in protectionism'. (The case for this has been well argued by another Japanese economist, Dr. Nobutane Kiuchi, in a paper entitled 'Steps towards a desirable new World Order'.)

(iii)   (By the IMF) a re-examination of the rules governing SDR issues to cushion the poorest economies against the drying up of development funds;

(iv)   (By the IMF) expansion of the system of compensatory payments for primary producers; NB: this despite Mr. Secretary Baker's opposition;

(v)   (By all - see Harold Lever quoted above) creation of international surveillance on the terms of lending to keep misdirection of resources as low as possible.

At the micro-economic level

(vi)   (By the World Bank, IDA, national aid agencies and non-governmental organisations - ngos) concentration on and increased generosity for agricultural development schemes where poor countries are not self-sufficient in food;

(vii) (By receiving governments) overhaul of their marketing systems, especially agricultural, to ensure that farmers are given timely and reliable advice on the farm gate prices they may expect for their products;

(viii) (By major companies involved or interested in work in heavily indebted countries) examination of the debt/equity formula which enables companies to relieve the receiving country of some of its debt by taking over portions of it in the form of equity in local companies unable to operate because of their debt burden; this encourages technology transfer as well as removing the obstacle caused by debt to development and increased earning.

Forgiving of debts in special circumstances is advocated by some e.g., Senator Bill Bradley in the Washington Post of Sunday 5 October 1986, ('Squeezing the Debtors will make things worse for Them and Us') and Jeffrey Sachs in The New Republic of 28 October 1985 ('How to Save the Third World - forgive some debt, forget protectionism, and trust the IMF').

It is not, however, included in the above list of proposed actions. The IMF's strategy of voluntary rescheduling allied with conditionality, worked out in 1982, and predicated on US-led world recovery remains in place despite the dashing of so many intermediate hopes and the US failure to deliver. Nevertheless the possibility is not ruled out that other banks may follow the example of one of their number which decided to treat interest payments from a Central American debtor country as reductions in the principal owed.

These are pragmatic suggestions based solely on the facts and capacities of the current international financial system. They amount to the starting point of a programme which can be extended. It is not suggested that new financial institutions should be created. That battle was fought out in the late seventies and early eighties and the existing complex was not changed. The moral arguments are barely mentioned. But, of course, in this world of ours, although it is thought unseemly among the financial *literati* to speak of moral considerations, they are what weigh most in the hearts of men of goodwill. And those who support this effort can begin now to spread the ideas of this paper with the aim eventually, possibly in 1988, of getting launched a major conference to discuss the establishment of a 'Marshall Plan' for the Third World.

W Peters, 26 February 1987

Appendix 2

Hope in a World of Tension, Caux 1 Sept 84

Since coming to Caux I have had several opportunities of sharing with friends here a concern which has been deepening over the past months. It is about the failure of the international financial community to deal with the increasing desperation of many Third World countries. They find their development halted and even the ability to feed their people denied them. Ambassador Gamini Correa, from his ringside seat as Secretary General of UNCTAD had some wise but disturbing words to say on the subject when he was here. Our talks in Caux encourage me to speak of the problem as a major source of world tension and to look for signs of hope in ways of tackling it.

Perhaps I can best illustrate the problem by describing the recent economic experience of one Third World country, Malawi, where I was High Commissioner for 3½ years until May last year. Malawi's President, Dr Banda, is not everybody's favourite African leader. Some of his neighhours regard him as a maverick because he openly prefers dialogue to confrontation. During the Rhodesian crisis and in his relations with South Africa he has always kept the lines open. More recently he amazed the diplomatic world by inviting North Korea to open an embassy in Malawi although South Korea already had one there. He said he was merely following his policy of contact and dialogue. If the two Koreas had missions in Malawi they might even get talking there! But whatever differences may exist about Malawi's political policies, opinions do not vary that her economic policies have been highly pragmatic and successful.

The country was one of the few in the world to sustain an average rate of growth of GNP of 7% from 1963 to 1979. I first visited Malawi in 1968 and so can compare what conditions were like then and, say, in 1982. In 1968 the signs of malnutrition, children with swollen stomachs and glazed eyes, were all too frequent. People were often poorly dressed and many houses in the villages were in a ruinous condition. The journey from Zomba to Lilongwe took six excruciating hours and we ate much red dust on the way. Now it can be done in 2½ comfortable hours. The children are well fed, the people dress smartly and the villages look well-kept. The education system works through most of the country, accessible to all and there is a good network of hospitals and clinics. The obvious improvement results from sensible policies consistently applied, notably concentration on bettering agriculture and the choice of hydro-electricity, to which the land is adapted, rather than more costly sources of energy. By 1982 Malawi was exporting maize not only to neighbouring countries like Zambia, Mozambique and Zaire, but also to South Africa. Her reputation for honest use of aid funds was so high that all the international financial institutions were happy to lend to her as well as many individual countries on a government to government basis.

But in 1980 a drought reduced the maize crop below national needs and oil-price rises put up the cost of imports for that part of the energy requirement still based on oil. The IMF had to support Malawi's foreign exchange imbalance with a stand-by credit and the World Bank gave a loan on IDA terms to help cover the budget deficit. Development continued because from IDA and other international sources capital for major projects continued to be available. 1979-82 were, moreover, the years when private or commercial bank lending was running at $2.4 billion world-wide and Malawi had a small share of this. But in 1982/83 bank lending dropped to $800 million where it has remained and this means that at best new loans do no more than equate the interest payments due on earlier loans, a net outflow for countries like Malawi. As this source dried up, so the availability of funds from the IMF, the World Bank and the IDA became more difficult.

Malawi behaved according to the precepts of the institutions. There were two heavy devaluations and foreign debts were rescheduled. But the terms of trade for Malawi moved from a base of 100 in 1975 to 32 by 1982. In other words, for the man in the village or in the small farm it was necessary to use up three times the amount of his produce for the same imports as seven years earlier. Development is now virtually frozen and children with swollen stomachs can again be seen in the villages. In a tour of 20 villages served by a leprosy assistant last May I saw people who were going to be dead in a matter of weeks. They are now dead. The case of Malawi is much better than those of Zambia, large parts of Zimbabwe and Zaire, and Mozambique.

In these grievous circumstances why has there not been more help from the International Financial community? The Bretton Woods institutions were set up partly to help poor countries through hard times. But the total burden of Third World debt means that the resources of these institutions have to be spread much thinner. Worse, the resources available to the institutions from some richer countries are being reduced. High rates of interest and very large budget deficits in some industrialised countries - deficits inflated by very high levels of defence expenditure - have meant that available resources are
continuously sucked into those industrialised countries to cover their deficits and maintain their defence expenditure. So the last IDA replenishment was only about half what had been planned and much-needed development projects by the score have had to be deferred or abandoned in the Third World.

The consequence of this is that bitterness and disillusionment about the international financial system is growing. One African country has already reneged on its debts, an example which, if followed, would spell disaster for the economic stability of large parts of the world. Third World leaders who have been prepared to accept sound principles and favour the open systems of government in the West are now pondering their preference. They ask themselves whether those systems can be so much better than the closed systems fostered by Marxism/Leninism if the result is the starvation of their compatriots. The outcome in terms of world balance could be profound. The danger in my view is even greater than that arising from nuclear confrontation.

What is needed? After the Second World War men of vision saw that orthodox economics applied to a ruined Europe would not suffice. Reparations on the lines agreed at Versailles in 1919 would only compound the problem. So the Marshall Plan was devised. Europe restored went on to achieve unprecedented levels of growth and improvements in living standards for all. The Third World needs something like a Marshall Plan which will revitalise the Bretton Woods institutions and provide the resources to allow the World Bank, the IMF and IDA to do the work for which they were intended. One small but significant adjustment would be a two-tier interest structure with countries below a certain level of GNP qualifying for rates they could more easily tolerate. News has come out recently of a group of Swiss bankers which had offered to denominate some Third World debts in Swiss francs rather than dollars, thereby reducing the debt burden of the countries concerned by a considerable amount.

I believe that here in Caux a start can be made. I am prompted to say that a number of us with God's guidance should seek to talk with those who take the crucial decisions in and relating to the international financial institutions and encourage them to begin devising new schemes within the existing framework to enable development funds to flow once again. Anything less will lead to the alienation of the Third World. Self-interest dictates change. But, much more, God-guided change could open the way, not only to continued existence but to a better life for millions around the world.

W Peters

Caux, 1 September 1984

Appendix 3

Press Release: Third World Debt (Jubilee 2000), Caux 1 Sept 1984

Mr Bill Peters, a former British diplomat, today called for something like a 'Marshall Plan' that would revitalise the Bretton Woods institutions and remove the present serious restrictions on lending to poor countries of the Third World. He was addressing the international Moral Re-Armament conference in Caux, Switzerland.

'The failure of the international financial community to deal with the needs of the Third World is a major source of world tension,' he said.

Mr Peters drew on his experience in Malawi, latterly as High Commissioner, where from 1968 to 1983 he saw a dramatic improvement in nutrition, clothing, transport, educational and medical services. By the end of the period Malawi had started to export surplus maize, even to South Africa. However, after the drought of 1980 and oil price rises Malawi had to appeal to the World Bank and other agencies for foreign exchange and budgetary aid. During the 'Eighties aid had become progressively harder to obtain, he added. Also, between 1975 and 1982 the terms of trade for Malawi had fallen so that they had to export three times as much to keep up the same level of imports. 'Now hunger can be seen again in Malawi and people's standard of living is falling,' said Mr Peters.

He continued, 'World-wide, development projects by the score have been abandoned. Bitterness and disillusionment are spreading through the Third World. One country has already renegued on its debts. If this spread it would spell disaster for economic stability in large parts of the world.' He also felt that disillusionment with the Western system could alter the balance of power in the world. This danger was, in his view, no less than that arising from nuclear confrontation.

Marshall aid had lifted Europe out of recession and destruction after the Second World War, said Mr Peters. Now the leading financial experts and people who run the international financial institutions should be encouraged to work out new mechanisms to make the Bretton Woods arrangements effective once again in lifting Third World countries out of poverty.

One possibility might be a two-tier interest rate system so that countries in dire need could borrow at a lower rate.

'Self-interest dictates change,' said Mr Peters. 'But, much more, if we allowed God to show us how to change the system this would open the way not only for continued existence but also to a better life for millions of people around the world.'

Caux
1 September

Appendix 4

High Level ILO Meeting, 23-25 Nov 1987
Final Document: Conclusions

The international community, through its competent bodies, has in recent months agreed on the main difficulties confronting the world economy which particularly affect the developing countries.

Bearing in mind these agreements, the urgency of the world economic situation and the growing interdependence of the countries of the world, the High Level Meeting adopted the following conclusions.

1. The number of unemployed and of the poor in the world is unacceptably high and, according to latest forecasts, rising. The crushing problem of international indebtedness is affecting all countries. Efforts must be made, by combined and concerted measures both national and international, to achieve employment-generating growth. There is general agreement on what these measures should be, but action is now necessary. Large imbalances remain in the world economy, as evidenced by the recent instability on financial markets, threatening, in an increasingly interdependent world, the prospects for future growth. These imbalances must be reduced and, linked to the promotion of more dynamic and non-inflationary growth, a major effort of world-wide structural adjustment is needed. This can be a painful process and its burden should be shared both among countries and within them. The poorest and most vulnerable groups, including particularly women and young people, should be protected against sharp falls in their levels of income and social protection, while adjustment policies would be designed in such a way that they lead to a growth of employment and incomes.

2. In order to promote sufficient growth to bring about fuller employment and a reduction of poverty, concerted action is needed on the part of the industrialised countries both as regards macro-economic and financial policies and as regards policies for expanded trade, capital flows and aid, backed up by appropriate policies in the developing countries. International organisations should support and facilitate action by governments to this end.

3. The maintenance and extension of an open world trading system is a necessary prerequisite to the efficient and effective promotion of growth, employment and the improvement of living standards. Protectionism in all its various forms will delay needed adjustment and reduce the scope for growth in the world economy. It is unacceptable because it exports unemployment from one country to another.

Appendix 5

The High Level ILO Meeting on Employment and Structural Adjustment

In the meeting at Caux on 28 August 1987 on International Debt and its Social Implications, Francois Blanchard, Director General of the ILO, said that to deal with the enormous third world debt problem (over $1000 billion) and the problem underlying that, the slow progress of and drying up of funds for development in Latin America, Africa and Asia, a concerted effort was required by the entire international financial community. Hitherto a fragmented approach had been adopted with the three main aspects, financial, social and trade treated separately. The conference he planned in November under his own ILO aegis would be the first attempt ever to tackle the problem from all sides in a single comprehensive approach. He likened this to a mountaineer's premier. He even dared to hope that a successful conference would be a turning point.

The Meeting's Context

The ILO High Level Meeting took place in Geneva from 23 to 25 November. It came very soon after the first stock market crash of 1987 which had concentrated the world's mind on the weaknesses of the market economy system. It came at a time when several of the principal parties, notably the governments of the USA, West Germany and Japan were clearly at odds, failing to concert action which might deal with the prevailing instability without causing a depression. Not wholly unrelated to this, however, the two superpowers were nearing an I.N.F. agreement with Shultz and Shevadnaze meeting in Geneva right next to the ILO building and further advances in disarmament were in prospect, being approached with an openness until recently unimaginable.

Participants

Four groups of participants were invited to the High Level Meeting -

Governments, International Organisations involved in social and economic fields, representatives of employers organisations and representatives of workers organisations. Among the governments those from the Third World, who had more directly at stake, showed no reluctance to send imposing delegations. That from Brazil, for example, was led by the Minister for Labour supported by six senior officials. Algeria, Cameroon, Cuba, Ghana, India, Philippines, Syria, Tanzania, Yugoslavia and Venezuela all sent delegations headed by Ministers or Ministers of State. From the Eastern bloc, Hungary sent the State Secretary for Labour and Wages, accompanied by five senior officials. The most notable absentees were from the industrialised countries, particularly the USA, West Germany and Britain. (I had myself made an unsuccessful attempt to secure the attendance of a British official delegation. I was told that the staff who would have to prepare the briefing was too heavily engaged on other matters). But France, Italy, Canada, Australia and Norway sent delegations led by Ministers, and Japan sent the Assistant Minister for International Labour Affairs supported by the Counsellor of their Mission in Geneva.

Among the international organisations, significantly, all were represented and in four cases the delegation was led by the top men ('the crowned heads' as Blanchard put it). These were the Secretary General of the United Nations Conference on Trade and Development (UNCTAD), the President of the International Fund for Agricultural Development (IFAD), the Director General of the General Agreement on Tariffs and Trade (GATT) and the Secretary General of the Organisation for Economic Co-operation and Development (OECD). The World Bank and International Monetary Fund (IMF) both had two-man delegations, the first led by the Director of the Strategic Planning and Review Department in Washington and the second by their top man in Geneva.

The organisations of employers and workers added useful facets to the meeting. Mr. A. Katz, President of the United States Council for International Business and Mr. L. Kirkland, President of the American Federation of Labour and Congress of Industrial Organisations (AFL - C10) ensured that American voices were heard. In a similar category was Mr. E. Breit, President of the German Confederation of Trade Unions. The Australians were strong on all fronts with Mr. J. Clark of Broken Hill Propriety (BHP) representing employers and Mr. S. Crean, who took a leading part in all the meetings including those of the drafting committee, representing workers; he is President of the Australian Council of Trade Unions, successor to Mr. Bob Hawke, now the Australian Prime Minister.

Some old friends like Sr. Jones Santos Neves of Brazil who took a leading role in the Caux meeting, and Naval Tata from Bombay, were among the employers' representatives.

The Plenary Sessions

Plenary sessions of the high level meeting occupied 23 November and most of the 24th. The record is rich in references to the interdependence of the world economy, the need for greater commitment of resources to the World Bank and the IMF to enable structural adjustments to be made in the economies of countries overburdened by debt and to secure minimum standards for the poorest - possibly as many as 80 million now live in absolute poverty - and action to bring about employment - creating growth in industrialised as well as in developing countries. Frequent references were made to protectionism as a principal obstacle to the world-wide free trade, a requirement for interdependence, provoking a sharp response from one US spokesman (Mr. Kirkland) that he was no less opposed to protectionism than any other delegate provided the definition of protectionism covered all its forms. The Brazilian Minister said that the only real solution was the creation of a new international economic order; this theme, recalling earlier unsuccessful attempts to devise a world strategy for debt and poverty, remained in the air but did not appear in the conclusions.

Particular attention was paid to the contribution of the World Bank, the IMF and Japan. The first two both said more resources should be committed to their organisations to enable them to fulfill their respective roles. Both also acknowledged the need to broaden the base of international economic discussions to take in social and employment aspects, as proposed by the I.L.O. Mr. Nakamura traced Japan's course from a defeated and wholly dependent nation to its present position of strength. The change had been wrought by Japan's own efforts and with generous external, primarily American, support, and the boost to demand favouring Japanese industry given by the Korean war. He implied that Japan's example could be followed by other countries now dependent and suffering hardship; nevertheless, he said, his government honoured its obligation to assist developing countries.

Drafting Drama

At the end of the plenary meetings a drafting committee got down to the task of extracting conclusions from the two-day discussion. Its task was not easy and, despite intensive debate until 4.00 am in the morning of 25 November, its first draft was not acceptable to all Committee members. After further debate through the morning and afternoon of 25 November a final version was considered in plenary and, subject to the deletion of one sentence,* unanimously adopted, within minutes of the deadline set by several delegations because they had to catch planes that evening (and departed while the closing formalities were still in progress).

The Conclusions

The conclusions begin by recalling the agreements reached in recent months in the competent bodies of the international community on the main difficulties, particularly those which affect developing countries, now confronting the international community. Foremost among them is the section in the Final Act of UNCTAD VII which says

> The debt crisis is complex and an equitable, durable and mutually agreed solution will be reached only by an approach, based on development within the framework of an integrated, co-operative, growth-oriented strategy that takes into account the particular circumstances of each country. The response to the debt crisis should continue to evolve, through continuous dialogue and shared responsibility, and the strategy should be implemented with flexibility in an environment of strengthened international co-operation.

They also recall the ILO's charter responsibility 'to consider and examine economic and financial policies and measures in the light of their impact on employment and social conditions.'

Action is now urgent, bearing in mind the alarmingly high and rising numbers of the unemployed and poor in the world, to accelerate employment-generating growth the more so as recent instability in the financial markets had emphasized the imbalances which threaten the prospects of future growth. The pain of adjustment should be equitably shared both among countries and within them, with special concern for the most vulnerable groups. Expanded trade, capital flows and cash from the industrialised countries need to be matched by appropriate policies in the developing countries, both being supported and facilitated by international organisations. An open world trading system and the renunciation of most forms of protectionism was another requirement.

The conclusions then go on to specify policies and programmes for more dynamic adjustment and growth in first the industrialised countries and second the developing countries. Next the conclusions formulate the problems common to all countries in building the social consensus necessary for the pursuit of policies that enable adjustment to the changing conditions of an interdependent world economy. Finally there is a detailed examination of the potential for joint action by the international organisations, and in particular the role of the ILO, in promoting socially oriented problems of dynamic adjustment and growth.

The conclusions are concise, specific and wide-ranging and should be read in full to obtain their full impact.

Assessment

The most important feature of the High Level Meeting was that it took place. Moreover, despite the unfavourable financial and economic background, authoritative delegations from a wide variety of governments participated as well as a complete roll of the competent international bodies, four at the level of Director-General or equivalent, and an impressive selection of representatives from employers' and workers' organisations. The discussions were in the main constructive and relevant and the conclusions provide a comprehensive base on which further action can proceed at global level to work out an equitable programme, country by country, for alleviating the burdens of unemployment, poverty, financial instability, economic maldistribution and advancing technology.

Next Steps

The meeting thus sets the scene for a gigantic enterprise. It envisages nothing less than the careful formulation of a highly complex plan to address the problems of debt, poverty and unemployment. This must be acceptable to all the concerned governments, international bodies and employers' and workers' organisations. The difficulties ahead were well illustrated at the meeting through the near failure because of reservations by important delegations to arrive at conclusions which could be accepted by the plenary body.

The Pope sent a message to the Meeting expressing his interest 'in all negotiations aimed at ensuring the dignity and well-being of human beings.' Earlier, during his October visit to the USA, he stressed the need for a global approach to the financial, economic and social issues which confront the world community. This is in line with the paper, 'An Ethical Approach to the International Debt Question' produced by the Pontifical Commission 'Justitia et Pax' and commended to us at Caux on 28 August by Monsignor Mullor Garcia, Papal Nuncio in Geneva. Francis Blanchard's hope, then expressed, that the High Level Meeting might be a turning point will be fulfilled if the conclusions formulated on 25 November generate action across the widest possible spectrum on the lines they suggest. To bring this about much sustained work is needed in many places, not least to ensure that a leavening of the principal actors gives full weight to ethical considerations as well as to the pragmatic and technical ones which produce their decisions.

W Peters
Geneva
3 December 1987

* The excised sentence is 'The ILO should stand ready to explore with the other international bodies concerned the promotion of the observance of basic international labour standards as a factor contributing to the reduction of trade tensions.'

Appendix 6

International Debt Question, Caux, Switzerland, 25-27 August 1988,

'Make sure what would have the Lord's approval' (St Paul - Ephesians, 5.10)

Background

Following the introduction of the theme of Third World indebtedness at general meetings in Caux in 1985 and 1986 when the interest in the topic of a wide cross-section became evident, a meeting to deal specifically with debt was arranged in August 1987. This satisfied a wish expressed by the Director General of the ILO, M Francis Blanchard, to discuss the human and social consequences of the debt with interested persons 'in the atmosphere of Caux'.

Later, several Caux participants attended the High Level Meeting organised in November 1987 by the ILO at M Blanchard's initiative. The meeting drew in for the first time significant representation from all the international organisations whose work is touched by the debt issue (as well as governments, employers' organisations and trade-union federations) and concluded, *inter alia*, that the debt issue could not be realistically processed without attention to the social and human consequences of the debt and the link between international trade and employment.

At the August 1987 meeting in Caux, His Excellency Bishop Mullor Garcia, Head of the Holy See Mission in Geneva, introduced the paper by the Pontifical Commission *Iustitia et Pax* entitled 'to the service of the human community : an ethical approach to the international debt question'. This was taken as the background text for further meetings in Caux on 25, 26 and 27 August 1988 which considered Third World indebtedness. The meetings ran parallel with discussions on the theme 'Men, Money and Morality' by the Industrial Forum, which itself followed a Round Table on economic topics for senior businessmen from Japan, Europe and North America.

The attached annex gives a list of persons who attended, *inter alia*, the 1988 Caux Debt meetings.

Progress achieved

At his request this group gave Mgr Mejia, Vice-President of the *Iustitia et Pax* Commission, their view whether progress had been made in dealing with indebtedness since publication of the Commission paper. The answer was affirmative, with the following especially noted:

a) The IMF's Structural Adjustment facility for loans in concessional terms to poorer developing countries with severe balance of payments facilities had increased by some $8,000 million.

b) Some governments, including those of Britain and Canada had converted old aid loans into grants for a group of sub-Saharan African countries. This debt forgiveness, although limited in scale and in practice, operated through the Paris Club mechanism in association with debt rescheduling, represented a new departure.

c) Active consideration was now being given to multi-tier interest rates on the debts of the least developed countries together with other alleviations for debt rescheduling of LDCs, such as longer grace periods.

d) Co-responsibility for debts was now widely acknowledged while the examination of short term (emergency) measures had produced better co-operation between governments and international financial institutions. (A great need remained for more progress in medium and long term adjustments.)

e) MIGA (The Multilateral Investment Guarantee Administration) had been established as an arm of the World Bank under a Japanese, Mr Yoshio Terasawa.

f) A substantial menu of alleviatory measures had been constructed from which debtor countries could choose the items most appropriate to their circumstances (eg debt/equity swaps).

g) A measure of international exchange rate control had been achieved.

h) The recession feared in October 1987 after the stock market crashes had not materialised and anxieties over the world banking system had not been fulfilled. However, before credit-worthiness could be restored, essential conditions to be fully satisfied embraced

    (1) Improved policies by many debtor country governments,

    (2) Identification of substantial sources of finances,

        a. Commercial for new developments in LDCs,

        b. Non-commercial (IFIs and governments) for new development and for debt adjustment,

(3)   Amelioration of conditions in the international financial system.

Discussion

In general discussion it was acknowledged that a grave complication of the debt issue was the lack of new income-earning development in many debtor countries. Its absence exacerbated the difficulty of repaying debts and in some cases even servicing them. New loans for development would come only when confidence in debtor countries had been restored; they would need to be insulated from the debt servicing and repayment processes. Substantial resources for debt/equity and other similar swaps were unlikely to be forthcoming and might, in any case, prove unsatisfactory if organised on too large a scale. It was also submitted that the reforms would require substantial changes of attitude and moral conduct in industrialised and debtor countries.

To the question whether positive new flows of resources from developed to less developed countries are desirable, however, a simple affirmative answer was necessary.

Once that was acknowledged, positive progress to achieve the desired result could be devised, provided the political will was there. That, in turn required restoration of confidence in the economies of debtor countries and transparency in some activities of governments and international financial institutions.

In examining the role of Caux in continuing attempts to solve the debt problem, the group recognised that it was not their function to attempt to devise solutions. They were not qualified to do so. In any case, solutions were the responsibility of those in the international community charged with the relevant functions. Caux could be of value as a sympathetic location in which parties directly involved might be brought together, including the Pontifical Commission, should they decide to continue their involvement. The group thought the Holy See should do so because it was eminently well qualified to emphasize to Christians the ethical aspects of the problem and its solutions, as well as the antecedent factors which had contributed to the problem, such as capital flight.

Caux could also function as a centre for efforts to prepare informed public opinion for the steps which governments, bankers and international financial civil servants would have to take to resolve the problem. In 1989 a conference at Caux on the debt issue might be timely in relation to the global conference on new world economic balance which President

Mitterrand had indicated he might organize in France in 1990. Its value could be enhanced if it could be organised around a few well known personalities.

Further initiatives considered

At the end of the session on 25 August, Mgr Mejia asked the group for answers to the following questions:

a)   As a sequel to their publication of 'An ethical approach to the international debt question', should the Holy See engage in further exchanges with the World Bank and possibly the IMF?

b)   Should they, further, become involved with senior commercial bankers on the same topic?

c)   Would a further initiative by the Holy See on the New International Economic Order be timely?

The group offers answers to these questions as follows:

a)   It is highly desirable that the Holy See should increase its exchange with senior World Bank and IMF personnel. The stimulus of 'An ethical approach to the international debt question' has been entirely beneficial. It would be all the more effective for being directed also to policy makers in debtor and creditor governments and banks. The Bank of International Settlements, Basel, might also be drawn into their exchanges. A prime objective would be the opening of windows of communication between parts of the international financial structure which do not at present communicate, to the detriment of the effort at globalization.

b)   It is also desirable that the Holy See be involved in exchanges with senior commercial bankers. To this end, the group records a proposal made by Mr Rinaldo Brutoco, President of the World Business Academy and participant in the Caux Round Table. He is currently engaged in consultations about a paper on the international debt issue which emphasizes the higher efficiency of solutions founded in moral considerations. He has offered to correspond with some members of the Group about holding a conference in New York at which those interested in the moral aspects of the problem might meet a substantial cross-section of senior commercial bankers. The group thinks this might provide an opportunity for

Pontifical Commission exchanges with the bankers to whom this question relates and was ready to offer the help of their members if needed. It is for consideration whether Europeans and Japanese bankers should be drawn into a New York conference, or a separate conference in Europe. (Muslim, Buddhists and other non-Christian bankers also need consideration.)

c)   The concept of a New International Economic Order is highly volatile and subject to widely different interpretations. One thought discussed by the Group is that in the search for a global solution the concept of bankruptcy, with a clean slate being established after company breakdowns, might be integrated at the international level (ie in relation to national economies). A global solution would have to embrace trade flows and terms of trade. An issue of immediate concern is the lack of congruence between European and American views on the trade in cereals.

Conclusion

While the Group considered that Caux should not be involved in the formulation of technical solutions to the debt problem, it was felt that Caux could play a positive role in providing a sympathetic location where parties directly involved could meet, in clarifying and underlying the moral dimension of the problem and in formulating questions relative to social and human aspects which could be put to protagonists to assist them in their task.

The 1989 programme for Caux should be drawn up with the above discussion in mind. Depending on the responses received to this paper planning might be centred on a more structured but still limited discussion of the debt problem in 1989, possibly in association with a further Round Table conference.

WP/MS 29.06.88

Annex: List of Participants

Mgr Jorge Mejia, Vice-President of the Pontifical Commission *Iustitia et Pax*.
Mr Jean-Michel Servais, from the office of the Director-General of the ILO, representing M Francois Blanchard
Mr Maurice Hel-Bongo, from the staff of ILO
Mr Eduardo Wiesner, head of the Geneva office of the IMF
Mr Jean-Loup Dherse, formerly from the World Bank
Mr Chris Barrett, from the Institute of International Finance, Washington
Mr Pierre Lanquetin, former Governor (until April 1988) of the Swiss National Bank
Mr Arnold Smith CH, former Secretary General of the Commonwealth
Mr Neville Cooper, Chairman of Institute of Business Ethics, London
Mr Otacilio Canavarros, President, Confederation of Industry for the State of Mato Grosso
Mr William Peters, former British Ambassador to Uruguay
Mr Archibald R J Mackenzie, former British Ambassador, from the staff of the Brandt Commission
Mr Allan Griffith, former adviser to the Prime Minister of Australia
Mr Gherhard Grob, President of the Moral Re-Armament Foundation, Lucerne
Mr Daniel Mottu, from the Moral Re-Armament office in Geneva

Appendix 7

The Hon Helen Liddell MP
Economic Secretary to the Treasury
Treasury Chambers
Parliament Street
London SW1P 3AG

JUBILEE 2OOO
A debt-free start for a billion people

27 August 1997

Dear Economic Secretary

*   *   *   *   *

It is the intention of Jubilee 2000 and the Jubilee 2000 Coalition to build pressure worldwide for the comprehensive remission by 2000 of the unpayable public debts on a case-by-case basis of some 50 highly indebted poor countries already identified in the HIPC Initiative. We and our allies in other countries are extending our already wide appeal globally, recruiting supporters for our petition on an inter-continental and inter-faith basis. The aim is to assist decision takers in governments and IFIs to summon the necessary political will. The precise formulation and its justification are available, as I said, in Jubilee 2000 papers which your Department already hold. We emphasise that by pressing for a detailed remission package for each debtor country we address the matter which you mention of the need for 'balanced economic reform programmes to ensure (sustainable) economic development leading to lasting poverty reduction' and for 'policies in debtor countries which promote economic and social development'; as we envisage them, those 'conditionalities' framed in the wider context will be more palatable to debtor governments than anything that has so far emanated from the IMF or the World Bank.

The debate in the House of Lords initiated by my friend Richard Harries, the Bishop of Oxford, has, if they were needed, provided many arguments in favour of a more generous and timely remission of debts than the IFIs proposed. Winding up that debate for the Government Lord McIntosh of

256

Harringey was generous in setting a high value on the work of Jubilee 2000 and Christian Aid in raising awareness in the UK of the debt problem. His suggestion that we use the next couple of years to exert pressure internationally is very well taken. We are seeking to encompass just that. May I add that we have constructed a political case on realpolitik grounds showing creditor governments that they will serve many of their own interests, mainly non-economic, by generous and timely remission. No doubt your staff can fill out similar ideas, but they are welcome to ours if they should wish to have them. Suffice to say here that these grounds include low intensity conflict, economic migration, drug production, environmental protection and unemployment in industrial countries. Lord McIntosh touched on some of these last, recognising that 'there are economic costs for us all in world poverty as well as the costs of instability - we benefit from successful development of the poorest countries.' (It would be interesting to know whether the Treasury economic model has been applied to assessing the effects on HIPC economies and our own of substantial remission. It seems obvious that a globalised economy which is fully active would be healthier than one in which two fifths of the whole are non-functioning. Lord McIntosh also cited among a range of helpful measures 'opening our own markets to the exports of poor countries'. There are currently EU limits on such exports; does his remark foreshadow a stronger effort by HMG to reduce these limits? Will they also oppose continued dumping of agricultural surpluses?)

In describing the HIPC Initiative as one among several 'available to us', Lord McIntosh opens up wider vistas. Jubilee 2000's objective for the remainder of the decade centres on a sustained effort, using political as well as economic arguments, to move the IFIs and fellow members of OECD from their present reluctant attitude to debt remission to one which allows a genuine liberation for the poorest elements in the indebted countries - as our slogan says 'a fresh start for a billion people'. We think this can be achieved in an important respect by demonstrating to creditors that the benefits of generous remission are more than enough to justify the sacrifices they are asked to make; (at net current values the costs to them will be much less than the recorded figures, and the IFIs hold resources which could meet a considerable proportion of those costs without endangering their triple A status and the integrity of their principal operations. The responses of our supporters suggest that at grass roots there is a readiness to accept a share of the sacrifices). We believe that, as a riposte to generous treatment, a detailed declaration is possible from the debtor countries, factored by leaders such as Mandela, of intention *inter alia* to avoid future unsustainable debt, to limit corruption, to concentrate on sustainable development with balanced social provision and to maintain transparent accountancy and audit procedures.

We realise that politics is the art of the possible; HMG is constrained to work within the limits which OECD members and the IFIs can tolerate. But we hope that our own efforts in building support internationally for generous remission will enable you to hold out for exceptional terms, leaving aside such polarities of language as remission v. relief, which could close a large part of the gap between our expressed objective of a one-off clearing of the slate and your requirement to work within the bounds of financial practice (and prudence) and the need to maintain a common front among the creditors. This hope is reinforced by the facts that political realignments among G7 members are changing and that there is much convergence of principle between the White House and No.10.

*   *   *   *   *

Yours sincerely

W Peters
Co-Founder, Jubilee 2000

Appendix 8

Redemption from Debt Bondage
for a new-start UHURU

Accra Declaration.

We, *participants from Afrika, Asia, Europe, Latin America and North America, attending the Jubilee 2000 Afrika launch in Accra, Ghana from 16-18 April 1998,*

Having *reflected on and discussed the debt crisis in Afrika and its effects on the people of the Continent*

CONSIDERING

That *the root causes of these debts lie in the history of slavery and colonialism*

That *the debt issue is a function of the unjust system of international trade and investment and of unaccountable government*

That *the conditions and policies that constitute the framework for the repayment of these debts are unjustified instruments of control of the destiny of Afrikan people*

That *Afrika has paid by way of debt servicing far more than the original loans contracted and that currently for every $1 in grant to Afrika, the developed world takes out of Afrika $3*

NOTING

The *general failure of IMF and World Bank policies and prescriptions in Afrika.*

That *the international financial institutions are inefficient, undemocratic, non transparent and unaccountable in their dealings with Afrika and undermine our sovereignty*

That *these debts are simply unpayable and that Afrika will continue to be in economic bondage and its ability to develop be blocked unless the debt burden is eliminated*

CONCERNED ABOUT

The *inability of governments in Afrika to alleviate, let alone eliminate mass poverty*

CONVINCED THAT

Writing *off these debts, as was the case with Britain and Germany after the Second World War, would have negligible impact on international financial institutions and markets*

HEREBY DEMAND

(1) The immediate and unconditional cancellation of Afrika's external debts

(2) That all the gains from debt cancellation be re-channelled into social services, in particular, education, health and housing

(3) That good governance, accountability and responsibility in Afrikan States be part and parcel of the conditions before new loans are contracted

(4) That accountability, transparency and democracy be established in the structures and operations of the international lending institutions

(5) That the current system of international trade and investment be restructured so that Afrika can be free to develop its resources for the benefit of its people

(6) That organisations of civil society be actively consulted and involved by both lending institutions and Afrikan Governments in loan transactions

TO THIS END WE CALL:

For *the formation of Jubilee 2000 National Coalitions across the Continent embracing the whole spectrum of civil society and its organisations in Afrika to spearhead the active mobilisation of Afrikan people in the campaign to eliminate the debt burden.*

On *religious bodies to stand up to their moral obligation and fulfil their prophetic mission of defending the voiceless*

On *other Jubilee 2000 Coalitions to sustain and deepen their solidarity with the Jubilee 2000 Afrika Campaign*

FINALLY:

We dedicate ourselves to the Jubilee 2000 Afrika Campaign for the elimination of the debt burden so that Afrika will have the opportunity of harnessing its human and natural resources for development and transformation as we enter the 21st Millenium

ACCRA, 19th APRIL 1998

Appendix 9

A Jubilee Call for Debt Cancellation and Economic Justice
Rome, 17 November 1998

At the dawn of the third millennium people all over the world hear the Jubilee call for a new beginning, aware that two thirds are impoverished by the global economic and political system. People have transformed the world before and it is time to do so again. Nourishing hope, we continue in our determination to overcome world-wide injustice to establish equitable relationships between all who share this planet. As one necessary step, we are committed to justice in resolving the debt crisis. We insist that current initiatives for debt relief are not just, comprehensive, or effective in addressing the problems of the debt crisis and of development.

We are gathered in Rome as 38 national Jubilee 2000 campaigns from all continents and 12 international organisations. We come from diverse contexts and experiences combining our efforts to participate in a common movement for debt cancellation: Jubilee 2000. Our diversity is a strength in this campaign.

We are united in the call for debt cancellation by the year 2000, including:

1) Unpayable debt, which is debt that cannot be serviced without placing a burden on impoverished people.
2) Debt that in real terms has already been paid.
3) Debt for improperly designed policies and projects.
4) Odious debt and debt incurred by repressive regimes.

Creditor governments, international financial institutions and commercial banks, which are chiefly responsible for the debt crisis, should not set the conditions for debt cancellation. Civil society in the South must play a significant and influential role in a transparent and participatory process which will define and then monitor the use of resources released by debt for the benefit of the impoverished.

Lending, borrowing, and debt negotiation must reflect a just relationship between debtors and creditors. Transparent and independent arbitration should be available to cancel debt.

This is a call to urgent action. Lives have been destroyed and damage has been done. On the eve of the new millennium, the time for a new beginning is now.

Rome, 17 November 1998
(Adopted at the first Jubilee 2000 International Conference, Rome, 17 November 1998)

Appendix 10

Declaration in Support of the Southern Africa Apartheid Debt Campaign, Rome, 17 November 1998

Gathered in Rome as 38 national Jubilee 2000 campaigns and 12 International Organisations from around the world, we declare our full support for the campaign to cancel the odious apartheid debt of South Africa and the odious apartheid-caused debts of the Southern African region.

Denounced as a crime against humanity, apartheid is now forcing its victims to pay twice over for their suffering. Apartheid devastated the whole of Southern Africa, not just South Africa. The apartheid regime sponsored wars and economic destabilisation throughout the Southern African region, forcing the region into heavy debt. This debt continues to drain huge amounts of money which seriously limits efforts by the region to recover from the apartheid legacy.

The struggle against apartheid continues until all apartheid's debts have been cancelled in Southern Africa. The world-wide Jubilee 2000 coalition calls for the cancellation of the odious apartheid debts by the year 2000.

(Adopted at the first Jubilee 2000 International Conference, Rome, 17 November 1998)

Appendix 11

International Network - Jubilee 2000

The Jubilee 2000 petition has been signed by people from all of the following countries:

Algeria	Finland*	Niger
Angola*	France*	Nigeria*
Argentina*	Georgia	Norway*
Armenia	Germany*	Pakistan
Australia*	Ghana*	Papua New Guinea
Austria*	Greece	Peru*
Belarus -	Guadeloupe	Philippines
Belgium *	Guatemala	Poland*
Benin	Holland	Portugal*
Bolivia*	Honduras*	Romania
Botswana	Hungary	Russia
Brazil	Iceland	Rwanda*
Burkina Faso*	India*	Slovakia
Cameroon*	Indonesia	Solomon Jslands
Canada*	Iran	South Africa*
Cayman Islands	Italy*	Spain*
Chad	Japan*	Sri Lanka
Chile	Kazakstan	St Vincent
China	Kenya*	Sweden*
Colombia	Lebanon	Switzerland
Congo (DRC)	Lesotho	Taiwan
Costa Rica	Malaysia	Tanzania*
Cote d'Ivoire*	Malawi	Trinidad
Cuba	Malta	Turkey
Czech Republic	Mauritius	Uganda*
Denmark*	Mexico	Ukraine
Ecuador*	Micronesia	Uruguay
Egypt	Morocco	United Kingdom
Eire*	Namibia	USA*
Estonia	Nepal	Venezuela
Ethiopia*	New Zealand*	Zambia*
Fiji Islands	Nicaragua	Zimbabwe

* Countries with coalitions established (countries that have coalitions but have not yet sent petitions are Mozambique, Guyana & Haiti)

264

Appendix 12

A Background Paper for the Bishops' Meeting on the International Debt Crisis, July 1994

JUBILEE 2000

We are talking about countries which the World Bank calls 'Seriously Indebted Low-Income Countries' (SILICs). Most of them are in Africa. There, only countries like Botswana, Cameroon and South Africa escape this classification. In Asia countries like Bangladesh, Nepal, Cambodia and Myanmar fall into it. SILICs' indebtedness began to be insoluble around 1982 when capital flows, resulting from the enormous surpluses of petro-dollars from OPEC countries, prodigally farmed out via Western banks to their own advantage, began to dry up. These debts added to debts owed to the international financial institutions (Bretton Woods - World Bank, International Monetary Fund, Regional Development Banks) and to OECD governments. The total indebtedness of the Third World to the three types of creditor now stands at well over $1 trillion (one million million dollars).

Alleviations have been attempted, some through the Bretton Woods institutions. The principal method is the rescheduling of debts carried out in Paris (the Paris Club) at separate sessions, involving all OECD creditors on one side and the debtor on the other. The rescheduling adjusts principal and interest repayments, generally extending the term of repayment, ensuring unavoidably that the debtor remains in debt for the foreseeable future. Structural adjustment programmes must be undertaken by the debtors, almost invariably involving devaluation of their currencies and severe reductions in service budgets for health, education and social support. In human terms this means that the deprivation already suffered by the poorer sections of the debtor countries' population is multiplied, leading to starvation and death at worst (which are very common), and unimaginable - for any OECD citizen - deprivation at best. In SILICs, on average, one fifth of the minuscule income *($650* p.a. mean) of a peasant farmer goes to service this debt. At the same time the value of his product, if sold for money, has diminished steadily through global pricing of commodities which, on market principles, reduces the return to producers and the cost to (OECD) consumers. The price movement of essential products from OECD countries, like fertiliser, is strongly in the *other* direction. The debt payments of SILICs are more than the total they spend on health and education combined; and that, proportionately, is 4% of what is spent in OECD countries for those purposes.

Other alleviations have been outright remission of government-to-government loans, in which HMG has taken a leading part (the Trinidad terms), and American schemes (the Baker and Brady plans) skewed to the wealthiest indebted countries (e.g. Argentina, Brazil, Mexico) and designed to provide them with development credits to increase their revenue earning and debt repayment capacity. The effect of the G7 decision, taken in Naples on 9 July by participating governments, to remit on select conditions two-thirds of the debt owed to them by SILIC Governments, remains to be seen.

There is growing, general recognition in international financial circles that this outflow of resources from the poorest areas of the earth to the richest cannot continue much longer. Increasingly it is acknowledged that after 50 years the Bretton Woods' structures, supporting the rich and penalising the poor, need radical overhaul. Since 1986 the Vatican has been restating 'the priority to be granted to people and their needs, above and beyond the constraints and financial mechanisms often advanced as the only imperatives' *(Justitia et Pax Commission - 'At the service of the Human Community')*. More recently Gorringe says *('Capital and the Kingdom')* 'The assumptions behind the world economy, dictated by the economic superpowers . . threaten us all with disaster.' Kairos Europa has just ended a widespread (three continents) campaign calling into question the Bretton Woods structures.

At the beginning of the last century it was argued against the Abolitionists (of slavery) that their campaign, if successful, would undermine the established economic order. The same is now being said of those who campaign about Third World debt. The two obscenities - slavery and debt slavery - have much in common. To demand of a man with a family and an income, if he is lucky, of $650 p.a. to pay $385 per head to liquidate debts which have done him no good **without feeding, clothing or housing him** is not very different from treating him as a maintained chattel; some would say even worse. *Jubilee,* first envisioned in Deuteronomy and Leviticus, aimed, as an act of higher justice, to remove their burden from the most economically oppressed among the ha-pi-ru. Economists are wrong to reject the possibility of acts of international altruism just as Adam Smith was wrong to name self-interest as the only economic motive worth considering in economic theory. Steps are already being taken to have the year 2000 recognised by U.N. as a year of Jubilee, for the remission of the unrepayable parts of Third World debts (with necessary conditions to cover corruption, malversion, sloth and theft).

As the nineteenth century churches swung the balance in favour of the Abolitionists, so now a coalition of the churches and non-government organisations might do the same for debt slavery, by encouraging at the grass roots an outcry against the slavery of debt. Let them question financiers, bankers and politicians, from Ministers down, about Third World debt. Let them make it clear, to the last named especially, that they and their congregations don't want a world system which starves the poorest and engrosses the rich, even if this means abandoning promises to voters of continually rising living standards. Let them challenge the orthodox structures laid down by the World Bank and the IMF, particularly those protecting their own credits. Let them back strongly the vision of an 'acceptable year of the Lord', as valid for 2000 A.D. as it was for those who recorded it in Leviticus.

Bill Peters, Deal, Kent
July 1994

(Circulated at the request of the Bishop of Dover)

Appendix 13

The Third Fisheries Project in Bangladesh

This example is the Third Fisheries Project in Bangladesh, which ran for the first few years of this decade. It is unusual in that in concept and technology it was really a superb project. The principle contractors were also excellent. Briefly it involved breeding and buying millions of fish fingerlings (carp varieties), and inserting them into the rice fields just after planting, as the rice fields flooded at monsoon time. The fish and the rice benefited each other during growth, and when the floods subsided, both rice and fish were harvested.

The price of these fingerlings before the project began was 60 takas per kilo, and it was known that the price should drop to 45 takas. Instead the price rose to 120 takas once the World Bank's funds flooded the market. As the producers of fish fingerlings were poor peasants, only literate in Bengali, the sensible way to buy the fingerlings should have been through numerous small contracts written in Bengali.

However, such a straightforward procedure was not normal for the World Bank. Nor was it deemed transparent. Instead it insisted upon its standard documentation in English and limited the number of possible contractors to 9, each winner being therefore responsible for the supply of a large tonnage of baby fish. Documentation included a 40 page pre-qualification process preceded by advertisement, which all lasted several months. This was followed by further advertisement for the actual bidding. Bidding documents had to be purchased after those who had previously pre-qualified answered. Award of contracts started with press publicity and public opening.

Unsurprisingly the eventual winners were not the actual breeders of fish, but turned out to be 'musclemen' or 'mastans'. These men cornered the market, went about armed, and fixed the prices by cornering the actual breeders. They operated at a distance from the specified paddy fields, and fish mortality was high. In subsequent years the procedure was repeated exactly, with no rating allowed for the quality of previous performance. The excellent consultants employed for this project, wishing to correct the situation, eventually decided to issue contracts to some actual breeders in a small way of business, whose prices were proved to be lower and quality higher. They then told the World Bank what they had done, which reacted with horror, and told them to go back to the prescribed methods.

Ancillary contracts were handled with the same insensitivity. At a critical stage the fingerlings had to be dropped into the water and held in a small net for an hour before being released. This required a cheap temporary structure made of bamboo and corrugated iron. It only needed to last one month but again a 40 page bidding document in English with drawings was called for, with the same drastic effect upon price. The project required the supply of certain goods such as scales and lifts, and the purchase of these was started as soon as the project began. Once again the full World Bank documentation was deemed necessary, the contract winner being a middleman in Dhaka who subcontracted to another middleman in Singapore, who performed the actual buying. Prices paid were inflated, and goods only began to arrive when the project was 2/3rds completed.

Bibliography

African Development Bank, (1997), *African Development Report, 1997*, Oxford, O.U.P.

Annan, K. (1998), 'The Causes of Conflict and the Promotion of Durable Peace and Sustainable Development in Africa', *Report of the UN Secretary-General to the Security Council*; United Nations.

Arrowsmith, S. and Davies, R. (ed.), (1998), 'Public Procurement: Global Revolution', Klauser Law International, The Hague Chapter by T. Tucker: 'A critical analysis of Procurement Procedure at the World Bank'.

Atherton, J. (1992), 'Christianity and the Market', *Christian Social Thought for Our Time*, SPCK, London.

Atherton, J. (1996), 'Jubilee & Justice'. U.S.P.G. Thinking Mission No. 32.

Blackburn, R. (1988), *The Overthrow of Colonial Slavery, 1776 to 1848* Verso, London.

Bowlby, Rt. Rev. R.O. (1996), *Third World Debt, What are the Ethical Issues?* Unpublished lecture, Essex University, January 1996.

Brandt, W. et al. (1980), *North-South: A Program for Survival*, Pan, London.

Bread for the World, (1998), *Hunger in a Global Economy*, Silver Spring, Maryland.

Brookings Dialogue on Public Policy (1989), *Third World Debt, the Next Phase*, Brookings Institute, Washington.

Brown, B.M. (1997*), An African Road to Development: Are we all Romantics?* Leeds African Bulletin, No.62, 1997.

Buxton, C. (1849), *Memoirs of Sir Thomas Fowell Buxton*, John Murray, London.

Christian Aid (1991), *Banking on the Poor, the Ethics of Third World Debt*, London.

Christian Aid (ed) Willey, E. and Bank, J. (1998), *Proclaim Liberty*, Christian Aid, London.

Cohen, B.J. (1980), 'Developing Country Debt a Middle Way', published in *Essays in International Finance*, No. 173, the Department of Economics, Princeton University.

Commons, House of (5 May 1988), *Report of House of Commons International Development Committee on Debt Relief*, HMSO, London.

Commonwealth Secretariat (1987), *Persistent Indebtedness: The Need for Further Action*. A Study. London.

Davis, J. (ed.) (1993), *World on Loan*, Bible Society, London.

Donmen, E. (1989), *Righting the Debt Burden – Some Sidelights from History*. UNCTAD Review Vol.1, No.1

Duchrow, U. (1995), *Alternatives to Global Capitalism, Drawn from Biblical History, Designed for Political Action*, International Books, Utrecht.

Duchrow, U. and Springe, C. (1991). *Beyond the Death of Socialism. Visions from Germany on Alternatives to Capitalism.* Trans. Keith Archer, The William Temple Foundation. Occasional Paper No.19.

Etchegaray, R. (Cardinal), (1996), 'Millenium Jubilee; Church Event Challenge to Society' *Pope VI Memorial Lecture,* CAFOD and Tablet, London.

EURODAD (1996), *World Credit Tables - Creditors' Claims on Debtors Exposed,* EURODAD, Brussels.

Finer, S.E. (1998), 'Ancient Monarchies and Empires' *History of Government from the Earliest Times, Vol. 1,* Oxford University Press, Oxford.

George, S. (1989), *A Fate Worse than Debt,* Penguin, London.

George, S. (1989), *The Debt Boomerang,* Penguin, London.

George, S. and Sabelli, F. (1994), *Faith and Credit: The World Bank's Secular Empire,* Penguin, London.

Gonzalez, J.L. (1997), *Faith and Wealth; a History of Early Christian Ideas on the Origin and Use of Money,* Harper and Roe, San Francisco.

Gorringe, T.J. (1994), *Capital and the Kingdom: Theological Ethics and Economic Order,* SPCK, London.

Gorringe, T.J. (1996), *Debt and Mission.* U.S.P.G. Thinking Mission No. 27.

Government of Switzerland, (1994), *The Swiss Debt Reduction Facility: A New Instrument of Development Cooperation.* Federal Office for Foreign Economic Affairs paper for Seminar on External Finance for Low Income Developing Countries: The Debt Dimension, Geneva, 19-20 May 1994.

Green, D. (1995), *The Silent Revolution: the Rise of Market Economics in Latin America.* Latin American Bureau.

Green, D.G. (1993), *Reinventing Civil Society: the Rediscovery of Welfare Without Politics.* I.E.A., Choice in Welfare No. 17, London.

Gutierrez, G. (1974, revised edition 1988, reprinted 1993 and 1996). *A Theology of Liberation.* SCM Press, London.

Hanlon, J. (1998), *What will it Cost to Cancel Unpayable Debt?* Jubilee 2000 Coalition, London.

Holy Bible, esp. Deuteronomy, Leviticus, Isaiah, and the Gospel according to Luke.

Holy Q'uran, esp. Chapters 2, 3 and 90.

Hussein, I. and Diwan, I. (eds.) (1989), *Dealing with the Debt Crisis,* World Bank, Washington

Hutton, W. (1995), *The State We're In,* Vintage Books, London.

Joseph, M.P. (1991), *Third World Debt, First World Responsibility,* Centre for Theology and Public Issues, Edinburgh.

Killick, T. (1995), 'Solving the Multilateral Debt Problem: Reconciling Relief with Acceptability'. A Report to the Commonwealth Secretariat.

Kraske, J, et. al. (1996), *Bankers with a Mission,* OUP, New York.

Lever, H. and Huhne, C. (1986), 'Debt and Danger, the World Financial Crisis', *Atlantic Monthly Press,* New York.

Logan, P. (1997), 'Biblical Reflections on the Political Economy of Jubilee'. Occasional Paper of Southwark Diocesan Board for Church in Society, London.

Miller, M. (1991), *Debt and the Environment, Converging Crisis,* United Nations Publications, New York.

Mistry, P.S. (1989), *African Debt: the Case for Relief for Sub-Saharan Africa,* Oxford International Associates.

Mistry, P.S. (1991), *African Debt Revisited: Procrastination or Progress,* Fondad, The Hague.

Mistry, P.S. (1995), *A Response to the IMF and the World Bank. The Multilateral Debt Problem: Lurching towards Resolution?* Oxfam Seminar on Multilateral Debt, Sept '95.

Mistry, P.S. (1996), *Regional Integration Arrangements in Economic Development: Panacea or Pitfall?* Fondad, The Hague.

Mistry, P.S. (1996), *Resolving Africa's Multilateral Debt Problem.* Fondad, The Hague.

Novak, M. (1991), *The Spirit of Democratic Capitalism,* IEA Health and Welfare Unit, London.

Nyerere, J. (1987), Introduction, *The Challenge of the South.* South Commission, OUP, Oxford.

ODI. *Africa's Multilateral Debt: A Modest Proposal.* All Parliamentary Group on Overseas Development. (1994)

Parkinson, W. (1980), *This Gilded African,* Quartet Books, London.

Pettifor, A. (1996), *Debt, the Most Potent Form of Slavery,* Debt Crisis Network, London.

Pettifor, A. (1998), 'The Economic Bondage of Debt and the Birth of a New Movement; How We Surrounded G8' *New Left Review, 230,* July - August.

Pettifor, A. (1996), *Jubilee and the Remission of Debt, a New Fight Against Slavery,* unpublished evidence to the Bossey Conference on Jubilee.

Pettifor, A. and Joyner, K. (1997), *The United Kingdom as Creditor to the World's Poor.* Debt Crisis Network.

Pettifor, A. and Wood, A. (1996), *A Fresh Start for Africa,* Debt Crisis Network, Inter-Church House, Lower Marsh Street, London.

Pontifical Commission *'Justitia et Pax'* (1992), *At the Service of the Human Community: An Ethical Approach to the International Debt Question.* Social and Ethical Aspects of Economics. Vatican City.

Pope John Paul II (1994), Tertio Millennio Adveniente (Apostolic Letter) Catholic Truth Society.

Preston, R. (1991), *Religion and the Ambiguities of Capitalism,* SCM, London.

Richardson, K. Hollis, Rt. Rev. R. Reid, Rt. Rev. G. (1996), *Churches Together in England,* Church House, London.

Rowland, C. (1988), *Radical Christianity: A Reading of Recovery,* Polity Press, Cambridge.

Rowland, C. and Comer, M. (1990), *Liberating Exegesis: the Challenge of Liberation Theology in Biblical Studies.* SPCK, London.

Selby, P. Rt. Rev. (1997), *Grace and Mortgage,* Dartman, Longman and Todd, London.

Sen, A. et al. (1992), Social and Ethical Aspects of Economics. Vatican City.

The Debt for Development Coalition Inc. (1993) 'Debt for Development Conversions in the Context of the Debt Reduction Facility for IDA-only Countries', Prepared for the Project Financial Group of The World Bank.

Short, C. (1997), 'Eliminating World Poverty'. *A Challenge for the 21st Century.* White Paper on International Development.

Spray, P. (1991), 'The Abolition of the International Debt Trade' *Third World Debt, First World Responsibility.* Centre for Theology and Public Issues, Edinburgh.

Stein, H. (1998), *Rethinking Stabilisation & Structural Adjustment in Africa: Towards a Critique of Classical Development Economics.* Lecture delivered in Cambridge on 26 October 1998.

Stewart, F. and Daws, S. (1996), *Global Challenges: The Case for an U.N. Economic and Social Security Council.* Christian Aid, Viewpoint Series 10.

Stiglitz, J. (1998), *More Instruments and Broader Goals: Moving Towards the Post-Washington Consensus,* Wider Annual Lecture delivered in Helsinki 7 January 1998.

Strange, S. 'The New World of Debt', *New Left Review,* 230, July-August 1998.

Taylor, M. (1995), *Not Angels, but Agencies: the Ecumenical Response to Poverty - a Primer,* SCM, London.

Taylor, M. (1996), *Jesus and the International Financial Institutions.* Selly Oak Colleges, Occasional Paper, No. 17.

Temperley, H. (1972), *British Anti-Slavery,* Longman, London.

Thomas, H. (1997), *The Slave Trade,* Picador, London.

Thirlwall, A. (1990), *How to Escape the Debtors Prison,* Foreign Focus, 23-24, March-April 1990.

Thirlwall, A.P. (1993), *An Analysis of Changes in the Debt Service Ratio for 96 Countries 1986-90*: Banco del Lavoro Quarterly Review 84: Italy, 1993.

U.N.D.P. (1997), *Human Development Report.* New York, O.U.P.

U.N.D.P. (1998), 'Overcoming Human Poverty'. *U.N.D.P. Poverty Report 1998,* New York, O.U.P.

Vajiragnana, Pandith M. (1997), Unpubl. correspondence on the Dhammapada and other Buddhist scriptures.

Williams, D. *The Specialised Agencies of the United Nations,* Hurst, London.

Wolfensohn, J.D. (1998). *The Other Crisis.* Report to the Board of Governors of the World Bank, Washington. 6 October 1998.

World Bank, (1994), *Reducing the Debt Burden of Poor Countries: a Framework for Action,* Washington.

World Bank, (1998), *The Structural Adjustment Participatory Review Initiative (SAPRI),* Washington.

World Bank Annual Reports, (1992), (1993), (1994), (1995), (1996), (1997), (1998), Washington.
World Bank Debt Tables, Vols. 1 and 2 (1992), (1993), (1994), (1995), (1996), (1997), (1998), renamed Global Development Finance (1999), Washington.
World Bank Development Indicators, (1997), Washington.

Published and unpublished works by Dent, M. and Peters, W.

Dent, M.J. (1990), *Why We Are Starting Jubilee 2000.* Short photocopied paper circulated at lunch on Jubilee 2000 Campaign, Keele University. (Unpublished).
Dent, M.J. (1999), 'Jubilee 2000, a New Start for the Debt Ridden Developing World'. Paper presented to conference on Jubilee in Jerusalem to be published in *Finance and Common Good* (1999), Observatoire de la Finance.
Dent, M.J. *Jubilee 2000 and Lessons of the World Debt Tables 1992-3 and 1993-4.* Published by the author, Department of Politics, Keele University.
Dent, M.J. long letter to Sir Leon Brittan explaining the relevance of Jubilee 2000 to the agenda of the EU and world trade, in response to his request for copies of my pamphlet 'Jubilee 2000 and Lessons of the Debt Tables'.
Dent, M.J. (April 1993), 'The Role of Unselfish Motivation in Successful Movements for Beneficial Change' (a comparison of the Jubilee 2000 campaign and the anti-slavery movement in Britain 1820 to 1834) in report of *Tirley Garth Consultation,* held at Tirley Garth Conference Centre, March 1993.
Dent, M.J. (1996), 'The Mechanics of the Operation of Jubilee 2000, Problems of Implementation', unpublished paper presented at Convention of the International Studies Association, San Diego, April.
Dent, M. and English, C. (1992, reprinted 1994), 'Jubilee 2000; Lifting the Burden of Debt'. Summary of the above pamphlet published in *Journal of Modern African Studies* (Review article by M.J. Dent on Africa's debt, 1994, vol. 32).
Dent, M.J. and Peters, W. (February 1995), 'The Need to Create a Coalition' for *Jubilee 2000,* a paper circulated to Debt Crisis Network and elsewhere, London.
Dent, M.J. and Peters, W., 'Poverty and Debt in the Third World', *Conflict Studies,* 310, June-July 1998, Research Institute for the Study of Conflict and Terrorism, Leamington Spa, Warwickshire.
Dent, M.J. and Peters, W. (1998), 'Lessons of ECGD Annual Report & Trading Accounts 1995/96 and 1996/97' and Interviews with Senior ECGD Personnel, London.
Dent, M.J. and Peters, W. (1998), *Malawi Debt: Cause of Great Suffering and Impediment to Development – Means of Removing the Burden.* Journal of the Society of Malawi. Blantyre, Malawi. Vol.50, No.2
Peters, W. (1971), *Diplomatic Service: Formation and Operation.* Longman Green, London.

Peters, W. (1971), Confidential Record ed. Commonwealth Heads of Government Meeting, Singapore, January 1971. Commonwealth Secretariat.

Peters, W. (1989), *Mountain of Debt.* U.S.P.G. Network. April 1989. (1994).

Peters, W. (1991), *Central Asia & the Minority Question*, Asian Affairs XII, June 1991, 152-7, Royal Society for Asian Affairs, London.

Peters, W. (1993), *Unselfish Motivation & Beneficial Change*, Economics & Unselfishness. Tirley Garth, March 1993.

Peters, W. (1994), *Notes on Jubilee 2000,* Journal of Modern African Studies, Vol.32, No.4, December 1994. (1995)

Peters, W. (1994), *An Introduction to the Jubilee 2000 Campaign for International Debt Remission.* Pub. Jubilee 2000.

Peters, W. (1995), *An Introduction to the Jubilee 2000 Campaign for International Debt Remission*, with comments by Charles K. Wilber and Barend de Uries. Bulletin of the Association of Christian Economists (U.S.). Issue # 26, Fall '95.

Peters, W. (1995), *Jubilee 2000*, Comment, Methodist Church, Issue 13, Autumn, 1995.

Peters, W. (1995), *Jubilee 2000*, Christian 95/4 New Economics Issue, Michaelmas 1995.

Peters, W. (1996), *Jubilee 2000 Update*, Christian 96/4, Michaelmas 1996.

Peters, W. (1996), *Report of a Visit to the United States and Canada*, 15.4.96 – 4.5.96. Jubilee 2000.

Peters, W. (1996), *Grass Roots Mobilisation for Debt Remission*, pub. The Jubilee 2000 Coalition.

Peters, W. (1997), *Objections to Jubilee 2000 answered – The case for creditor government remission.* Pub. The Jubilee 2000 Coalition.

Peters, W. (1997), *Jubilee 2000.* Oxford, Nov 1997 Vol. XLX No.2. The Oxford Society.

Peters, W. (1997), Report on Lobbying at the 1997 Commonwealth Heads of Government Meeting at Edinburgh, 23-24 Oct 1997. Jubilee 2000.

Peters, W. (1998), Report of a Tour of New York, Washington, Vancouver (Ottawa) & Chicago 25 June – 8 July 1998, Jubilee 2000 Coalition.

Peters, W. (1998), *The World Bank & Unpayable Debt* – Paper addressed to President James Wolfensohn, World Bank, with letter, signed by Bishop P. Selby & 21 other bishops from the Lambeth Conference 1998.

Index